William Wilberforce Juvenal Colville

Dashed Against the Rock

A Romance of the Coming Age

William Wilberforce Juvenal Colville

Dashed Against the Rock
A Romance of the Coming Age

ISBN/EAN: 9783744673457

Printed in Europe, USA, Canada, Australia, Japan

Cover: Foto ©Thomas Meinert / pixelio.de

More available books at **www.hansebooks.com**

DASHED AGAINST THE ROCK

A Romance of the Coming Age

W. J. COLVILLE

EDITOR OF "THE PROBLEM OF LIFE"
AUTHOR OF "SPIRITUAL THERAPEUTICS," "STUDIES IN THEOSOPHY,"
"ONESIMUS TEMPLETON," ETC.

"Happy shall he be that taketh and dasheth thy little ones against the rock"
Psalm cxxxvii. 9 (Revised Version)

BOSTON
COLBY & RICH, PUBLISHERS
9 BOSWORTH STREET
1894

TO

MY VERY DEAR FRIEND AND NOBLE BENEFACTOR

G. F. T. Reed

THIS BOOK IS RESPECTFULLY AND AFFECTIONATELY

DEDICATED

IN LOVING MEMORY OF A MUNIFICENT

PHILANTHROPIC EARTHLY CAREER

AND IN SINCERE CONVICTION

THAT THOUGH UNSEEN BY EYES OF FLESH

THAT GRACIOUS LIFE

IS STILL EXPANDING IN STRENGTH AND USEFULNESS

.

W. J. COLVILLE

INTRODUCTION.

In presenting to the public the following extraordinary romance, I wish it to be distinctly understood that I am not in any sense the author of the scientific dissertations and tables which form a considerable portion of the volume.

In "Onesimus Templeton" I gave to the world the outcome of some truly wonderful experiences which came under my notice, and arrested — I may say, literally *compelled* — my attention during the summer of 1885, when my time was divided between France and England. That wonderful phenomena did indeed occur, that the most remarkable cures were accomplished, through a subtle agency defying exterior analysis, I was then thoroughly convinced; but at that time I had not in my possession the mysterious — and yet I daresay altogether natural, even though spiritual — statements concerning exact science which I now introduce into these pages, not for any one's blind acceptance, but as a challenge to whoever may desire to investigate, or even seek to disprove.

We are certainly living in an age of scientific inquiry and marvellous mechanical achievement, — an age, moreover, which, despite its vaunted agnosticism, is to an extent deeply interested in the mysteries of the psychic *realm* or *borderland*, to use the most popular terms at present.

The scope of a novel of ordinary dimensions does not of course permit of much more than a bare, unelaborated recital of facts, introduced in the almost transparent guise of assumed fiction. Some readers may object to the extreme plainness of speech of some of the leading characters, and doubtless there are those who would have liked to suppress all contrast between *genuine* and *spurious* occultism; but, in my opinion, to show only one side of a subject is misleading and unfair. There are far too many people yet who never reason or discriminate; therefore they class all real knowledge concerning spiritual things with the veriest chicanery and dishonesty. To such — if any of them read this book — it may be a revelation to find that in the same narrative the most positive expressions of entire confidence in the reality of the spiritual are placed side by side with the most unmistakable uncoverings of fraud.

The time has now certainly come to unveil — to all who are in any way prepared to profit by such unveiling — the subtle operation of universal Force through the action of unchanging Law.

It is also decidedly a *privilege* as well as *duty*, devolving upon all who are somewhat acquainted with the facts of genuine SCIENCE to discriminate plainly and boldly between *scientific* teachings which are purely THEISTIC in their entire trend and *sciolistic bombast*, which in the mouths of the conceited and ill-informed is made a pretext for denying the very being of Supreme Intelligence, and heaping ridicule upon all who sin-

INTRODUCTION. 5

cerely trust in the immortality of man as a spiritual reality.

The unusual and distinctly technical terminology employed in some of the most important sections of this story may be considered out of place in a tale containing some *amusing* incidents and ostensibly published as a novel; but, whatever may be the appropriateness or inappropriateness of introducing such matter into a romance, I had no alternative but to do what I have done or suppress this priceless knowledge altogether, for I have only received it on trust from a friend who is its custodian in a sense that I am not. For the sake of this superlative information many will read the story, and again, because of the story, some will have their attention turned to this astounding revelation.

I know beforehand that no "critic" will have a word of praise for so unconventional a style as the one I have adopted; but, as the book is written for public edification, not to please the fancy of cynical know-it-alls, the mission of the volume will be fulfilled if any one anywhere, no matter what his or her position in the world may be, receives light from its pages; and even those who get only entertainment may not have read in vain, for to be entertained is frequently to be cheered and uplifted, and he who is himself upraised becomes in turn, whether he knows it or knows it not, an uplifter of others.

The really singular feature of "Aldebaran's" science and philosophy is the deep spiritual-practical lesson clearly taught through even the abstrusest portions. The name given to the mystical scientist intentionally conveys the idea of a bright cluster of stars, not of a single luminary; the title is therefore absolutely true in its suggestiveness, for no single person on earth is the sole possessor of important truth concerning the universe. Special discoveries along particular lines are made by eminently qualified individuals, who are in relation spiritually with great centres of knowledge in the unseen; but there are in all parts of the world to-day, men and women who are entitled to bear the glorious title of *Brothers and Sisters of the* PERPETUAL LIGHT. I do not mean to say that they are organized into societies bearing that name; I only mean that such a title by right belongs to them; and I further declare, and that most emphatically, that these truly illumined men and women are not located in any special part of the world, nor is there any other way of joining their number, save through inward growth and the qualification resulting therefrom.

I am sure that many of my readers will be speculating as to where in the story I introduce my own particular opinions. I do not care to afford any clue to my private views on any subject in the course of the narrative, and this for two reasons. First, inquisitive prying into an author's private predilections is certainly not a profitable occupation; therefore I have no intention of deliberately setting people to work at it. Second, one of the greatest weaknesses of humanity is the widespread, almost universal disposition to adopt the views of some person rather than to weigh statements, look at a subject from all possible points of view and then arrive at one's own unbiassed conclusion. I do not pose as a teacher; I am in these pages only a recorder, and as such I must appear before the world, in company with all novel-writers in this age of the novel, who discover that the deepest philosophy and most glorious science must be introduced in the guise of fiction if it is to be considered extensively.

A few special students read professedly scientific and philosophical works, but everybody reads "light literature." I believe conscientiously in the influence for good both of the novel and the theatre, consequently I will say that I accord most cordial assent to the statements made by some of my characters regarding the possibilities of these great popular modern institutions.

It will be quite useless for any one to inquire of me for further information concerning the deepest questions raised in this volume. I have disclosed all I can reveal for the present, and when I am at liberty to make further disclosures I shall publish another book; but all attempts at private interviews with myself will prove utterly fruitless. I expect very soon to be travelling in Europe, and possibly in other continents; I have, therefore, no address save that of my publishers.

I shall read, I daresay with great interest, the various comments upon the singular revelations with which these pages abound, and I shall, of course, be made acquainted with the extent of the sale of this somewhat new departure in the line of romantic literature. Works treating of "occult" themes are indeed plentiful, but, we hear some one exclaiming: Whoever *did* hear of introducing "Scale of the Forces in Octaves," and that to a positively *bewildering* point — utterly incomprehensible, by the way — into a *novel*, positively a NOVEL? I know this is a singular proceeding, dry, uninteresting, unintelligible to the drawing-room young lady and the moustache-twisting dude, but for them the book contains decidedly other features, in which even they may condescend to be mildly interested.

The scientific world will, however, pay its respects or disrespects to this unpretending volume, and it would indeed be worth a large price of admission, if only for amusement's sake, to see the wiseacres shaking their heads and rubbing their foreheads as one says to his crony, "But where in the name of possibility did the author get it from? Novel-writing is, I daresay, easy to one who has a command of words and an eye for incidents, but whoever could invent such extraordinary tables must either be possessed of an *inexplicable* imagination, or else be actually in possession of some very peculiar knowledge."

I have an intimation within me that this book will make a stir in scientific circles by reason of the parts which I have not written and could not write. To fulfil its strange mission, whatever that may be, I commit it to the *wide, wide world.*

W. J. COLVILLE.

Easter, 1894.

N.B. I beg most earnestly and respectfully to call the reader's *especial* attention to the plates or diagrams, which I am convinced will serve to illustrate, and I hope *elucidate,* some of the most difficult problems in science.

W. J. C.

DASHED AGAINST THE ROCK.

CHAPTER I.

It was a Sunday afternoon in London, an unusually bright beautiful day near the end of June, when a hard, cold, set face might have been observed gazing hopelessly and disdainfully toward the great cathedral of St. Paul, whose massive gates were still wide open; the throng who had been in attendance at the imposing service had not all left the spacious interior of this somewhat gloomy but nevertheless magnificent monument to the genius of Sir Christopher Wren.

Claudius Regulus Monteith, the sad-eyed cynic who is now gazing so mercilessly upon the departing worshippers, sightseers, and musicians,— who all congregate in St. Paul's to see the building, listen to the splendid choral service, and some to pour out their honest hearts in true aspiration toward the Supreme One whom no church can contain or limit,— is a well-built man about forty-five years of age; his frame is strong and sinewy, his eyes are deep set and of a dull leaden hue, though occasionally rare gleams of sunshine flitting through them prove the slumbering presence of a soul not dead but deeply sleeping; his head is massive, with heavy beetling brows, and thickly covered with a heavy iron-gray thatch of rather wiry hair; his whole aspect might be described as peculiarly uninviting by a chance passer-by, but a second glance would surely reveal to the thoughtful observer the presence of a mighty even though perverted intellect, struggling against almost overwhelming pressure from without, to yield to the persistent voice of the tempter, "Curse Heaven, then die." As he gazes he ruminates: "What humbug religion is, and worse than humbug — what hideous barbarity is it that calls together three thousand men, women, and children on a summer afternoon, and then to the accompaniment of a superb organ and in unison with the voices of an almost perfect choir, composed largely of thoughtless boys, invites this multitude to chant the 137th psalm, which finishes a wail by the waters of Babylon with a vile imprecation, and ends with a promise of happiness for those who curse their enemies and practise to the full the law of retaliation, — which the New Testament distinctly condemns. Then to cap the climax of absurdest incongruity, — even barbarism might be logical, — one of the white-surpliced priests of this heathenish cult, miscalled Christianity, reads words ascribed to a supposed divine-human Saviour flatly contradicting the entire spirit of the psalm sung only a few minutes before; for this gospel lesson emphatically commands us 'to bless, and curse not.' Are the clergy mad? Are all the people idiots? And this religion, as they term it, is said to be heaven-appointed to establish the reign of universal peace and goodwill on earth, — such is the inconsistency they claim. Pshaw! such ridiculous mummeries are enough to convince any thinker that this wretched world is a vast madhouse where nearly all the inmates are hopelessly insane; and yet the one woman who was and is to me the *beau ideal* of nature's fairest beauty and goodness believes in this religion — no, not in *this* religion, thank reason, but in a religion widely different from this; for she always declared the letter killeth though the spirit giveth life — but, oh! that elusive *spirit*, what is it? where is it? can anybody see, hear, taste, smell, or touch it? What does it weigh and measure? how can science grapple with it? Alas! alas! such dreams as fairy maidens dream are but beautiful conceits woven of charming fancy, but like the *mirage* in the desert, fleeting and false. 'Blessed shall he be who taketh thy little ones and dasheth them against the rock.' What could Lavinia say to that, she who loved children so dearly and never could pass a weeping child without a word of comfort to still its cry? Spirit, they say, is immortal; but where does it keep itself? what is it, anyway?" Thus darkly cogitating he hears a soft low voice. Was it the slanting sunbeam which spoke, was it the voice of a passer-by, was it "*unconscious cerebration*"?

Whatever it may have been, Claudius Regulus Monteith, cynic and agnostic, heard, or thought he heard, within his ear a voice so soft and sweet that its dulcet notes carried him back to the halycon days of his earliest manhood, and to the lemon groves of Sicily; for the words were those which had fallen twenty years ago from the dying lips of the adored Lavinia, who, as she yielded up her fair body to the embrace of death, smiled radiantly with eyes full of triumph, as she uttered words which had ever been her life talisman: *Semper credo in vitam æternam.* — Always do I believe in the life eternal.

Guided by an irresistible, or at all events an unresisted, impulse, the man who hears these words of undying faith ringing in his doubting ear, goes back to the cathedral steps, and again mounting them enters the sombre interior just as the last of the congregation file out through the heavy door which the verger is now closing, but which he does not lock, as another service will commence at seven, and it is now considerably after five. The organ is now silent, the choir stalls are vacant, the chairs, which were all occupied half an hour ago, are now completely deserted, and the great church seems vainly endeavoring to recover from the excitement of the fashionable choral service so recently ended, and become what a church should ever be, — a haven of rest for the myriad toilers who are invited through its constantly open doors to rest beneath the imposing canopy of its majestic roof and dome. Sleep, that ever-welcome guest to those who are weighted with care, falls tenderly, softly, suddenly, over the weary intellect of the hopeless doubter, as he throws himself into a chair near the chancel rails and sets to work to puzzle out if possible the cause and meaning of the strange but sweet *hallucination* which has just overtaken him. But he cannot think; his reasoning faculty seems totally benumbed, his materialistic theories have all deserted him, and for the space of fully an hour he and his beloved are together,— where or how he does not know and cannot decide. Once again *semper credo in vitam æternam* falls upon or *into* his ear, and he wakes with a start to find the gas-jets lighted and a congregation assembling for the second evening service.

Having no desire to hear repeated the ecclesiastical ritual of the afternoon, Professor Monteith strolls out through the side entrance on to Cheapside and walks aimlessly, and yet it seemed to him for some definite end, in the direction of Argyle Square, where, though not to his previous knowledge, is situated one of the largest Swedenborgian places of worship in London.

On reaching the square and coming unexpectedly in front of the New Jerusalem Church, his attention is at once attracted by the words, "Dashed against the Rock," which is the topic announced for the discourse on that particular evening, as one of a protracted series of sermons on "Dark Sayings of Holy Writ." The service has already commenced, and feeling strangely impelled to enter, the professor, who begins to think himself haunted by that awful text, takes a seat in the rear of the handsome, well-filled church, and soon becomes impressed with the earnestness of the minister's tone, who is reading the same lesson from the Gospel according to St. Matthew he had heard at St. Paul's a few hours earlier. This time the clear, wonderful, though simple words did not seem the mockery they had appeared before to this world-weary listener; for the well-modulated intonation of the reader carried with it the conviction that the man who was then reading them desired to be true to their spirit in his own life and teachings, and also to help others to become true likewise to the noble precepts therein contained. Fine music and hearty prayers led up to the sermon, which was a perfect revelation to at least one of the listeners; for with all his learning Professor Monteith had never read Swedenborg, and was totally unacquainted with that wonderful teacher's remarkable theory of *correspondence* as applied to the text of much of the Bible. Dr. Presland spoke directly to the point, and as this was the seventh in a series of twelve lectures on a general theme, he spent no time on elucidating the doctrine of the interior sense of Sacred Scripture, but launched at once into the depth of the assertion that whenever *rock* or *stone* is mentioned in Holy Writ, it signifies foundation principle of truth.

"The Jewish Law contains," said this eloquent pastor, "an inner meaning which the Gospel discloses. When Christ condemns self-righteous Pharisees by convicting them of their personal transgressions through arousing within them a sense of right and purity, he abrogates the harsh letter of Mosaism, but fulfils the Law in love. The letter vanishes from sight when its work is completed. The woman taken in the act of adultery is to be *spiritually*, not *literally*, stoned. Our enemies, my friends," continued the preacher, "are not our personal foes, they are our own illicit appetites; the children of the daughter of Babylon are the offspring of an iniquitous mental state, and when these results of error are brought into collision with the rock of truth, sin dies, and man is new-born to righteousness."

After an earnest plea in favor of mercy as the inseparable associate of divine justice, the speaker dismissed his hearers with the assurance that the darkest parables of Scripture are full of goodness and truth, as they emanate from infinite love and wisdom.

"Well, here at least is consistency," mused the professor, as he slowly wended his way to his chambers in Russel Square, Bloomsbury, where he lived in bachelor apartments, a lonely, loveless life, cheered only by the chill moonbeams of physical research. His laboratory interested his intellect, but it never satisfied his emotions, and despite his cynicism, affection was to him what light and air are to flowers and birds. This man's intellect was suffocating his affection; for he saw only a barren waste of boundless territory ruled by an iron force he vaguely described as Law; to his sad, discontented mind the universe was totally unlighted by even a solitary beam of beneficence, save only when such an experience visited him as had come that very afternoon; and that was the sweet, lingering *reminiscence*, so he termed it, of an idol of his youth who had promised him on her deathbed that were it possible she would reveal herself to him as his deathless friend and guardian. And now he questions more seriously than ever; had that promise been fulfilled? had she really spoken within him twice that day? was it possible that he and she had spent an hour together in dreamland while he was sleeping after evensong in the cathedral? and could it have been she who directed his steps to the church in Argyle Square in order that the tumultuous passion against religion in his brain might be stilled by a new suggestive inference drawn from a long-detested text?

Be this as it may, Claudius Regulus Monteith was less a cynic when his head touched his pillow that night than he had been for the past twenty years. "After all," he murmured as he fell asleep, "love is better than hate; faith is better than despair, even in this old sad world where the shadows so far outnumber the sunbeams; and if it is only a delusion, well, the cheat is so comforting it may be best sometimes to give way to our illusions, but anyway I'll learn whatever I can of this new philosophy I have heard so ably expounded. I'll call to-morrow morning on the brilliant novelist, Visalia Discalcelis, whom I met at Dr. Ferguson's Literary Matinee last Thursday. I know I acted like a bear when I told her she wrote silly ghost stories and tried to dress them up in the livery of science; but she was not at all offended, and only said: 'Well, we shall have time to discuss that question if you call on me next Monday, when I shall receive a few friends from two till six; but if you desire comparative privacy for your talk, make your visit at eleven in the morning.'

"This Madame Discalcelis," he pondered, "is a very curious woman; she frequently turns away in haughty coldness from her flatterers and then makes instant friends with old boors like myself who have positively insulted her. She is a strange being and evidently sincere; if any one could make me believe in immortality, it would be some one like that woman. Well, anyway, we'll see what to-morrow brings forth." And he fell asleep.

CHAPTER II.

FAITH *vs.* AGNOSTICISM.

SINCERITY *vs.* SHAM.

The morning of the day following rose bright and clear; all nature seemed to smile and sing in opposition to the pessimistic plaint of the poor professor, to whom the world had for twenty years appeared nothing but a dreary wilderness, with here and there a faint tiny oasis of illusory brightness. To-day his mood is slightly sweeter than its accustomed wont; he has had no more remarkable dreams, but his sleep has been profound, and the hour of waking found him less restless than usual; though he with long-accustomed habit has determined to shake from him, as far as possible, the glimmering faith which surely dawned, even though but faintly, in his soul the night before, telling him of the real presence of a spiritual universe, where the living die not, and where his dearest angel dwelt, untouched by the ravaging hand of mortal dissolution.

"Well, I'll go and see her," decided the professor; and as to carry a mental determination into immediate action was his life-habit, eleven o'clock found him ringing the bell at the door of a charming villa residence in the most delightful part of Bayswater.

Madame Visalia Discalcelis was domiciled during the London season with her most intimate friends, the Eastlake-Gores, at whose hospitable home in Hants she always spent Christmastide, and indeed a considerable portion of the winter. Mrs. Gore, a widow in middle life, received Professor Monteith in her private sitting-room, which was a *rendezvous* for the entire family at any time; for, though a lady of true refinement and tender susceptibilities, Mrs. Gore was literally without nerves, *i.e.* nerves in a pathological condition.

"Can I see Madame Discalcelis? I believe she resides with you. Eleven in the morning seems an unseasonable visiting hour, but she wrote in pencil on her visiting-card, a few evenings ago at Lady Porchester's, 'come at eleven in the morning when you want to talk with me.' I have read her latest book, *Askalon*, with deep interest, and was much pleased to meet the authoress of so wonderful a story; but though I am sure her talent is marvellous, I told her frankly the other evening that her conclusions relating to man's spiritual life here and hereafter were utterly unsupported by science; and we, who are giving our entire lives to scientific researches, can scarcely be expected to credit as sober realities the dream-creations of our poets."

"Pardon me, my dear sir, I do not in the least know why we should not; poets are the greatest scientists alive," broke in suddenly the ringing, happy voice of Mrs. Eastlake-Gore's only son, the pride and joy of her motherhood.

Arthur Selwyn Eastlake-Gore was one of those exceptional young men who strike people at once as being thoroughly normal. Extremely handsome in personal appearance, erect in bearing, perfectly dressed, and absolutely well-bred, he was nevertheless what the world calls a mystic and a dreamer. Though an Oxford graduate with high honors, and a perfect athlete, he could demonstrate almost every phase of "mediumship" that is really genuine, as easily as he could solve a problem in Euclid. But instead of spurning society and going into a tomb to develop psychic qualities, he had from early boyhood been distinguished for his love of all that makes life attractive to the young and healthy. Coming as it did from a stylish young gentleman of extremely aristocratic bearing, this tribute to the veracity of the Muses struck the devotee of "exact science only" as strikingly incongruous, and the only reply he vouchsafed was: "My young friend, twenty years from now, you will have learned to distrust the poets."

At this juncture Visalia Discalcelis entered the room, accompanied by the daughter of her hostess, — a girl fully as handsome as her brother and about three years his junior, with all the manifest traits which show near relationship in mind as well as body. As the two young ladies entered together, they formed a striking tableau: the authoress, the elder of the two, would, according to physical measurement, be called a small woman, for she was neither tall nor stout; but her intense individuality, sparkling but not obtrusive, made it impossible for any one to doubt the unusual size, or at least quality, of her intellect. Unlike most Italians, she was fair rather than dark; her skin was pink and white, natural roses and lilies, her light, wavy chestnut hair disported itself in spontaneous little curls all over her well-shaped head, while her deep hazel eyes looked into you and through you, as though she could read the very depths of a human soul.

The glance she gave Professor Monteith was grave and kindly, though there was a touch of rebuke in it, as she extended her hand, saying: "Let us be sure our science *is* exact before we proclaim it as such."

"My dear madam," began the professor, after he had learned that Madame Discalcelis was ready for a two hours' confab with him regarding the mysteries of the universe, "you state that man can *know* that his spirit is immortal, and in your latest book you tell us it is our own perverse blindness and nothing else that bars the gates of paradise against our outward life; but how can this be true, when, during the past twenty years, I have been seeking everywhere for light, and have found only darkness?"

"Have you been seeking only for truth, or have you not rather been striving to confirm certain vague though ironclad opinions, such as the exploded vagary of spontaneous generation, for example? Believe me, my friend, the vision you enjoyed yesterday was a million times more real than all the objects we discern with our mortal eyes. I do not profess adherence to the tenets of Swedenborg to the extent that those good people do, whose church you attended last evening; but I speak from *knowledge* when I tell you that the sermon you heard last night was worth a million so-called scientific discoveries as a contribution to the world's peace and general welfare."

"My very dear madam," remonstrated the professor, excitedly, "*you* use a woman's emotion, while *I* employ a man's intellect to defend a position; but how did you guess at my dream of yesterday, and then also at my visit to Argyle Square later? Do you profess clairvoyance, may I ask? Dr. Closingshell, at the Polytechnic, told us only a few weeks ago that we should in fifty years from now have elevated clairvoyance to the rank of a science. I disagreed with him at the time; but if you tell me your informant as to my whereabouts yesterday was your own 'psychic sense,' I shall certainly be compelled to reconsider my decision."

"*Compelled*, did you say? Oh dear, no, not in the least; we are *compelled* to do nothing; the foolish belief in necessity is in my opinion a relic of barbarism rapidly becoming effete; you can accept or reject the evidences of the soul exactly as you desire. I simply relate to you an incident, and you can credit or discredit it as you please. Acceptance or rejection of proffered evidence is purely voluntary; we can believe or disbelieve whatever we choose."

"My *dearest* madam," literally shrieked the professor, now utterly beside himself with protest, "what are you dreaming about? Science *proves;* I say it *proves* that man has no more liberty to elect his course than your slippers have to decide whether they will or will not be placed upon your feet; we are all the abject slaves of environment, and have not a particle of freedom; the theological fiction of human free agency is one of the ghastliest mockeries ever imposed by designing priests upon credulous humanity."

"Doubtless, so it appears to you," rejoined the fair Visalia, who fastened her piercing though kindly eyes directly upon her visitor, as though she could and would penetrate to the very core of his nature; "that is why you are at this hour a self-confessed failure, a restless spirit, complaining against what you term 'cruel, relentless fate.' It is the soul within you which is ever urging upon you the necessity, not of yielding to the supposed inevitable, but of conquering destiny by your might as man."

"Conquer destiny?" literally screamed the now almost frantic disciple of blind Necessarius; "destiny is immutably fixed in the constitution of the universe. *Conquer destiny*, madam? You can, maybe, when water and fire cease to seek and find their respective levels; or when oranges grow on pear-trees, and lemons are produced from thorns. I cannot conceive it possible that a woman possessing the education which is undoubtedly yours can, for a single instant, question the absolute immutability of law. Pope may have been wrong when he said, 'Whatever is, is *right*'; whatever is may be *wrong*, for all I know, but it is certainly *inevitable*."

"Poor fellow, I am heartily sorry for you," was the only response which this tirade elicited from Madame Discalcelis, who in her quite brief career as a popular authoress had met and corresponded with hundreds of just such cases, all of which she regarded as distinctly pathological specimens, needing more thorough and skilful handling than she felt personally able to bestow;

she therefore never sought to pose in the rôle of a great teacher, but only strove to help the really honest ones who came to her, as best she might, to a clearer apprehension of the truth she herself was only, as she felt, just beginning to learn.

"The wheel of the law, my dear, the wheel of the law," harshly broke in upon the momentary silence which followed Visalia's expression of sorrow for the mental attitude of her interlocutor; and turning in the direction whence the rasping voice proceeded, the assembled company beheld standing in the doorway Madame Sanskrita Bromleykite, an English resident of Calcutta, who had married an Oriental and was now with her husband occupying the adjoining villa to that rented for the season by the Eastlake-Gores, who were almost the only people whose residence afforded Madame Discalcelis what she considered a *home*.

"The Gores *live* in a *home;* other friends of mine *exist* in *residences*, and I prefer the former to the latter, infinitely," was Visalia's invariable response, when she was asked why she always resided with the same family when so many pleasant and fashionable houses were open to her.

Mrs. Bromleykite had just *dropped in*, to use her own phrase, — which was admirably descriptive of her peculiar movements, — to ask, *as a great favor*, the loan of a few plates, cups and saucers, and spoons, for a theosophical *soirée* to be held at her rooms that evening; also to request everybody to request everybody else to sell tickets for the illustrious Pundita Kamadevacha's lecture on "The Secret Doctrine," to be given under

Mrs. Bromleykite's own distinguished auspices, at St. James' Hall on the ensuing Monday evening. Mrs. Bromleykite was a wonderful talker; her quotations from ancient Sanscrit documents were truly amazing, and — whenever the conditions were favorable — the massive silver collar would be removed, by "occult agency," from the neck of Lady Porchester's pet pug and placed in the pocket of that worthy lady's constant and devoted friend and companion, Miss Katherine Poyntz. This phenomenon, however, was very rare, and could only be produced when the "masters" gave special, though reluctant, permission.

Any one who is at all familiar with modernized Orientalism will experience very little difficulty in surmising the exact nature of the conversation which ensued during the next half-hour between the highly excited professor and the no less enthusiastic, though far less gloomy and despondent, Madame Bromleykite. At length Madame Discalcelis, availing herself of a break in the buzz, said in clear, decided tones, — and when she was particularly decided she was decidedly majestic: —

"Your blind quibblings over destiny are but as the froth upon the surface of the lightest table beer; you are right and you are wrong; there is *Necessity*, but it is *Divine Order;* God is the Source of all Law, and therefore your freedom and mine, real though it be, is God's will concerning us. You, my studious professor, will have further spiritual visions; and you, Mrs. Bromleykite, had better study the New Testament as well as the Vedas."

"Study the New Testament, indeed," contemptuously sniffed Mrs. Bromleykite; "haven't I been *made* to study it from the time I was a little girl, when my father literally *forced* me to learn a whole chapter every Sunday afternoon? If you Englishwomen are going to cling with such stupid obstinacy to your old Gospels, no wonder our *illustrious*, but too often, alas, *rejected*, pundits, make the return voyage to India without having secured more than two, or at most three, converts to Esoteric Buddhism. I have read *Askalon*, and I must say you hit some hypocrites pretty hard, but you are not the right kind of a theosophist by any means; and as for my dear husband, who is *thoroughly* familiar with Sanscrit, he says you are still infatuated with idols and psychologized by priests, though you do once in a while give your readers a fraction, somewhat distorted though, of our sublime Oriental doctrines."

At this point the Anglo-Indian proselyter became eloquent and strident, and turning to Professor Monteith — who was secretly enjoying this strange woman's presumptuous uppishness — said to that gentleman: —

"And you, sir, though you do well to criticise the Christian religion as you do, are not yet acquainted with Esoteric Buddhism; but we will gladly initiate you. My dear husband can give you the mystic key to the Vedas in twelve lessons, and it will only cost you fifty dollars, — that is, ten pounds in English money; he has taught sixty classes in America, composed of the leading physicians, lawyers, merchants, journalists, and all the big guns in the largest cities; after you have taken his course of instruction you will be indeed a *saved* man. Professor Bromleykite is a name honored wherever truth is prized."

When the impetuous advocate of her own and her husband's peculiar pet form of "esotericism" had ceased this volley of conjugal eulogy, Mr. Gore, who had been quietly leaning against the mantelpiece reading the voluble speaker's character pretty thoroughly, suggestively remarked: —

"Lady Porchester, with whom I believe you are well acquainted, knows a genuine mystic, who is in the privileged possession of actual knowledge of many of the hidden sources of life; he lives in almost complete retirement, devoting his whole time and energy, and that incessantly, to the demonstration of palpable proof of the spiritual constitution of the universe. If you, my dear professor, are honestly in search of light, I will intercede with Lady Porchester to procure for you an introduction to this extraordinary young man, who, strange to say, considering his accumulated knowledge, is scarcely over thirty years of age; he, I am convinced, can show you the *practical* side of theosophy, while,— pardon the suggestion,— from what we know of reputed theosophists in general, we are sure they can but vaguely theorize at best."

The conversation soon became general, and as Madame Discalcelis had an appointment with her publishers at half-past one, she soon made her adieux, and accompanied by Mrs. Gore set out in her exquisitely appointed brougham in the direction of Oxford Street.

Subsequent to their departure Mrs. Bromleykite soon realized the necessity of her superintending the cooking and serving of the stewed cabbage and fried onions, which would constitute the early dinner of these devoted *cheelas*, who professed to regard the eating of meat as a terrible sin, if partaken of at their own table and paid for with their own money; in other people's houses, when they were invited, porter-house steak, boned turkey, and even *pâte de foie gras* were perfectly legitimate articles of diet, so they apparently had been informed by a *supreme judicial authority;* "delayed *karma*" was so considerate of their bodily infirmities, that though it was really very wrong to kill animals or birds for food, it was quite right to satisfy the present needs of a semi-carnivorous appetite, provided always the banquet was furnished by other people and eaten out of one's own apartments. This theory of morality, as applied to diet, was mercilessly ridiculed by Madame Discalcelis; but then, she was a "scoffer," and her opinions did not merit attention in "occult" society.

Professor Monteith had accepted Mr. Gore's cordial invitation to a little bachelor lunch in that young gentleman's private "den." And during the meal, it was with more than ordinary interest that he expatiated upon the need of absolute *physical* proof of the existence of the human soul, if such an existence could ever be accepted as a reality; and though the two gentlemen did not by any means agree, either in their premises or conclusions, the hour they spent at the lunch table was a profitable one for both. The bright, healthy, hopeful, happy young man, full of glorious life and noble aspirations, exerted, even though unconsciously, upon his elder companion, an electric influence of such an uplifting character that the poor professor, who had been for many years a martyr to dyspepsia, enjoyed a hearty meal without fear of indigestion, and felt a hundred per cent better for it two hours after he had eaten it.

Arthur Selwyn Eastlake-Gore was a gifted young man, of a type far too rare in modern society; for were there more like him, interest in true religion would not be at the shockingly low ebb it now is among college-bred young gentlemen. Professor Montcith, cynic and sceptic though he had long been, was deeply impressed and strongly influenced by the evidently perfect sincerity of his genial host. Noble characters can wear broadcloth and fine linen, and appear with well-trimmed nails and well-brushed hair, with much greater likelihood of influencing the world for good, than though they foolishly arrayed themselves in tattered robes, and made a virtue of dirty hands and unkempt locks.

"I shall not forget the introduction," said Mr. Gore pleasantly, as the strangely assorted pair bade each other a temporary adieu.

"Thanks a million times," responded Professor Monteith; "it may be my salvation."

The young gentleman retired to his dressing-room to prepare for Lady Porchester's "At home," which was always on Monday afternoons, while the elder man, deeply impressed, but not yet by any means *converted*, gave himself to speculation concerning what might possibly occur as the result of his anticipated introduction to the mysterious "Aldebaran," whose workshop at Tower Heights, Islington, had once been mentioned to him as the most wonderful laboratory of "*alchemy*" to be found in all Great Britain.

CHAPTER III.

LADY PORCHESTER'S RECEPTION.

Lady Porchester's house in Grosvenor Square was one of those commodious old-style mansions tenanted, during the "season" at least, by that portion of high society in London which prefers the traditions of the forefathers, in the matter of dwelling, to the new-fangled freaks of the young bloods of English aristocracy. Comfort was unmistakably suggested by the quiet, roomy massiveness of the house, whether regarded from within or without. Ground-rents were evidently not nearly so high as now when Grosvenor Square came into existence; for in all the residences in that substantial abode of solidity there is ample room for families to spread themselves at will through suites of ample apartments, each room in which can be devoted to the special purpose for which it was designed.

In a house of twenty spacious rooms, exclusive of servants' quarters, Lady Porchester lived nearly the whole year round, with her faithful and beloved protegée, Miss Katherine Poyntz, attended by at least a dozen well-trained and, for the most part, rather ancient, servants. In June, however, the house was not so bare of occupants; as, within certain clearly defined limits, Lady Catherine Aurelia Clavering Porchester was given to hospitality. All through the year — save during the short intervals when her ladyship deserted the metropolis for Brighton and sea air, which was usually during October and November — her handsome, though decidedly old-fashioned, drawing-rooms were thronged on Monday afternoons with as curious an assemblage of human beings as could well be met with anywhere; for, though fastidious to a degree in the keeping up of many family traditions, this elderly dame of an ancient régime was so completely carried away with every novelty connected with the amazing progress of Spiritualism and Occultism, that she attracted to her house, her person, and her fortune almost every visitor to London who laid any claim at all to being a clairvoyant, clairaudient, telepathist, occultist, or aught else that savored of the mysterious or the theosophic. Among this motley throng were persons of the greatest probity; but these were well-balanced by schemers, who found the excessive credulousness of their hostess an open sesame to the furtherance of their unrighteous plans to defraud the unsuspecting, under pretext of a heavenly revelation.

As the Bromleykites had heard of Lady Porchester's hospitality and also of her amazing gullibility, very shortly after their arrival in London, and their *fame*, or to speak truly, *notoriety*, had reached that good woman's ears through the medium of her favorite newspaper, *The Psychic Eye-Opener*, edited by Jarvis Montressor Palgrave, P.Q.R., H.E.F., etc., etc., she had not only sent them a cordial invitation to be present at her weekly "At homes," but had even despatched a special confidential messenger, in the person of the ever-faithful Katherine, *urging* them not only to attend the "functions" in her drawing-room, but to dine, lunch, sup, or anything they pleased *en famille* with her ladyship, whenever their *numerous* and *pressing* engagements would permit of their straying as far as Grosvenor Square from the *delightful* suburb where they were so *charmingly* domiciled.

The face of Miss Poyntz was truly luminous with cordial greeting as she delivered this delicious invitation, with Lady Porchester's own expressive accentuation. Of course the Bromleykites responded, and on the first Monday after its receipt they were in Lady Porchester's drawing-room among the earliest of the visitors. They arrived before three; Mr. Gore dropped in about four; and as the guests and visitors had heard of nothing but the doings of Professor Bromleykite while in India, for over an hour, they were not sorry when Mr. Gore's entrance changed the conversation, but without leading it away from its pivotal Occultism.

"By the way, my dear Lady Porchester," said the new arrival, "my mother and I are deeply interested in Professor Regulus Monteith, who seems, despite his scepticism, to be really in earnest in his desire to know something of the discoveries of that remarkable scientific mystic whom we only hear of in a vague way through a mutual friend as Signor Aldebaran; if he is open to visitors, I think he would be glad to meet Professor Monteith, and I may also say on behalf of my mother's particular friend, Madame Discalcelis, that she also would like an introduction."

"My dear Eastlake," responded the hostess, "nothing would give me greater pleasure than to put you in the way of seeing him; but I understand he is very seclusive, — quite a hermit, I should judge, — living in a tower, where he has a complete alchemist's outfit; really a romance of the Middle Ages in *anno domini* 1893." Then addressing Miss Poyntz, "Katherine, my dear, write at once to Lady Tomlinson and request two letters of introduction to Professor Aldebaran; one for Madame Visalia Discalcelis, the noted authoress, the other for Professor Regulus Monteith, professor of *all* the natural sciences: that sounds inclusive, and I cannot designate his specialty."

With Miss Poyntz, to serve Lady Porchester was a delight; the two women loved each other truly, and the younger served the elder — though not without liberal compensation, however — from pure devotion and gratitude. Miss Poyntz could do everything; she could play the piano, sing, recite, write a good letter, direct the affairs of a household, collect rents, and overlook wardrobes; she was indeed a treasure, a domestic woman as well as an artist, but she had never married; possibly she had been crossed in her affections; but were that the case, no one suspected it, and she and Lady Porchester were positively inseparable.

While the letters were being written at an *escritoire*, in a palm-shrouded recess, the clatter of voices became louder and more incessant, as carriages were now arriving rapidly, filled with the *élite* of Belgravia, who felt it to be a duty to always look in upon *dear* Lady Porchester on Monday afternoons.

As Mr. Eastlake-Gore was one of her ladyship's favorites, — and, oh, how she wished his eyes might rest lovingly on her companion, though twenty years his senior, — she cordially invited him to remain to dinner, which she declared she always took on Mondays alone with *dear* Katherine in their cosey boudoir, and then — and here her voice sunk to a whisper — the Bromleykites were going to join them, and Mrs. Bromleykite had confidentially informed her that sometimes, when conditions were *exceptionally* favorable, and the gas was lowered at dessert, and the footman dismissed from the room, bracelets, brooches, watches, and other articles of value were transported to India to be blessed by "T.H.E.M.," and returned to their respective owners when "T.H.E.Y." saw fit.

Though too much of a gentleman to laugh while her ladyship was speaking, Mr. Gore was simply *compelled* to cough and take out his handkerchief; nevertheless, he graciously accepted the invitation, and this the more readily as Lady Porchester had telephoned to his mother and their guest that if they could drop in about half-past eight they might possibly witness some of the most wonderful feats of occultism ever presented to the world.

Six o'clock came, and the other visitors had all departed. Lady Porchester and Miss Poyntz had left the drawing-room, and Mr. Gore was left alone with Mr. and Mrs. Bromleykite, who at once endeavored to enlist the young man's sympathy in an endeavor to raise, through courses of lectures, entertainments, etc., a fund of not less than fifty thousand pounds, to build theosophical headquarters in the metropolis. Assuming the attitude of a frenzied prophet, his long, thin, grizzly hair fluttering below his collar as he gesticulated, his lean long arms extended like the wings of a bat, his shiny threadbare broadcloth contrasting soberly with his yellow, frayed linen, Professor Sanskritikus Bromleykite looked every inch a wizard.

Seated in a commodious arm-chair near by, his wife carefully scanned the face of their acquaintance as they eagerly sought to enlist this promising young Englishman as one of "T.H.E.I.R." disciples. Mrs. Bromleykite, fully as shabby and ragged as her spouse, her dyed-black hair and artificial chignon contrasting painfully with her sallow cheeks and sunken eyes, looked ghastly in the subdued lamplight which mingled with the light of day, which still streamed brightly in through the partly curtained windows.

The professor was no orator, he was not even eloquent, but he was impassioned; and when he talked of the ashes of "B.P.H." and their removal to India, tears flowed in torrents down his livid cheeks as he finished an address on the absolute altruism of theosophy, with a harrowing allusion to the bitter persecutions meted out by a *lacerating* world to the "reincarnate John the Baptist," whom "Occidental perfidy had stretched bleeding on its infernal rack of torture, and gloated over the iron which had entered the marrow of his veins."

"Not moved by this recital of the greatest suffering of the ages!" shrilly screamed the professor's wife, as Eastlake-Gore quietly turned over the pages of a recent periodical, when the professor had ceased speaking; "are you a man of stone,—though I should not take you to be such,—that such inexpressible emotion as my darling husband's fails to move you? Why, when he lectured last April in New York, the halls — the largest and finest in the city — were thronged to suffocation; women rushed out in hysterics, men fainted and fell over the gallery railings; it was a Pentecost of fire; my husband literally *asphyxiated* them."

"How very awful," was Mr. Gore's sole comment.

"*Awful*, AWFUL, did you say?" pursued Sanskrita, who, by this time, had risen and taken the attitude of a menacing pythoness; "I called it *glorious*, HEAVENLY, and" — here her voice was lowered to a stage whisper — "I am sure 'T.H.E.Y.' were with him."

"I know not, nor do I care, who or what may have been the direct or indirect cause of so execrable a pathological phenomenon; no wise or benevolent power throws men and women into convulsive paroxysms of aggravated hysteria; I believe yet in the old-fashioned counsel, 'Judge the tree by its fruits,' and the fruits you seem to have on exhibition are to my mind diabolical."

"*Diabolical* results, when *my husband* is the speaker! this is too much; dear Lady Porchester cannot know your principles, young man, or she would ostracize you from her circle." But fearing her endeavors might react against her own and her husband's future interest, she instantly took refuge in loud, wailing sobs, and between her fast-flowing tears succeeded in feebly articulating with choked utterance: "Oh, Mr. Gore, you don't know us; we are angels, and you think us devils; but those whose mission is so *very* exalted must expect to be misunderstood; even Buddha was maligned by ignorance, booh! booh! booh-h-h!" and the poor woman broke down utterly.

Hating a scene, as all healthy people do, Mr. Gore sought to quell the ire and sorrow of the offended Bromleykites by politely remarking, "Well, doubtless you are well-meaning; if I have misinterpreted your meaning, I gladly offer my apologies."

"My young friend," responded Mr. Bromleykite, now quite recovered from *his* emotion, "you are like thousands, nay, millions of others; you know not 'T.H.E.M.' — would that we might initiate you."

The announcement that it only wanted fifteen minutes to seven, at which hour dinner would be served, put a happy termination to this ludicrous and rather embarrassing interview, as the claims of the toilet demanded the attention of all who had engaged in it; and when they reappeared from the dressing-rooms, dinner was served, and conversation became animated on the side of Lady Porchester, who regarded the Bromleykites as valuable acquisitions to her coterie of intimates, while Mr. Gore and Miss Poyntz discussed quite amicably a new picture which had just been exhibited in Bond Street. Miss Poyntz was quite an intellectual woman, and were it not for her uncompromising submission to every one of Lady Porchester's fads, she would doubtless have expressed her views far more decidedly on the transportation of trinkets; as it was, she respectfully acquiesced in her ladyship's decisions, and permitted her own faculty for scrutiny to remain in customary abeyance.

Professor and Mrs. Bromleykite, though *strict vegetarians on principle*, ate very heartily of turtle soup, salmon cutlets, roast duck, and kidney *sauté;* and though pillars of *total* abstinence, they freely imbibed hock, moselle, and burgundy, with evidently the keenest relish; but they were not at home, and out of their own house it was no sin to indulge at other people's expense in these luxuries, the sin of flesh-eating and wine-drinking consisting only in buying wine and meat with one's own money, or in preparing and eating it in the private apartments of "consecrated *cheelas.*" Mrs. Bromleykite distinctly declared that "T.H.E.Y." permitted violations of the strict rule of "Yoga" when "holy probationers" were accepting hospitality from less initiated "thresholders."

Just as the walnuts were passing round, Mrs. Eastlake-Gore, Madame Discalcelis, Mrs. Fitzcraven-Spottiswoode, Mr. Clarence Fitzcraven, and Professor Regulus Monteith were announced as already in the drawing-room. This was the signal to commence the *serious business* of the evening, for at Lady Porchester's urgent request *dear* Professor Bromleykite and his *darling* wife had graciously consented to try a few experiments in hypnotism; and if these proved successful, then it *might be possible* that a *few* articles of jewelry would disappear by magic from the persons of the sitters.

Mrs. Spottiswoode and her brother, Mr. Fitzcraven, were quite distinguished literary personages; Mrs. Spottiswoode's articles on the Passion Play of Ober-

Ammergau were the talk of literary circles; Mr. Fitzcraven was literary and dramatic critic for the *Belgravia Eagle;* and as Mr. Gore was a *reviewer* for the *Kensington Lion,* the two gentlemen had often met in the course of the discharge of their respective obligations. Mrs. Spottiswoode impressed every one who met her as a woman of *will;* her tall, majestic figure, stately, commanding voice, and handsome dress all conspired to give an air of queenliness to her ample person, and her brother was scarcely less conspicuous with his fine military bearing and faultless evening attire. Professor Monteith looked inquisitorial and only partly at his ease; Madame Discalcelis and Mrs. Gore presented a beautiful tableau; they might easily have been taken for mother and daughter, they appeared so much alike in quiet dignity and unobtrusive strength of soul. Mrs. Gore's quiet pale gray silk contrasted peacefully with the snowy muslin of the younger lady's robe and the amber and black costume of Mrs. Spottiswoode. Mr. Gore and Mr. Fitzcraven were about of a height and not dissimilar in build, but the perfectly easy, unaffected grace of the one differed widely from the decidedly "got up" appearance of the other. Lady Porchester looked fiery, in spite of her serene amiability of disposition, in the scarlet satin she insisted upon wearing on a warm summer evening, though "sweet Katherine" suggested pale blue in preference, and received in consequence the gift of a beautiful dress of that color for her own use from her ladyship.

Professor Bromleykite suggested "exercises" to "thrill the circle into sympathy with the occult vibrations of Devachanic rest."

Madame Discalcelis, who was an exquisite pianist, readily complied with an invitation — she was utterly unaffected — to render one of Schubert's Nocturnes and then two Beethoven Sonatas, which she rendered with such perfect shading that a holy hush really did seem to fall upon all the listeners. A perfect accompanist is always a much-to-be-desired acquisition at a reception where music is introduced, and in this rôle the fair Visalia was peerless; Miss Poyntz was consequently so greatly aided when she gave "The Song that reached my Heart," and "One Morning, oh, so Early," — Lady Porchester's particular favorites, — that Mr. Fitzcraven, even though a professional critic, condescended to exclaim, positively *la diva*,— a compliment which Katherine was not slow to accept at far more than even its face value.

When the company was sufficiently harmonized and tranquillized, Professor Bromleykite, introduced by her ladyship, delivered a grandiose address on the marvels of hypnotism, in which he freely quoted from Bernheim, Charcot, and other authorities, and paid his half-complimentary respects to Mr. Stead's "automatic writing." Experiments were of course suggested, and as no one but Lady Porchester appeared a willing subject, and she was anxious to be thrown into the "subconscious ecstasy" wherein her "sub-self" might satisfactorily convince its auditors that human beings really have two minds, — the inner of which is far more luminous than the outer, — lights were lowered till only the outline of figures could be discovered easily; then in a loud sepulchral whisper Professor Bromleykite recited an incantation. Madame Discalcelis and the Gores shuddered at its blasphemy; Professor Monteith regarded it as an interesting revival of an ancient superstition, and watched its possible "magnetic" effect with the critical eyes of a nineteenth century scientist, to whom the convolutions of the gray matter of the brain and the emanations radiating therefrom constitute a fascinating topic for rigid scrutiny; Mrs. Spottiswoode and her brother were amused rather than interested; Miss Poyntz was careful to watch Lady Porchester's respiration, fearing that there might be danger to an elderly lady whose heart was none too vigorous, in such a pastime; Mrs. Bromleykite assumed the attitude of a motionless sphinx gazing into a crystal which one of "T.H.E.M." had blessed for her especial use.

"Guru-Mahatma, permit this candidate, tyro though she be, to gaze into the impenetrable and reveal the secret of the unconditioned," spake the now rising voice of the acrobatic hypnotist, who, breathing seven times upon her ladyship's white lace neckerchief, at length snapped his fingers, shook his head, and muttered: —

> "O the rook in the eagle's nest,
> O the dog in the river,
> O the shadow of monkeys[1] blest,
> O the mystical shiver."

Her ladyship apparently could not resist the charm of so sublime a stanza from the "holy Mantras," and lifting her eyes slowly from the floor to the ceiling she

---

[1] Monkeys are the sacred animals in the temples at Benares.

uttered in an oracular tone, entirely unlike her own accents and without a shadow of resemblance to her natural style: —

"The temple shall be built; I hereby pledge myself to donate to its erection one thousand pounds sterling, payable on demand of Professor and Mrs. Bromleykite, and I hereby inform you all, that whosoever shall say a word against this sacred project shall be condemned of — "

Here her voice failed, and she sank into a restful slumber, in which she remained for about five minutes, the professor and his wife meanwhile retaining an attitude of. apparently sublime forgetfulness of all terrestrial affairs, when suddenly Lady Porchester's voice and manner changed, and she spoke swiftly and loudly these impressive words: —

"Now shall it be done, now shall the unbelieving witness the power of Indra, now shall the *gurus* of the plains teach the dwellers in Babylon of their secrets; even now do I declare to you this house shall be the place, and this hour the time, when matter shall yield to spirit, and muscle be made to obey the force of will."

Relapsing into silence, a serene smile playing upon her kindly features, Lady Porchester leaned back in her chair as though nothing had happened, and thus she remained, breathing regularly, for fully ten minutes, Miss Poyntz holding her hand.

"Well, what do you think of it?" said the guests, one to another.

"Hypnotic influence, without a doubt," declared Mrs. Spottiswoode; "but as to the source of the intelligence conveyed through the subject's lips, it is unquestionably the Bromleykites. Such manifestations are not at all uncommon; my brother and I have witnessed them in our own house repeatedly. They are not imposture in one respect, for they clearly prove the influence exerted by one mind upon another. The Bromleykites are clearly hypnotists. but how any one with the smallest share of reason can believe that any power superior to the 'operator's' has anything to do with the result, I for one cannot imagine. My brother, who loves a joke dearly, has in more instances than one sent a ludicrous mental telegram across the Atlantic; and as he and Mrs. Wolf Katzenheimer — an eminent lecturer in the United States — are on terms of almost intimate friendship, he was able on one occasion to cause her to exclaim, 'You spiteful old cat!' to a very sober-faced old gentleman whom she was seeking to instruct in mental therapeutics, which is her specialty."

"I do not doubt it," added Madame Discalcelis; "such phenomena are easily accounted for, and when nothing but amusement, even, is the object sought, I see no special harm in hypnotism, though there is nothing whatever spiritually elevating about it; but I do not think it honest to seek to extort pledges of financial support for wild-goose projects by any such uncanny methods; and as to the incantation which preceded the farce this evening, it was an outrage."

Visalia cared nothing for the opinions of the Bromleykites, and she let them know it, though her tones were soft as ever and her manner perfectly ladylike. Mr. and Mrs. Bromleykite, on this occasion however, did not pretend to hear anything they would have wished unsaid; they had read and thoroughly digested Flammarion's *Urania*, and the part of that singular astronomical romance which they took most to heart, was the suggestion that on Mars there are inhabitants provided with ear-lappets, somewhat resembling eyelids, which enable them to open and close their ears, literally as well as figuratively, at pleasure. To hear and not to appear as though one heard is quite an accomplishment, but it is surely a far higher one to be able to so control one's sense of hearing that the very act itself becomes entirely voluntary. This was the feat which the Bromleykites most prided themselves in being able partially to accomplish.

The *séance* which followed the hypnotic exhibit was an almost dark one, though two shaded lamps shed a very subdued radiance across the room. Professor Monteith, who had long been a believer in animal magnetism, was not at all averse to table-tipping and such demonstrations of professedly occult power; he was consequently quite ready to accept a seat at Lady Porchester's right, while Miss Poyntz took her invariable seat at her benefactor's left, to prevent the dire possibility of untoward vibrations from strangers injuriously affecting her ladyship's heart. Mrs. Bromleykite insisted upon sitting between Mrs. Spottiswoode and Mr. Fitzcraven, as she distrusted them and wished to have hold of one hand of each of these possible opponents of occultism while the manifestations were proceeding. Mrs. Gore was placed between her son, who was appointed to sit beside Miss Poyntz and Madame

Discalcelis, who, by the way, highly disapproved of the sitting, but still consented to be a witness or auditor of what transpired. Mr. Bromleykite was, most inconveniently for himself, seated between that, calm, prepossessing lady and Mrs. Spottiswoode, between whom and himself he detected no shadow of affinity, though he was very polite to them.

Some one suggested singing a sacred song; but this was quickly vetoed by Mrs. Gore saying pointedly to her son: "Arthur, I am sure all our friends would like to hear that new ballad you have just received from America, 'A Sailor's Knot.'"

Arthur, knowing his mother's detestation of a travesty on holy things, at once responded, and in an exquisite tenor sang this charming nautical song by Homer Tourjée of the Chicago Musical Conservatory, in a truly enchanting manner.

The last refrain had scarcely ceased; "their hearts were tied in a sailor's knot" still reverberated on the air, when Lady Porchester enthusiastically exclaimed: "Oh, the dear spirits; they are carrying off my bracelets!"

"Illustrious lady," breathed a deep, guttural voice at her elbow, "not spirits, but *gurus;* your spirit friends are resting in peace ineffable in the perfect illusion of *Devachan,* and no discarded *shell* can babble forth in this pure atmosphere its siren tones of deep seduction to mislead the hungerers for living bread. But hush! the *Guru Padmonodonovarkootmohino* is removing now the diamond pendants from your ears, and when these gems return to you after their baptism in astral tears, shed by the all-immolated victims of the most unutterable *Grief*, they will convey to you, even from the skirts of 'T.H.E.M.' an influence redolent of Para-Quislamascha."

Lights were now permitted; conditions were not favorable for any experiments with other members of the circle. Lady Porchester was sleeping sweetly in her chair, with her wrists devoid of bracelets and her ears destitute of jewels.

Presently she awoke, whispering, "Oh, how divine are 'T.H.E.Y.'" She was evidently happy, no harm had befallen her; she was more than satisfied with the result of the *séance*, and none of her guests had anything to comment upon on their account.

"Well, what do you think of it?" questioned Professor Monteith of her ladyship's companion.

"I cannot answer you," responded Katherine; "I am quite a novice in the new doctrines of Occultism, though my experience with old-fashioned Spiritualism has been quite extensive."

"What do you think, my dear madam?" the professor continued, this time addressing Madame Discalcelis, and they were now in a remote part of the spacious drawing-room, far from the corner where the Bromleykites and Lady Porchester were constituting a mutual admiration tableau.

"Ventriloquism and conjuring, and not a very fine display of either," was Visalia's immediate reply.

"What, you say that who believe in the spiritual?"

"I emphatically say that, and as emphatically do I declare my *knowledge* of the spiritual," was the final answer of the lady addressed.

CHAPTER IV.

THE MYSTIC AT HOME.

IN a charming suburban residence about ten miles from Liverpool Street station, on a lovely June day, when the fashionable London season of '93 was rapidly nearing its close, Madame Discalcelis found herself in the presence of a modest gentleman about thirty years of age, plainly attired in the customary house-dress of men who attach more value to comfort than to display. Speaking with clear, measured accents on the subject which possessed his brain and evidently lay nearest to his heart, his fine lustrous eyes glowing with suppressed fervor, he uttered the following noteworthy statements concerning *the ultimate constitution of matter and the action of the force regulating its phenomena*,— statements which surely challenge the closest attention of the whole scientific world.

"First. Matter is capable of infinite subdivision.

"Second. In the aggregation of matter, force or energy is stored up or conserved.

"Third. In the dissociation of matter, force is liberated.

"Fourth. All matter is in a state of perpetual

activity, whether the substance under consideration be inanimate or animated, visible or invisible.

"Fifth. There is no dividing of matter and force into two distinct terms, as they both are ONE. FORCE is liberated matter. Matter is force in bondage.

"Sixth. All motion is synchronous; no sound or movement can be made but all that moves or sounds does so in harmony with something.

"Seventh. All structures, whether crystalline or homogeneous, have for their unit structures minute bodies called molecules. It is the motion of these molecules with which we have particularly to deal; as in experimental research and demonstration, when we produce an action upon one molecule we do so upon all the molecules constituting the mass operated upon.

"Eighth. These molecules have an envelope, rotating with inconceivable rapidity, formed of a high tenuous *ether*, whose place in the order of subdivision ranks third, the three divisions being, — first, molecular; second, atomic; third, atomolic! (For convenience' sake we will use the term *atomolic* in place of *etheric* in our subsequent definitions.)

"Ninth. This atomolic substance has a density approximately 986,000 times that of steel, enabling it to permeate steel as light penetrates glass; this rotating envelope of atomolic substance is in a *liquid* condition. There are four conditions of matter; viz. *solid*, *liquid*, *gaseous*, and *ultra-gaseous*. These conditions result from greater or lesser range of oscillation of the composing units individually: this is equally true, whether the units are molecules, atoms, atomoles, planets, or suns. *But one* LAW *governs all matter*.

"Tenth. This molecular envelope, rotating with such great velocity, holds in its embrace the next subdivision of matter, the atomic. There cannot ever be more or less than three atoms in any molecule. These are placed so as to form a triangle in the interior; they rest in a condition of substance, or matter, we will term inter-molecular. In this inter-molecular substance we find an enormous energy or force in bondage, held thus by the rotating envelope enclosing it. Were we to rotate a spun brass shell, say nine inches in diameter, at a very much less rate of speed than that at which the molecular envelope rotates,—say nine hundred revolutions per second,—its equator would first bulge out, then form into an oval disc. A solid block of wood subject to such revolution would swiftly fly to pieces. The rotating envelope of a molecule, unlike these, the greater its velocity of rotation, the greater is its compression toward the centre of the molecule. The rotation of this envelope is of such a nature as to produce an internal pressure upon every portion from every point of the molecule as a sphere. Were we to consider a rotating envelope as ordinarily understood, it would be one in which the envelope rotated around an equator having poles of no rotation; *i.e.* the poles would not possess the compressing force of the equator: the result would therefore be a compressed equator, and the inter-molecular substance would pass out without resistance at the poles.

"Eleventh. If it be possible let us conceive of an envelope with an equator, but destitute of poles, a number of these rotating over the sphere, this atomolic envelope possessing an almost infinite attractive force toward the centre of the molecule, pressing in the inter-molecular substance, where it is held until this revolving envelope becomes negatized by a certain order of vibration, when the enclosed matter rushes out to its natural condition of concordant tenuity, as in the case of gunpowder, dynamite, and nitro-glycerine. This force, we must see, has been held in the embrace of the rotating envelopes of the unit-structures, or where does it come from? This force at the time of an explosion was liberated by shock or fire, both being orders of imparted motion or vibration. How much greater the result would be were we to associate a scientific instrument now completed, and shortly to be given to the world, with such an agent as nitro-glycerine; one pound of nitro-glycerine would have its destructive force augmented beyond all possible control. These instruments are carefully concealed by wise masters from all persons save the few who are already prepared to study their potency with the exclusive end in view of aiding the real scientific progress of humanity; and, furthermore, it may be truly stated that a ferocious sensualist, however powerful his intellect, would be utterly unable to either comprehend or operate one of these marvellous constructions.

"Twelfth. Next in order of consideration is the second subdivision of matter — the atomic. The atom has the same rotating envelope as the molecule, governed by the same laws of rotation and compression. The rotating envelope holds in its embrace the inter-atomic substance and three atomoles resting in it, the atomoles within the atom being constructed after the same pattern as the atom and the molecule, obedient to the same laws; the atomolic being simply the third subdivision of matter. The threefold order is absolutely universal.

"Thirteenth. The atomolic substance is what is termed the ether which fills all space and is the transmitting medium for all celestial and terrestrial forces. This is the *liquid ether* of occult science.

"Fourteenth. The atomoles are made up of *atomolini* (singular *atomolinus*); the subdivision of matter from this point is beyond man's power, as at this point it escapes all control of apparatus, passing through glass and hardened steel as a luminous flame without heat, which is hardly seen before it vanishes, — a perpetual flame coldly luminous.

"Sixteenth. This again, from previous analysis, is made up according to the triple order, and may again be subject to subdivision, even to infinity."

"In my next interview with you," said Aldebaran to his visitor, "I shall endeavor to show you the law governing the triple aggregation of force and matter, which is, in brief, as follows: first, CREATIVE SOURCE; second, TRANSMISSIVE WAVE; third, EFFECT."

The mystical scientist then took a courteous leave of his visitor, and after seeing her to her carriage, hurried to the suburban station connecting with the underground railway to Aldsgate, where he had important business with a distinguished mechanical engineer.

CHAPTER V.

FURTHER REVELATIONS.

On the occasion of the next meeting between the lady and the scientist the latter gave utterance to the following remarkable truth.

Each molecule has three envelopes. The most external one the professor illustrated by an india-rubber ball on which he had traced a number of meridian lines. On another ball were represented the three envelopes. The outer hemisphere of one of the envelopes is removed to show the under envelope, the outer hemisphere of which is removed in still another part of the diagram to show the inmost envelope. A third diagram was then produced to show the position of the atoms which the rotating envelopes enclose. A fourth diagram showed the lines of interference of the rotating envelopes. There being three perfect envelopes, these of necessity must have six poles, to which add the neutral centre of the sphere itself, comprising the origin of the septenary of mysticism which is universal in nature. The fifth diagram exhibited showed the subdivision of matter into atomic, atomolic, and atomolinic. A black disc representing a sphere shows the negative atom; two white discs also representing spheres illustrate the two positive atoms in the triad, completing the tertiary aggregation forming the molecule. Each atom is in turn composed of three atomoles; in the negative atom are three positive atomoles, positive in the sense of activity; in the positive atom are also three atomoles, two of which are negative, *i.e.* passive, and one positive. The negative is always that which seeks the neutral centre; the positive represents the active radiating energy: for instance, the sun is a medium for transmitting radiant energy of positive order, which all the planets receive negatively, *i.e.* it focalizes upon their neutral centres. This order extends to infinity. The final diagram presented was simply intended to further elucidate the action of the rotating envelopes, illustrating the compressing force of the rotating spheral and the protection of the neutral poles. In the rotating envelopes force acts in the opposite direction to its action in the revolution of the earth, where the centrifugal action is greatest at the equator; and the greater the speed of rotation, the greater the centre-fleeing force.

In the case of the etheric envelope, however, the greater the speed of rotation, the more powerful is the centripetal (centre-seeking) force which compresses the atoms within; the pressure, therefore, is greatest at the equator and gradually lessens toward the poles. If there were only one envelope, the tendency would be for the atoms to be oblate, to fly out at the poles, where the pressure is least. A beautiful provision of nature obviates this, by providing three envelopes, rotating one within the other, like three shells; the line of greatest internal pressure in each one of which being protected by the equatorial lines, the line of greatest pressure covering the line of least pressure on the others. Each of the three atoms is placed directly under one pole of each of the three envelopes.

If the rotating envelope of the molecule were in any way checked in its motion, the enclosed matter would immediately burst forth, producing the phenomenon of integration, releasing from its previously pent-up condition a volume of matter many times as great as that before disintegration took place. Sound-force moving at certain rates of vibration negatizes the action of the rotating envelopes, producing conditions which result in their breaking up, followed by the separation of the atoms contained in those envelopes, and also of intermolecular substance occupying space not taken up by the atoms. By successive orders of vibration the atoms, atomoles, and atomolini are disintegrated, and so on to the luminous order, where all control ceases.

The human brain being formed of an inestimable number of spherical resonators, termed in medical science *nerve cells*, forming the gray matter of the brain, these minute spheres take up the *thought force* which permeates all space in endless waves, eternally active. This force we term *atomolic;* the cells are composed of *atomoles*, whose vibratory motions under the action of universal *thought force* result in the phenomena of thought, cognition, intellection, etc. Understanding this, no one should continue to feel surprise at the varying emotions and impulses of a human being in an undeveloped state, as only by developed WILL can the motions of this force be directed.

The entire human economy, in the action of all its functions, assimilations, and motions, is the result of differentiation of this unitary force, all tending to supply the instrument connecting the organism with this force (the brain) with certain gases whereby it sustains its ceaseless action from birth to death: these gases supply the rotating envelopes with necessary substance for their continued activity. Were this supply cut off, death would immediately ensue; it is a fact well demonstrated that the resonating brain-structure is the first to undergo decomposition.

In all embodied conditions of the manifested universe, the law of harmony reigns supreme; the cause of this manifestation is the result of the positive being stronger than the negative; the positive is everywhere the dominant order of the universe; this reality is perfectly embodied in the words I AM; it is the reason why annihilation is both inconceivable and impossible in the universe. The truth of this statement can be experimentally demonstrated; its law is found in all threefold aggregations, and there is a *universal* trinity composed of two positives and one negative. Eternal consciousness, immortal life, and an infinite order of beings is the result, whilst every provision is made in the order of creation for the happiness and enjoyment of all manifested beings. Conditions are also provided whereby satiety falls to the lot of none.

The eternally conscious entity — call it by whatever name we please — moves in cycles as eternal and infinite as itself; it oscillates and vibrates perpetually and is never unconscious of any present condition, be it pain or pleasure, joy or sorrow, shame or glory; like the pendulum of a clock or the sun, moon, or tides, it swings from the one to the other of these conditions, now in pleasure, now in pain, by its contact with the extremes of all varying conditions, like a child which throws up its head and laughing for joy exclaims, *I know I am.*

The professor, who was a most industrious toiler in nature's deep arcanum, smilingly exclaimed as he finished his discourse: "This is no theory or doctrine to be accepted on trust; it is the demonstrated result of years of experimental research, and as clearly demonstrable as any problem in mathematics."

DIAGRAM 1.

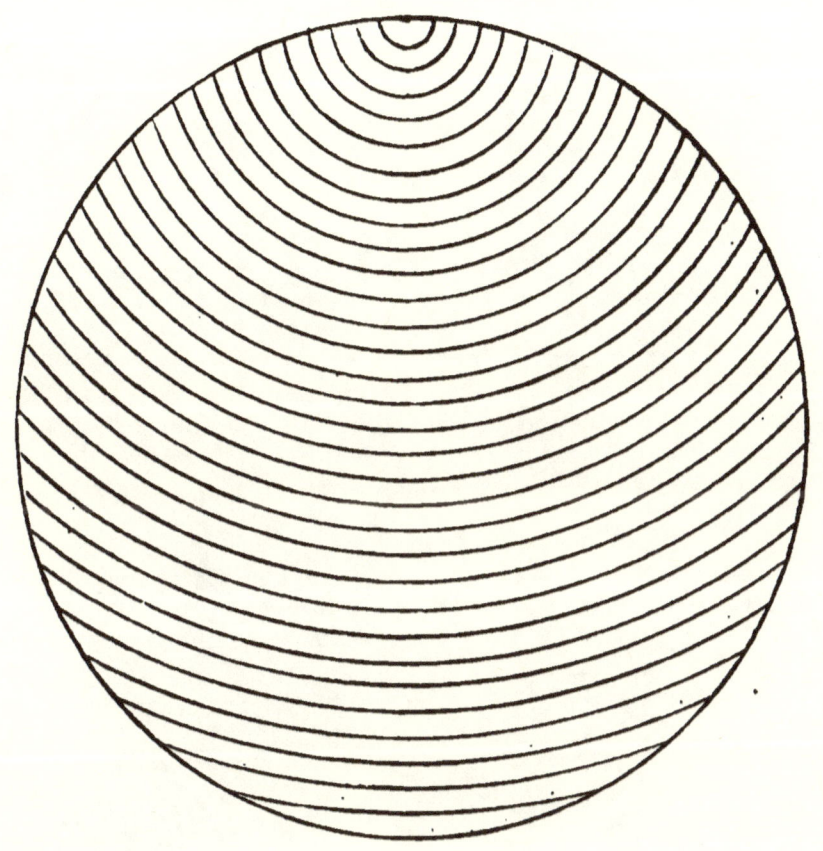

External View of Atom.

See page 51.

DIAGRAM 2.

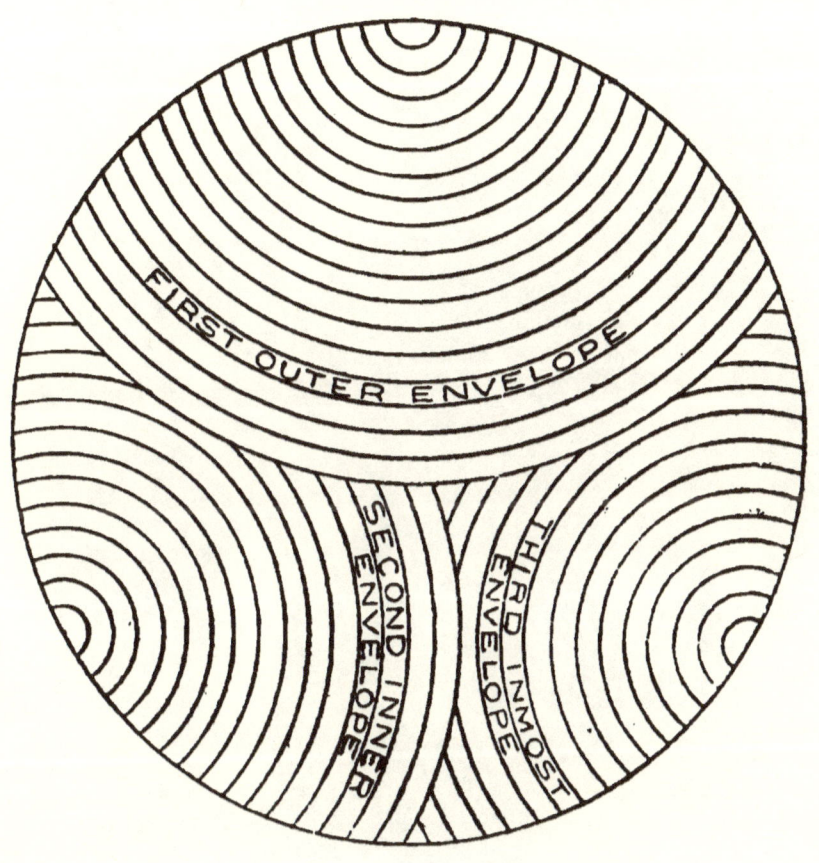

Showing Sections of the Three Envelopes.
See page 51.

DIAGRAM 3.

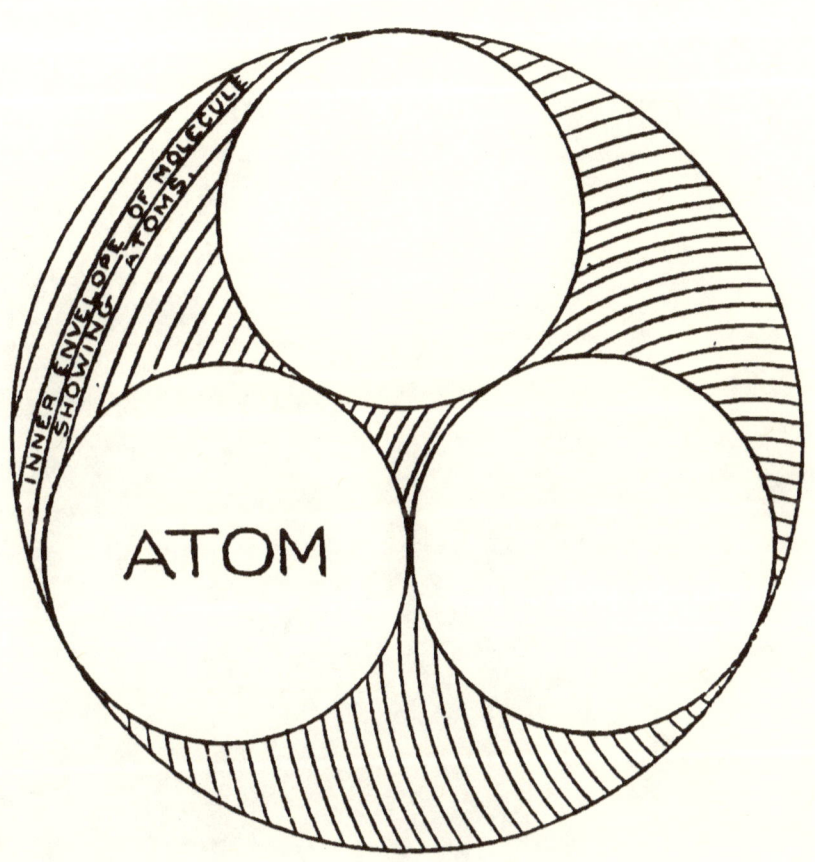

Showing Positions of Atoms in Inner Envelope.
See page 51.

DIAGRAM 4.

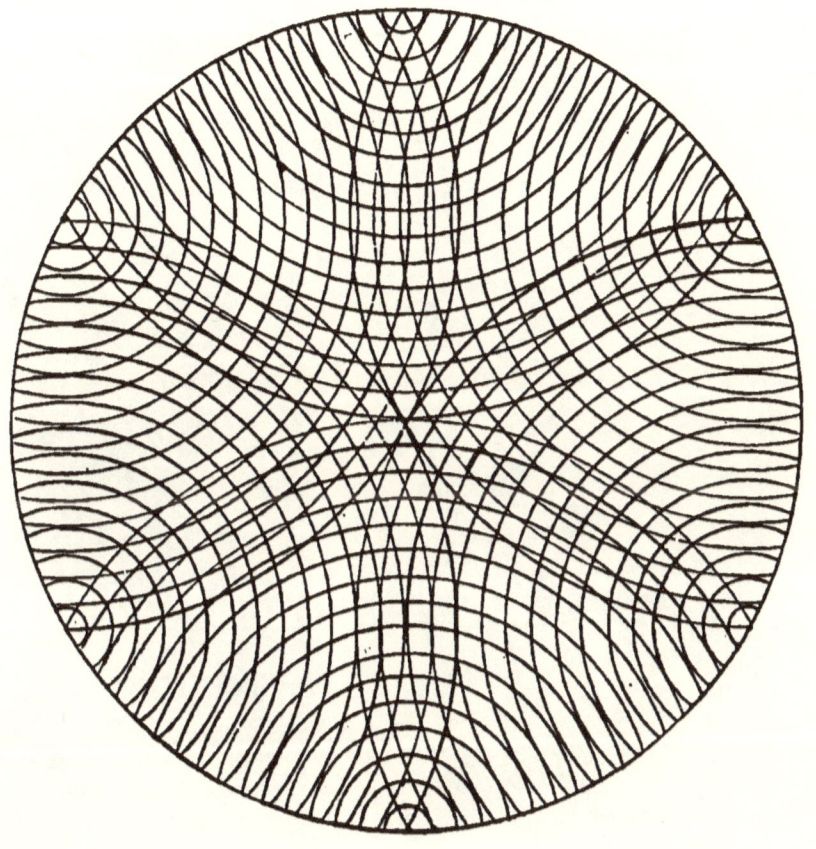

Showing Lines of Interference of Triple Envelope.
See page 51.

DIAGRAM 5.

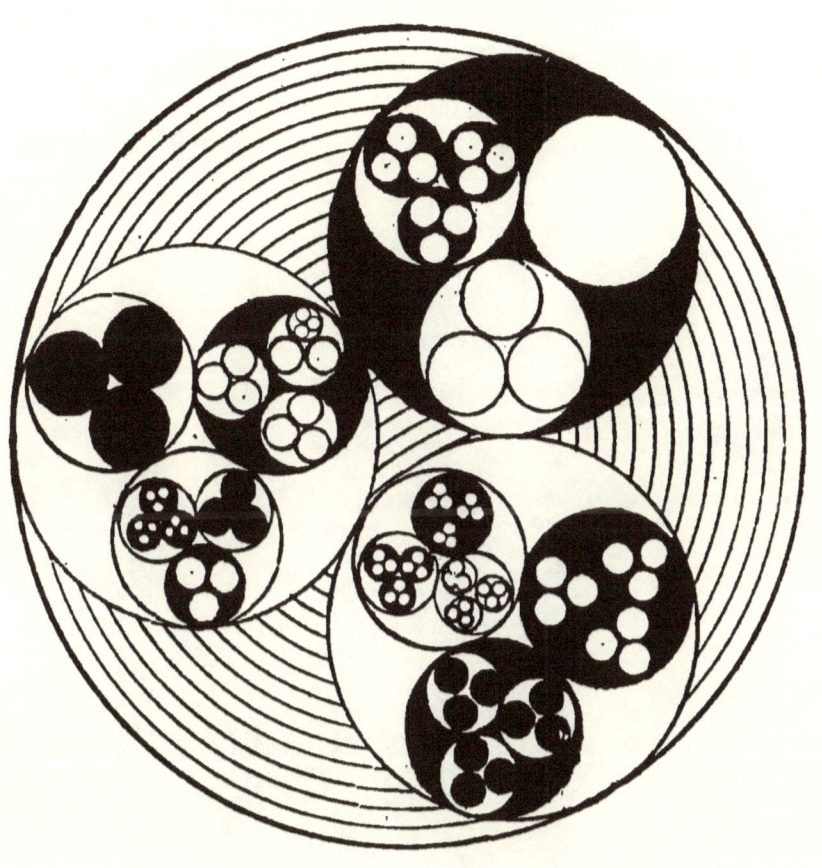

Molecule showing Subdivision of Matter.

See page 51.

DIAGRAM 6.

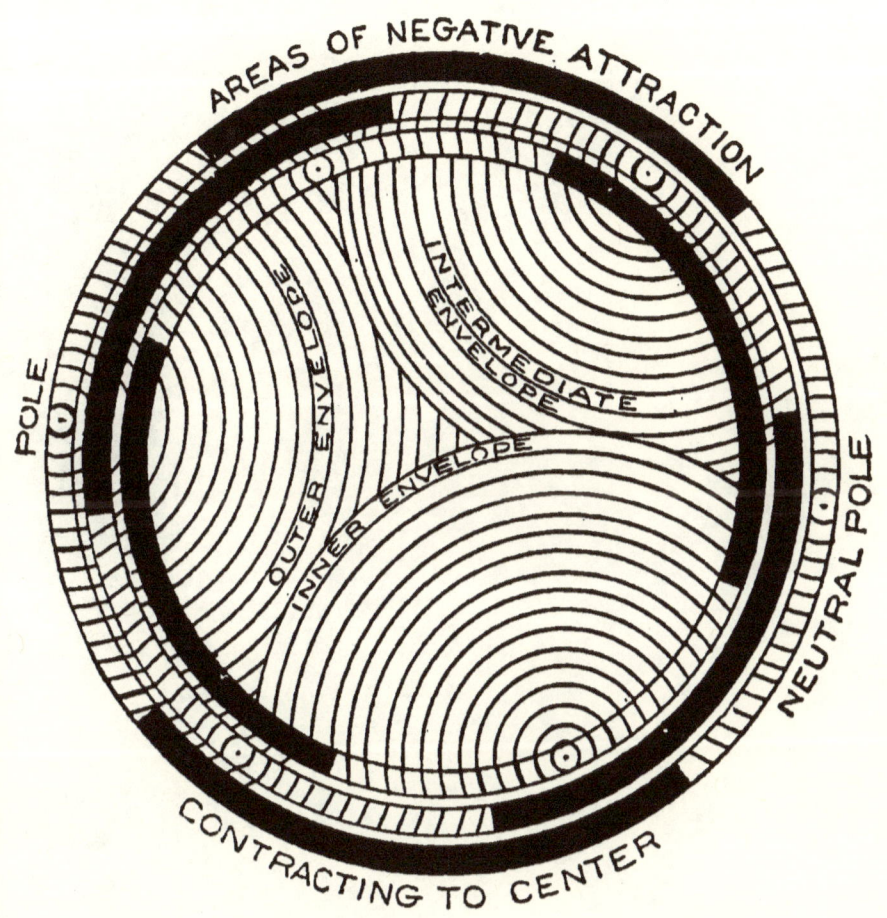

See page 52.

CHAPTER VI.

THE BASIS OF A NEW SCIENCE.

THE following extraordinary statements are given in the exact words of Aldebaran as he conversed with Madame Discalcelis on the marvellous work in which she found him ever tirelessly engaged, and she soon became a frequent visitor to his sanctum: she was one of the very few persons he always welcomed.

"The newly discovered forces, and laws governing all forces, make possible the processes herein described. Scientific investigations no longer consist in a blind groping after facts; an untried chemical combination can now be planned and its results predicted. Synthetical operations covering the entire domain of organic chemistry can be worked according to simple rules and methods deducible from these newly discovered laws and by the aid of these, to us, new forces. With a knowledge of these facts it is possible for man to work a wondrous change in his methods of manipulating matter.

"I shall be happy to present you with a table of definitions which I have written out as briefly and succinctly as possible; and though I doubt not the definitions will be well-nigh incomprehensible to the masses, you are at liberty to make any use of them you please in your literary endeavors to enlighten humanity."

Definitions.

Atomoles are elementary units of matter uniform in size and weight, and exist in solid, liquid, gaseous, and isolated forms.
Atoms are multiple combinations of atomoles, and they also exist in solid, liquid, gaseous, and isolated forms.
Simple Molecules are formed by the union of two atoms of the same kind.
Compound Molecules are unions of two atoms of dissimilar kind.
Complex Molecules are unions of molecules with other molecules or atoms.
Pitch is the relative frequency of vibration.
Vibration is the rhythmical motion of a body within itself.
Oscillation is a rhythmically recurring translatory movement.
Transmissive Energy is rhythmical motion of condensation and rarefaction produced by the vibrating or oscillating body in the medium in which it is immersed.
Attraction is the mutual approach of aggregates caused by concentrated waves of harmonic energy, tending to move in line of least resistance, by becoming the centre of one series of concentric waves instead of two or more series.
Harmony is the simultaneous vibration of two or more bodies whose harmonics do not produce discords, and whose fundamental pitches are harmonics of the lowest pitch, or are a unison with the resultant notes or overtones, or undertones, of any two or more of them.
Ether is an atomolic liquid 986,000 times the density of steel.
Electricity is the oscillation of the atomoles of an atom.
Induction is the transmissive force of the electric vibration in ether.

Magnetism is the mutual attraction of juxtaposed bodies vibrating at unison or harmonic electric pitches.

Gravity is the mutual attraction of atomoles.

Gravism is the transmissive form through a medium of atomoles in the fourth state, or a medium composed of atomolini.

Atomolini are ultimate units of atomoles, and when in a liquid state are the media for the transmission of gravism. The illimitable divisibility and aggregation of matter is a logical sequence.

1. Law of Matter and Force:

    Coextensive and coeternal with space and duration, there exists an infinite and unchangeable quantity of atomoles, the base of all matter; these are in a state of constant vibratory motion, infinite in extent, unchangeable in quantity, the initial of all forms of energy.

2. Law of Corporeal Vibrations:

    All coherent aggregates when isolated from like bodies, or when immersed or confined in media composed of matter in a different state, vibrate at a given ascertainable pitch.

3. Law of Corporeal Oscillation:

    All coherent aggregates not isolated from like bodies, oscillate at a period-frequency varying with the tensions that augment and diminish the state of equilibrium.

4. Law of Harmonic Vibrations:

    All coherent aggregates are perpetually vibrating at a period-frequency corresponding to some harmonic ratio of the fundamental pitch of the vibrating body; this pitch is a multiple of the pitch of the atomole.

5. Law of Transmissive Vibraic Energy:

    All oscillating and vibrating coherent aggregates create, in the media in which they are immersed, outwardly propagated concentric waves of alternate condensation and rarefaction, having a period-frequency identical with the pitch of the aggregate.

Scholium: All forms of transmissive energy can be focussed, reflected, refracted, diffracted, transformed, and diminished in intensity inversely as the square of the distance from the originating source.

6. Law of Sympathetic Oscillation:

Coherent aggregates immersed in a medium pulsating at their natural pitch simultaneously oscillate with the same frequency, whether the pitch of the medium be a unison, or any harmonic of the fundamental pitch of the creative aggregate.

7. Law of Attraction:

Juxtaposed coherent aggregates vibrating in unison, or harmonic ratio, are mutually attracted.

8. Law of Repulsion:

Juxtaposed coherent aggregates vibrating in discord are mutually repelled.

9. Law of Cycles:

Coherent aggregates harmonically united constitute centres of vibration bearing relation to the fundamental pitch not multiples of the harmonic pitch, and the production of secondary unions between themselves generate pitches that are discords, either in their unisons, or overtones with the original pitch; from harmony is generated discord, the inevitable cause of perpetual transformation.

10. Law of Harmonic Pitch:

Any aggregate in a state of vibration develops in addition to its fundamental pitch a series of vibration in symmetrical sub-multiple portions of itself, bearing ratios of one, two, three, or more times its fundamental pitch.

11. Law of Force:

Energy manifests itself in three forms: *Creative*, the vibrating aggregate; *Transmissive*, being the propagation of isochronous waves through the media in which it is immersed; *Attractive*, being its action upon other aggregates capable of vibrating in unisons or harmony.

12. Law of Oscillating Atomic Substances:

Coherent atomic substances are capable of oscillating at a pitch varying directly as the density, and inversely as the linear dimensions from one period of frequency per unit of time to the 21st octave above, producing the creative force of Sonity, whose transmissive force (Sound) is propagated through the media of solids, liquids, and gases, and whose static effect (Sonism) produces attractions and repulsions between sympathetically vibrating bodies according to the Law of Harmonic Attraction and Repulsion.

13. Law of Sono-thermity:

Internal vibrations of atomic substances and atomic molecules are capable of vibrating at a period-frequency directly as their density, inversely as their linear dimensions, directly as the coefficient of their tension from the 21st to the 42d octaves, producing the creative force (Sono-thermity), whose transmissive force (Sono-therm) is propagated in solid, liquid, gaseous, and ultra-gaseous media, statically producing adhesions and molecular unions, or disintegration, according to the Law of Harmonic Attraction and Repulsion.

14. Law of Oscillating Atoms:

All atoms when in a state of tension are capable of oscillating at a pitch inversely as the cube of their atomic weights, and directly as their tension from 42 to 63 octaves per second, producing the creative force (Thermism), whose transmissive force (Rad-energy) propagated in solid, liquid, and gaseous ether, produces the static effects (Cohesion and Chemism) on other atoms of association, or dissociation, according to the Law of Harmonic Attraction and Repulsion.

Scholium: Dark radiant heat begins at absolute zero temperature, and extends through light, chemical rays, actinic rays, and infra-violet rays, up to the dissociation of all molecules to the 63d octave.

15. Law of Vibrating Atomolic Substances:

Atoms are capable of vibrating within themselves at a pitch inversely as the Dyne (the local coefficient of Gravity), and as the atomic volume, directly as the atomic weight, producing the creative force (Electricity), whose transmissive force is propagated through atomolic solids, liquids, and gases, producing induction and the static effect of magnetism upon other atoms of attraction or repulsion, according to the Law of Harmonic Attraction and Repulsion.

Scholium: The phenomena of Dynamic Electricity through a metallic conductor and of induction are identical. In a metallic conductor, the transmission is from atom to atom, through homologous interstices, filled with ether, presenting small areas in close proximity. In crystalline structures, heat, which expands the atoms, by twisting them produces striæ, increases the resistance, etc. Between parallel wires and through air the induction takes place from large areas through a rarefied medium composed of a mixture of substances, whose atoms are separated by waves of repulsion of various pitches, discordant to electric vibrations; the said atoms sympathetically absorb the vibrations and dissipate from themselves, as centres, concentric waves of electric energy which produces heat and gravism.

16. Law of Oscillating Atomoles:

Atomoles oscillating at a uniform pitch (determined by their uniform size and weight) produce the creative force *Atomolity*, whose transmissive form, *Gravism*, is propagated through more rarefied media, producing the static effect upon all other atomoles, denominated *Gravity*.

17. Law of Transformation of Forces:

All forces are different forms of *Universal Energy* unlike in their period-frequency, merging into each other by imperceptible increments; each form representing the compass of 21 octaves. Each form or pitch may be transformed into an equivalent quantity of another pitch above or below it in the scale of 105 octaves. The transformation can occur only. through its static effect, developing vibrations of harmonic pitches above and below their fundamental vibration, or developing with juxtaposed aggregates, resultant and difference, or third order, as the case may be.

Scholium: A table of the intervals and harmonics of the normal harmonic scale will indicate the ratios in which the transformation of forces will occur.

18. Law of Atomic Pitch:

Atoms have each a different and definite pitch, at which they naturally vibrate.

Scholium: Atomic pitch is determined directly from its simple spectrum.

Scholium: Atomic pitch is determined by computations from its associate spectrum with all other atoms, as in known spectra.

Scholium: Atomic pitches are more important working data than atomic weights; tables of atomic pitches *must* be precise.

19. Law of Variation of Atomic Pitch by Rad-energy:

The higher harmonics and overtones of projected rad-energy are of a pitch sufficiently high to cause the atom to expand; by causing the atomoles to vibrate systematically the same influence will cause the atom to contract, and thus by changing the volume, atomic pitch is varied.

20. Law of Variation of Atomic Pitch by Electricity and Magnetism:

Electricity and Magnetism produce internal vibrations in the atom, which are followed by proportional changes in volume and, therefore, pitch.

21. Law of Variation of Atomic Pitch by Temperature:

Atoms in chemical combination oscillate with increasing amplitude *directly* as the temperature, and simultaneously absorb overtones of higher harmonics, producing expansion of volume and diminution of pitch.

Rule: The gradual approach of the temperature of harmonic combination can be observed by mutually comparing superimposed spectra; chemical combination commences when the fundamental lines of each spectrum bear harmonic ratios by linear measurement.

22. Law of Pitch of Atomic Oscillation:

Atoms not isolated and in a state of tension between forces

that oppose and increase the equilibrium oscillate bodily at a pitch that is a resultant of the atomic weight, atomic volume, and tension.

23. Law of Variation of Pitch of Atomic Oscillation by Pressure:
The frequency of atomic oscillation increases and diminishes inversely as the square of the pressure.

24. Law of Variation of Atomic Oscillation by Temperature:
The force of cohesion diminishes inversely as the square of the distance the atoms are apart, and the force of the chemical affinity diminishes in the same ratio. Heat increases the amplitude of the oscillations in a direct ratio to the temperature of the natural scale.

Scholium: New thermometers and accurate thermometric tables, on the natural bases, wherein doubling the temperature doubles the pitch of the transmissive energy, are required. Such a table of temperature will bear natural relations to atomic weights, pitches, specific heats, chemical affinities, fusions, solubilities, etc., and will disclose new laws. One table for each must be constructed.

25. Law of Variation of Atomic Oscillation by Electricity:
The electric current destroys cohesion and chemical tension directly as square of current in ampères, inversely as the resistance in ohms, inversely as the chemical equivalent, and conversely as the coefficient of the difference between the freezing and volatilizing temperature of mass acted upon.

26. Law of Variation of Atomic Oscillation by Sono-thermism:
Diminishes the tensions directly as the quantity of heat developed, and in antithetical proportion to the harmonics absolved.

27. Law of Chemical Affinity:
Atoms whose atomic pitches are in either unison, harmonic or concordant ratios, unite to form molecules.

Corollary: When two atoms are indifferent, they may be made to unite by varying the pitch of either, or both.

Scholium: This necessitates the construction of tables representing variation of atomic pitches by temperature, pressure, etc.

Scholium: Tables of all harmonics and concords, and harmonics founded upon a normal harmonic scale, are equally essential.

Scholium: Optical instruments may be made to measure pitches of energy.

28. Law of Chemical Dissociation:
If the pitch of either atom, in a molecule, be raised or lowered; or, if they both be unequally raised or lowered in pitch until the mutual ratio be that of a discord; or, if the oscillation amplitude be augmented by heat until the atoms are with the concentric waves of attraction, — the atoms will separate.

29. Law of Chemical Transposition:
New molecules must be harmonics of the fundamental pitch.

30. Law of Chemical Substitution (too complex for brief statement).

31. Law of Catalysis:
The presence of harmonics and discords.

32. Law of Molecular Synthesis and Combination (Organic):
The molecular pitch must be a derived harmony of the radicals.

Scholium: Reconstruction of electric units to represent pitches and amplitudes.

33. Law of Chemical Morphology:
The angle of crystallization is determined by the relation between the molecular pitch of the crystallizing substance to the vibration-density of the liquid depositing it.

34. Law of Atomic Dissociation:
Overtones of high rad-energy pitches produce separation of the atomoles and recombinations among the atomolic molecules of the atoms.

35. Law of Atomolic Synthesis of Chemical Elements:
    Harmonic pitches of atomolity produce association of etheric-atomolic particles to form atoms: the kind of atom is determinable by the pitches employed.

36. Law of Heat:
    Atoms under the tension of chemical combination oscillate with an amplitude directly as the temperature, inversely as the pressure, and as the square of the specific heat. Diminishing the pitch of oscillation inversely as the square of the distance of the atoms apart, and simultaneously increasing the vibrating pitch of the atom by absorption of overtones and higher harmonics.

37. Law of Electro-chemical Equivalents:
    An atom vibrates sympathetically under the influence of electric energy, such undertones of which are absorbed as are a harmonic or harmony of the electric pitch; the amount of energy absorbed being directly as the arithmetical ratio of the undertone of the fundamental electric pitch.
    Scholium: A table of electro-chemical equivalents on the normal basis will indicate the electrical conditions and amount of chemical change.

38. Law of Cohesion:
    The cohesion between atoms diminishes directly as the square root of the pressure and temperature, and as the square of electric intensity.

39. Law of Refractive Indices:
    A table of the refractive indices of substances indicates their molecular pitch; and in connection with *crystalline* form the phase of molecular oscillation.

40. Law of Electric Conductivity:
    Electric energy is transmitted through homogeneous bodies with a completeness in direct proportion as the atoms are more or less perfect harmonics of the electric pitch, but not at all through substances whose atoms are discordant to the electric

pitch; also through molecular substances, when their resultant notes are harmonics of the electric pitch, — the transmissions being *inversely* as the temperature, *directly* as the density diminished in proportion to the amount of crystallization, and inversely as the cube of the dyne, also directly as the reciprocal of the local magnetic intensity.

As we believe the above statements to be of priceless value to the world, in proportion as they are comprehended, we offer no apology to our readers for introducing so many technicalities, but publish them in the expectant hope that some struggling seeker after scientific verity may find in them a key to the solution of many perplexing mysteries.

CHAPTER VII.

THE AGNOSTIC AND THE MYSTIC.

HAVING been permitted by Madame Discalcelis to see some of the wonderful documents which Aldebaran kindly permitted her to carry home, Professor Monteith was in quite a flurry of excitement when the hour came that he was at liberty to present himself before the mysterious young man so deeply versed in occult knowledge.

With scarcely a preliminary, for time was precious, Aldebaran at once entered upon the following profound reply to the professor's first inquiry, which was: "I crave especially some light, indeed all you can give me, on the moral or spiritual bearings of your philosophy. By what term," inquired Professor Monteith, "shall we define that force which, when differentiated, expresses itself on the lower planes of manifestation as charity, self-forgetfulness, compassion, and the tendency of all illuminated ones to association in universal brotherhood?"

"I hold," responded Aldebaran, "that ONE SUPREME FORCE, which we may term the incomprehensible, holds within itself all these sublime qualities, as an octave embraces its many tones. This force expressed in the human organism, in the varied impulses already designated, has what may be termed CONCORDANT CHORD-SETTINGS dominated by one or other of the above-named differentiations of this supreme force. Now let us ask what makes human beings differ the one from the other. The reason we give for this striking natural phenomenon is that in one individual these chord-settings are allowed full amplitude in action, while in others they are suppressed, and by suppression rendered latent. To illustrate: we will picture a beggar asking alms of a richly dressed gentleman, who passes by entirely oblivious of the suppliant's needs; but here the wonderful law of sympathetic action intercedes, making the wealthy individual comprehend the necessitous condition of the pauper. At this point the *ego* enters the chamber of ordeal; here, in commonplace life, in every-day surroundings, man is tried; this is *initiation*. The well-to-do man goes on his way, not caring to stop, hurried perchance by the urgency of worldly affairs; the chord-setting representing that differentiation of infinite force called by us *compassion*, acting upon its concordant chord-setting, loudly proclaims to the *ego* what is right action, and the opportunity passing when it should be seized, powerfully exerts its force against the will of the personality that would suppress its action. Here is where the battle is fought; simple though the illustration may appear, it forcibly sets forth the actual conflict continually waging between divine wisdom and mortal error, carelessness, and ignorance. The man of wealth and position goes on, perhaps, for some distance, the battle all the while continuing; finally, he stops and turns back, he yields to the dominating influence of that chord-setting; he gives the beggar alms and goes on his way with the skies bright above him: he has won a battle he will not have to fight again. Understand that victory is won, not by the giving of alms, but by yielding to that divine force-differentiation. If this chord-setting had not retained its dominance, it would only require a few instances of the above type to render it latent, and when latent the person is no longer amenable to influences calculated to arouse compassion. In like manner, other centres may be rendered latent by repeated suppression, until we find a person so dead to all appeals from the various chord-settings that his whole course in life is represented by the sum-total of the antagonisms internally produced: results proving this are seen every day. You ask why do people commit such blunders and perform such acts as they do, all the while seemingly unable to help themselves. The reason is that they have rendered latent these centres which otherwise would have given them the power to rightly control their deeds instead of being, as they now are, dominated exclusively by the forces of aggregated matter which we usually call the self-will of the outer personality, as distinguished from the distinctly humane individuality which always responds to a divine appeal. It can be readily seen from this example that a man can mould himself practically as he chooses; though he may have to encounter many obstacles erected by himself in past periods of earthly existence, as he comes to earth anew with these chord-settings latent, or developed to the extent they were so, at the conclusion of his last earth-embodiment; a man has therefore only to carefully examine the condition of these settings to learn whether they are latent or developed: if latent, he knows well that if he yields to the dominance of the chord-settings of the supreme force — and he needs no monitor other than these to instruct him, their voice being loud-toned, full, strong, deep, and high — to carry him on to the consummation of his highest ideal, their suppression leading him to the lowest condition in which we behold that section of humanity which is dominated by the action of the blind forces inherent in aggregated matter, — forces which are at all times powerfully and intimately associated with every one who possesses a material body. The work of arousing to activity the latent chord-settings is sometimes equivalent to giving birth to an entirely new condition in the person, the intellect and the imagination having to actively co-operate in the endeavor to produce even the minutest degree of activity. In such persons their hardest experiences may be of the greatest benefit to them, if rightly taken; for it is through certain orders of experience — not unattended with suffering — that these centres are powerfully acted upon. The foregoing illustration of the merchant and the beggar introduces one in whom the action of these centres is to a certain degree active. In experiences where the emotions are *intensely* aroused their action is far greater, and we may see the result of the conflict, in the event of a person of hitherto unnoticeable traits being developed either into a person of crabbed, irritable disposition or into one of considerable moral beauty and attractiveness, and all because a centre hitherto dormant has been powerfully aroused or more completely suppressed. Who knows but that all the varieties of disposition we see expressed every hour in the persons of those about us is due to HABIT; in the case of the sweet and lovable, to the habit of constant yielding to the dominance of what we may term super-celestial force, while on the other hand, the sour and morose are but the suffering victims of their own habitual suppression of these same divine centres of radiation, which are continually dispersing the divine energy focalized upon them throughout the eternal ages of unwasting life. Concerning *circumstances* let it be most emphatically stated that they never need be permitted to suppress the upward tendencies of our nature; that they have, like *all* experiences, an opportunity contained within them, to act either for the more perfect dominance of the celestial or the terrestrial, none need deny; but it rests with every individual to *embrace* or *reject* opportunities as he will, to accept the honors of initiation or undergo the regrets consequent upon failure. Only the keen, sensitive soul can understand when these opportunities come and go, for only such have won this right by successive victories gained through yielding to these celestial streams of force, and the conqueror over himself is the victor *always*, though he may *seem* sometimes to yield obedience to a force greater than himself. Let the supreme desire of each one of us ever be that these resonating centres, permanent throughout measureless cycles of time, graduated by the all-wise builders of the universe to perfect concordance with the Divine Force which is in essence incomprehensible,— shall vibrate to fullest amplitude of action; so shall we each escape from the pains, sorrows, and disappointments associated with their suppression and *inevitably* resulting from it."

Here was what appeared to the professor, at least, the possible basis of a rational and yet religious philosophy, and the mystic's *scientific* attainments were unquestionably greater than his own; therefore, when bidding his patient, earnest preceptor a cordial *au revoir*, he felt within him that now at last *gnosticism vs. agnosticism* might win the victory in his consciousness, and he prayed that it might be so.

CHAPTER VIII.

A NEW SCIENTIFIC REVELATION.

AFTER this first pleasant interview between Aldebaran and Professor Monteith, visits between these singularly dissimilar men became quite frequent, and indeed so absorbed did the latter become in the teachings and demonstrations of the former that scarcely a day passed, provided both had some little leisure, without a renewal of the study of the subjects which lay nearest to the hearts of both. How they chatted, argued, calculated, demonstrated, could it be recorded, would fill many a bulky volume, and as it is impossible to follow the processes of their inquiring minds through all these subtle ramifications, we may best show the result of these wise and profitable deliberations by reproducing the amazing manuscripts which Professor Monteith brought to Lady Porchester's reception on the last Monday afternoon of July, just as the season was concluding. It was an occasion when several scientific celebrities were present, and was passed from hand to hand for their perusal. The Professor personally refrained from offering comment or criticism, and watched with intense interest the faces of his fellow guests as they read.

Mathematical Demonstration of the Size of an Atom. Its Weight and Volume.

A rectangular, or preferably, a circular, disc is suspended from the ceiling of a room in such a manner that vibrations cannot be communicated to it from the vibrating walls of the room. It is then experimentally determined to what fundamental note the metal plate sympathetically vibrates. Then, according to the law of linear dimensions, which is equally applicable to solids, liquids, or gases, it is mathematically determined what size of plate will produce successive octaves above that pitch, until a size of plate is obtained capable of producing a period-frequency corresponding to that of dark radiant heat, which we know is produced by the oscillations of atoms, and is termed *therma*. The vibrating atomic substance of the plate is capable of producing the transmissive force called sound and *sono-thermism*, which is propagated through atomic media by wave-motion, but which cannot be propagated through space devoid of atomic substance. But when the plate has been reduced theoretically to a size sufficiently infinitesimal to correspond to the maximum or minimum size of an atom, as determined by the atomic researches of Professors Tait & Clerk Maxwell, we reach vibration frequency so high that it can be propagated through a vacuum devoid of atomic substance, as a transmissive force called rad-energy, beginning with dark radiant heat. And be it carefully observed that period-frequency corresponds with that of dark rad-energy. The law of linear dimensions may be thus stated: The vibration-periods of two similarly circumstanced homologous bodies are to each other as their cubical contents, and therefore the vibration-frequencies of homologous metal plates are to each other as the inverse ratio of their linear dimensions. The octave of a given plate will be a homologous plate having $\frac{1}{8}$ of its volume. A circular disc twenty inches in diameter and one inch thick vibrates, e.g., 1024 times per second. The ten octaves from unity successively reducing the size of the disc by $\frac{1}{8}$, we get at each reduction the octave of the previous pitch, and at any given octave we have the volume, weight, and vibration-frequency of the vibrating atomic substance.

Ten octave, 1024 vibrations per second; metal disc, twenty inches in diameter, one inch thick. To get the cubical contents of this vibrating aggregate it is necessary to square the diameter; we multiply by 0.7854, which is equal to 314.16 inches in volume. Starting from this point, we progress through successive octaves upward, increasing in pitch and diminishing in size.

The Scale of Forces.

First octave (unity per second) is approximately the lowest frequency capable of producing waves of rarefaction and condensation in the air. The atomic aggregate oscillating at this pitch can be experimentally determined, and the aggregate vibrating at a pitch one octave higher will have a mass lying between $\frac{1}{8}$ and the cube root of the mass of the first-mentioned aggregate; the exact relation under varying conditions of gravity, magnetic saturation, and pressure, can be determined only by accurate measurements. But assuming a body of a size represented by x, with a pitch represented by 1024 per second, then a pitch of 2048 per second will be produced by a body having a volume of some mean between $\frac{1}{8}$ of x and the cube root of x. By accurately determining the pitch of a volume of any metallic sphere capable of oscillating at the pitch of, *e.g.*, the eleventh octave of *sonity* (1024 per second), under normal conditions of gravity, pressure, magnetism, and then successively diminishing its size by $\frac{1}{8}$ of itself, we get the successive octaves of pitches higher and higher in period-frequency until we pass the domain of *sonity* and enter the domain of *sono-thermity*. The point where the one form of energy merges into the other lies approximately at the twenty-first octave, and this pitch also marks the point where the air is no longer capable of vibrating at that pitch in waves of transverse form. This first *gamut* of $21\frac{1}{2}$ octaves consists of three forms; viz. *sonity*, *sound*, and *sonism*. The following is a tabulation of the pitches of *sonity* in octaves from one vibration per second to where the next form of energy commences.

Fraunhofer Lines.

The Fraunhofer lines represent the silences, or the places of invisible pitches between the luminous pitches of rad-energy. They cannot therefore be conveniently used as data from which to measure the fundamental pitches of the atoms undergoing examination. When a series of sound-pencils are projected upon a screen, they undergo a combination of overtones and undertones at the point of contact producing tones of a pitch either too low to be recognized by the human ear or too high to be called sound. The Fraunhofer lines are not therefore simply silences, but may be the higher invisible ultra-actinic rays. The fact is that some of the Fraunhofer lines are capable of producing a variety of chemical actions, when reflected and focalized. Observation thus far shows that these lines do not bear any definite ascertainable relation to the pitches producing them, but that they do bear some uniform relation from which the fundamental pitch could be determined cannot be doubted. The relation of the Fraunhofer lines to the luminous spectra are undoubtedly such as would enable one to compute the creative pitches producing them; but as yet no such determinations have been made. The accurate method of determining them is from the mutual relation of the harmonic pitches of the luminous spectra.

A table representing the harmonic overtones and undertones of simple vibrations, and the resultant harmonics of associate vibrations, will be of great convenience in making these determinations.

The natural unity of *sonity* lies above 1 per second, and below 2 per second, and for this reason the numbering of the octaves is accomplished by calling the end of the first octave No. 1 instead of No. 2. At the end of the twenty-first octave *sono-thermity* commences, and the bodies oscillating at this pitch are either correspondingly smaller by $\frac{1}{3}$ than the preceding sonitic aggregates; or larger aggregates undergo vibration in submultiple portions of themselves. In either case the originating oscillation of a *sono-thermic* pitch is that of an isolated or localized aggregation. This *first class* of forces, or first *double gamut*, is included within the range of about forty-three octaves. The bodies of the first *gamut* oscillate with a rhythmically recurring translatory pendulous motion and produce waves of a transverse form, while the bodies of the second *gamut* undergo internal nodal vibration and produce waves of a longitudinal form. Beyond the upper limit of the forty-third octave we reach bodies of a size (determined by the same method as in *sonity*) which we know to be about the size of an atom as approximately determined by various physicists to lie between eleven and twelve micromillimeters (hydrogen molecules), which gives the highest pitch of the known atoms, and from which can be roughly estimated the pitch of the heavier atoms. Starting with the approximate pitch of hydrogen as determined from its associate spectrum with oxygen, and working back to the size of the largest atoms, we again reach a pitch corresponding to the highest *sono-thermic* vibrations. Starting with the known temperature and pitch of a heated body, emitting definite rays of light, and working back to absolute zero, we again reach the pitch of the *sono-thermic* limit.

FIRST CLASS.

SCALE OF THE FORCES IN OCTAVES.

Sonity, Sound, and Sonism.

No. of Octaves. Unity per Second.	Period-frequency.
1st.	2.
2d.	4.
3d.	8.
4th.	16.
5th.	32.
6th.	64.
7th.	128.
8th.	256.
9th.	512.
10th.	1024.
11th.	2048.
12th.	4096.
13th.	8192.
14th.	16,384.
15th.	32,768.
16th.	65,536.
17th.	131,072.
18th.	262,144.
19th.	524,288.
20th.	1,048,576.
21st.	2,097,152.
Maj. 5th.	3,145,728.

Sono-thermity, Sono-therm, Sono-thermism.

22d.	4,194,304.
23d.	8,388,606.
24th.	16,777,216.
25th.	33,554,432.
26th.	67,108,864.

No. of Octaves. Unity per Second.	Period-frequency.
27th.	134,217,728.
28th.	268,435,456.
29th.	536,870,912.
30th.	1,073,741,824.
31st.	2,147,483,648.
32d.	4,294,967,296.
33d.	8,589,934,592.
34th.	17,179,869,184.
35th.	34,359,738,368.
36th.	68,719,476,736.
37th.	137,438,953,472.
38th.	274,877,906,944.
39th.	549,755,813,888.
40th.	1,099,511,627,776.
41st.	2,199,023,255,552.
42d.	4,398,046,511,104.

SECOND CLASS.

Thermism, Rad-energy, Chemism.

43d.	8,796,093,022,208.	Dark heat begins.
44th.	17,592,186,044,416.	
45th.	35,184,372,088,832.	
46th.	70,368,744,177,664.	Chemism begins.
47th.	140,737,488,355,328.	Infra-red. [begins.
48th.	281,474,976,710,656.	Major fourth (above). Light
49th.	562,949,953,421,312.	Below Major fourth. Light
50th.	1,125,899,906,842,624.	[ends.
51st.	2,251,799,813,685,248.	
52d.	4,503,599,627,370,496.	Limit actinic.
53d.	9,007,199,254,740,992.	
54th.	10,814,398,509,481,984.	
55th.	36,028,797,018,963,968.	Chemism ends.
56th.	72,057,594,037,927,936.	

DASHED AGAINST THE ROCK. 81

No. of Octaves. Unity per Second.	Period-frequency.
57th.	144,115,188,075,855,872.
58th.	288,230,376,151,711,744.
59th.	576,460,752,303,423,488.
60th.	1,152,921,504,606,846,976.
61st.	2,305,843,009,213,693,952.
62d.	4,611,686,018,427,387,904.
63d.	9,223,372,036,854,775,808.
64th.	18,446,744,073,709,551,616.
Maj. 5th.	27,670,116,110,564,327,424. Limit of thermism.

Electricity, Induction, Magnetism.

65th.	36,893,488,147,419,103,232.
66th.	73,786,976,295,838,206,464.
67th.	147,573,952,591,676,413,928.
68th.	295,147,905,183,352,827,856. Copper-zinc couple.
69th.	590,295,810,366,705,655,712.
70th.	1,180,591,620,733,411,311,424.
71st.	2,361,183,241,466,822,622,848. 50,000 volts.
72d.	4,722,366,482,933,645,245,696.
73d.	9,444,732,965,867,290,491,392.
74th.	18,889,465,931,745,580,982,784.
75th.	37,778,931,863,469,161,965,568.
76th.	75,557,863,726,938,323,931,136.
77th.	151,115,727,453,875,647,862,772.
78th.	302,231,454,907,753,295,724,544.
79th.	604,462,909,815,506,591,449,088.
80th.	1,208,925,819,631,013,182,898,176.
81st.	2,417,851,639,762,026,365,796,352.
82d.	4,825,703,278,524,052,731,592,702.
83d.	9,671,406,557,048,105,463,185,408.
84th.	19,342,813,114,096,210,926,370,816.
85th.	38,685,626,228,192,421,852,741,632.
86th.	77,361,252,456,384,843,705,483,204.

The limit of electricity and the beginning of atomolity.

CHAPTER IX.

HOW NATURE CURES. — A NEW FOOD-THEORY.

It was again a Monday evening, and this time Lady Porchester's drawing-rooms were filled to their utmost capacity. The occasion was one of the closing literary *soirées* of the season, at which Miss Pomona Merton, a young lady of great beauty, one of the reigning belles of the year, was to read an essay and then invite discussion on "The Natural Diet of Man."

Pomona Merton looked intensely charming, and withal marvellously healthy, as she stepped gracefully on to the raised dais which constituted the impromptu platform from which she was to address her eagerly expectant audience. The wonder was that she could look so blooming, considering that she had been "everywhere" during the past three months, and now, when other girls were utterly worn out with fatigue and fashionable dissipation, she was all aglow with the roses of perfect health and vigor. Her constitution was not extremely good to start with. Her mother had not been a strong woman; and when five years earlier she had (then in her sixteenth year) made the acquaintance of Drs. Frugus and Helena Moresden she was supposed by her physician to be tottering on the verge of incipient tuberculosis. Her sole diet for the past two years had been nuts and fruit, though for three years previous she had eaten sparingly of meat, and fish also, but all starchy compounds, including bread, had been eliminated from her dietary during the whole period of her association with the Moresdens, who were still making a decided sensation in the British metropolis, not only through the weekly organ of their movement, but also through series of public and private meetings at which distinguished disciples of the "Natural Food" doctrine spoke eloquently in its defence, and vigorously, though most politely and kindly, refuted opposition.

Pomona Merton was the chief advocate on the lecture platform; for, though young in years, she was old in experience and singularly well equipped intellectually and physically to introduce a new movement to the world. In clear, sweet, ringing tones, with perfect accent and exquisite modulation of pitch, she addressed the large company before her as — "Dear friends, all interested in human welfare, and all seeking to find the noblest path in life and steadfastly to walk therein." Instantly she was in touch with every listener, and though everybody expected to hear some extraordinary sentiments expressed, the speaker's majestic personality and winning smile, coupled with her radiant health and delightful though subdued vivacity, brought the three drawing-rooms — all open one into the other, and all crowded — figuratively to her feet.

"I may as well read to you the constitution of our society, that you may fully understand our principles," continued the graceful orator, and with this she launched at once into the very heart of her theme, prefacing her reading of a synopsis of the Natural Food System with three scripture texts: —

Yet his days shall be a hundred and twenty years. — GEN. vi. 3.

And Moses was a hundred and twenty years old when he died: his eye was not dim, nor his natural force abated. — DEUT. xxxiv. 7.

Every man that striveth for the mastery is temperate in all things. — 1 COR. ix. 25.

and then continued: —

"The Natural Food Society is founded in the belief that the food of primeval man consisted of fruit and nuts of sub-tropical climes, spontaneously produced; that on these foods man was (and may again become) at least as free from disease as the animals are in a state of nature. Physiologists unite in teaching that these foods are adapted to digestion in the main stomach, where, it is contended by this Society, the great bulk of our food should be digested, whereas cereals, pulses, bread, and in fact all starch foods, are chiefly digested in the intestines, and hence, it is maintained, are unnatural and disease-inducing foods, and the chief cause of the nervous prostration and the broken-down health that abound on all sides.

"We urge that all fruits in their season — including figs, dates, bananas, prunes, raisins, apples, etc., fresh and dried, each of many varieties — be substituted for bread and other grain foods and starch vegetables; and experience convinces us that this course will be found by a brief experiment highly beneficial, alike to the meat-eater and to the vegetarian.

"*All persons about to experiment with the non-starch food system are urged at first not to use nuts; but to use instead whatever animal food they have been accustomed to.* The central feature of this system consists in abstention from bread, cereals, pulses, and starchy vegetables, and in the substitution of food fruits.

"Invalids and all persons whose digestive organs have become so weakened that the use of so natural a food as fruit causes flatulence, irritation, or any other inconvenience, are advised at first to confine themselves to a diet of milk, fish, or flesh, until such a restoration has been accomplished as will enable them gradually, and with benefit, to add fruit to their dietary. Until such restoration has been accomplished, and until they can properly digest and assimilate a large proportion of fruit in their dietary, they are recommended to use daily a mild aperient.

"All persons not using fresh fruits in abundance are urged to use a liberal amount of water — preferably soft or distilled — and to use no other drink. A half-pint or pint a half-hour or an hour before meals is recommended; if taken hot, all the better.

"When I review the various reasons for which I believe in a fruit diet, I find the most potent to be the conviction that fruit is the only possible diet of a humane and truly civilized nation. Until I got hold of the idea of a fruit diet, I must confess that I could only give a very mournful sympathy to proposals of 'land reform,' etc. I know a charming Wiltshire valley full of trees and rich pasture. There are parts of it from which an extensive survey discovers no sign of cottage or other work of man, except, perhaps, a hayrick here and there. Cattle and sheep nibble peacefully, birds are unmolested, and squirrels leap from branch to branch. Now the ideal of some people is to see this and other similar spots — of which in this age of coal and iron there are none too many — cut up into potato patches, with square cottages and pigsties in the middle. Melancholy roosters innumerable are to vocalize victoriously, and abundant mangel-wurzels are to be hoed by future Joseph Hodges, bent as now into the shape of an inverted L.

"Many a time when nearing a town environed by allotments, with their plebeian potatoes and little eyesores of sheds, I have felt what a come-down they were (æsthetically) from the broad acres of waving wheat or crimson clover crops of the old-fashioned farmer. But better even than these would be the sight of a flourishing fruit land with pretty cottages peeping out amid a profusion of roses, jessamine, and honeysuckle. For it is quite clear that machine-harvested crops and pasture-fields will never require a large population on the land, and thus we are of necessity driven to fruit-growing — to the cultivation of trees and shrubs demanding intelligent labor, and converting the country into a fairyland of frost work in the winter, a paradise of blossoms in the spring, and a thing of beauty and a joy for ever all the year round. How much pleasanter such a sight would be from railway windows than bare fields, with impudent boards stuck up at frequent intervals to proclaim the virtues of proprietary pills. What man has done man may do, and what man has misdone man may, to a very great extent, *un*do. The operations of mining, manufacture, etc., will prevent some districts from ever being particularly pleasant, but under natural conditions much of the present output would not be required. Multitudes of quasi-invalids, whose roaring fires for warming and cooking contribute to thicken city fogs, would not exist. As regards my brother, who is no Spartan, I may say that he can live comfortably all the winter without fire for any purpose except lighting, temporary handiwork, etc., and that last season, with our windows as wide open as they would go, we escaped our customary colds for the first time in our lives. Furthermore, the number of appliances, artificial foods, drinks, etc., which mean so much work and smoke, and are useless to a natural liver, is really almost indefinite.

"A fruit diet is more radical than a root diet. That a man who should be content with a meal of raw fruit and nuts should wish to smoke a cigar after it is to us flatly inconceivable. At present our vices date from the cradle. Infants take milk through rubber tubes, and men imbibe smoke through wooden ones, and, what is still worse, the mammas and young ladies raise no objection to two such improper habits. Then come toffy and tarts, for which Harrow boys get two shillings a week pocket-money. Thus sweet-shops, which are the public-houses of children, and public-houses, which are the bitter-shops of men, will have to get themselves abolished, and I hope an enlightened generation will let down fine landscapes instead of ugly shutters, when they close whatever shops will remain. Another beneficial result of tree-planting will be the impossibility of 'sport,' at least in certain districts. I went over a kennel the other day, and was much impressed by the sight of sixty large dogs, howling, malodorous, and devouring huge quantities of red horseflesh with capital Scotch oatmeal boiled up for them in two coppers, superintended by a ruffian with a long whip. If there is some reason for the existence of a hunting instinct in Africa, I can see none for it in England.

"If those who do the Sunday preaching would lay a little heavier stress upon the imperative nature of natural law, how much more good might be effected than by the re-threshing of dogmas that have been spun and re-spun as often as Penelope's web. More kind severity and less spiritual soothing-syrup is what the people need. But no; men in office generally, and even most of our great writers, either ignore such subjects, or treat new discussions about them as worthy only of 'faddists.' Carlyle, with all his keen perceptions, found water 'the most destructive drug he had met with,' took castor-oil twice a week, and blue pill and brandy in proportion.

"A fashionable young lady does not know that it would do her more good to walk when she pays another young daughter of fashion a morning call, than to ride in a fine carriage with two fine bearing-reined horses, and two fine liveried flunkeys. A stylish young man does not know that it would do him more good to run himself than to watch horses running. What bishop has the courage to tell people so to their faces? All that bishops can do nowadays, as Emerson said, is to 'ask you to take wine.' But so it is, and I fear that women will continue to *dress* and men to *live* unhealthily for fear of Mrs. Grundy, for some time to come. Yet I believe the number of men and women who desire to live rationally increases day by day; hence I hope for better things. To bring these about, a fruit diet will be an important factor. Chewing raw beans and oats is eminently unpractical, either in our present social state or in any future state. Chewing raw apples and walnuts, I find both practical and pleasant, and thus, in spite of long-winded sermons on the merits of starch, I believe a natural diet to be the thin end of a very big wedge,— a wedge, moreover, which when once entered will open a massive door into the temple of health, peace, and gentleness."

"How extremely outspoken she is," whispered Mrs. Lispenard-Schermerhorn to her dearest friend and confidante, Mrs. Steuveyzante-Feesche, who was seated next to her; "she is unquestionably a splendid girl, but what outrageous sentiments she does express on the diet question. What should we, what could we, do to get up a dinner if all the world thought and acted as she does? And the marvel of it is she has been *everywhere* this summer, dined with *everybody*, and never once departed from her rule. Were I a theosophist and a believer in reincarnation, I should declare she was a re-embodiment of Daniel or one of his three companions, whom the Bible tells us never tasted meat or wine though they were entertained at a king's palace."

"What she said about the bishops was true, anyway," suggested a plain, tall spinster in gray, who was a rigid Nonconformist and made the disestablishment of the English Church her particular hobby; "I never could for the life of me see the good of a church, supported at vast expense to the nation, which never concerns itself in the least about the welfare of our bodies while it is always prating to us about abstention from vice. For my part I consider virtue physiological; no man or woman can possibly be really clean in thought who violates every law of nature physically."

"My dear Miss Velcherbeck, I must *totally* disagree with you, though I trust I am not a gourmand," broke in the penetrating tones of Mademoiselle Susette Kurle Klarke, who had darted in for five minutes on a round of engagements. She was a metaphysician of the most uncompromising type, and had been summoned the night previous to the bedside of the Hon. Mrs. Moheeneigh-Palankulus, president of six Hermetic Lodges, and one of the leading lights in the "Fraternity of the Ever-Occult," the most influential society of mystics at that time centred in London. "I have seen too much," continued Miss Klarke, "of this tampering with physical means to restore health, to believe anything in aught but pure SPIRITUAL SCIENCE; that is enough for me. In my treatments I find the cause of the ailment, and I — or rather the spiritual intelligences who work with and through me — expel the possessing demon of error, be it an entity who is obsessing his victim or a phantasmal error contained in the false beliefs of the sufferer."

"Pardon me, good friends," mildly but firmly protested Miss Merton; "I do not wish to ignore or undervalue the good offices of spiritual workers, and I am sure my dear teachers, the Drs. Moresden, would be the last to do so, for they are keenly alive to spiritual propositions themselves, but I must maintain that while embodied on earth the human spirit is dependent for expression upon the body, exactly as the pianist, even though he be phenomenal as Paderewski, is dependent on the piano. News has just reached us from America that the first serious break in the musical arrangements at the World's Fair, now open in Chicago, was owing to that eminent virtuoso not being permitted — at all events, not without angry protest on the part of the Directors — to use his own particular instrument, which he declared was absolutely necessary to the success of his recitals. I claim that food does make a very great difference in our condition and that my own physical welfare is largely, if not entirely, due to my present mode of living. If this is not so, explain if you please, or rather if you can, why so many really excellent, intelligent, kind-hearted, pious persons whose thoughts are pure and honorable are constantly ailing. I agree with you, my dear Miss Klarke, and with all who share your views in whole or in part, that mental treatment is extremely beneficial and often indispensable; but if we eat *anything*, why not eat the *right things?* I do not take it that you counsel us to eat *nothing*, on the plea that we are altogether spiritual; you and all your friends eat *something;* and if you eat at all, — as eat you do,— you must consider food a necessity in our present state of existence. I cannot see the force or logic of a position, to me utterly untenable, that *what* we eat makes no difference, when there are multitudes of things you would never dream of eating, while the special selections you make for the table are in my experience fully as unhealthy and inappropriate as the bulk of what you discard."

At this point in the conversation a very quiet, demure little woman, nicknamed Miss Mouse by almost every one who knew her, called attention to the great benefit a literary circle had derived from reading and studying systematically Dr. Morosden's great work, *How Nature Cures*, which comprises an entirely *new* system of hygiene, and explains in detail what is in truth the natural food of the human species. This extraordinary volume, though extremely unorthodox in its arguments and conclusions, is written by a man of science and letters whose standing as a physician is unsurpassed; he is indeed a veritable encyclopædia of psychological and physiological information, and if there should be anything he does not know at any time, his wife — also an M.D. of the first rank — is sure to be thoroughly familiar with it.

Miss Alice Mozier, *alias* Mouse, was therefore quite within bounds when she extolled this *new* system of hygiene so highly, and the word *new* certainly does sound fascinating in the ears of many. Old things have become so despicably threadbare, and old medical treatment has proved itself so wretchedly inadequate to cope with the real or imaginary ills of ailing humanity, that a novelty, even though it reach the point of human vivisection under the name of extremely scientific surgery, is cordially welcomed by the most delicate women, whose shattered nerves are consoled with the serene hope of *delightful spiritual visions* while under the influence of a poisonous anæsthetic during the period allotted to the sublime *scientific* work of butchering their distorted bodies, which would be in no condition to suggest the need of operating were they instructed from girlhood in the simple law of health and taught how to dress, eat, walk, and THINK in accordance with the ethics of the universe.

Because the system discussed that evening was said to be a *new* system, it did really make some impression on several who were present; so much so that Lady Porchester expressed a great desire that Miss Merton should visit her some day privately and discuss the whole matter with her ladyship's newly graduated medical grand-nephew, Dr. Erastus Pinchington de Tweeze, a young man already distinctly celebrated at the Royal College of Surgeons and the incumbent of a Chair at Vauxhall University.

"Erastus is *so* original, don't you know?" exclaimed his doting grand-aunt, who had paid all his college expenses and wild-oat bills out of her own personal income while he was matriculating at Shoddersfield; "his *alma mater* has simply heaped honors upon him, and I may say with reasonable, grateful pride that he has loaded the same fostering mother with dignity she scarcely wore before. I was sorry the other day that he and Mrs. Spottiswoode got along so badly. She, you know, is a Matteist; 'Electro-Homœopathy' is her darling fad; Count Mattei of Bologna is her idol, and she swears that his infinitesimals in which are fixed, according to her account, some mysterious *electric principle*, will cure *everything*. My nephew, of course, refuted her position and *scientifically demonstrated* that the whole system of Matteism is an exploded fallacy; but I noticed he winced considerably when Mrs. Spottiswoode, who is proverbially dauntless and uncompromising, showed him well-attested evidence that three important test cases, two of consumption and one of cancer, had been *perfectly cured* by this ridiculous parody on exact medical science."

"But, dear Lady Porchester, how did he answer her?" inquired Miss Merton and Miss Mozier in a breath.

"Answer her, my dears? why, what could he say? He just sniffed the air and petulantly ejaculated, 'Oh, another, or rather three others of those beastly coincidences; it's enough to make the very angels weep to see how quackery fattens upon an alteration in the mode of hysteria professed by the dupes of an infernal sensationalism.'"

"But," pursued the placid though inwardly mirthful Pomona, "how could such a ridiculously shallow and irascible exclamation be called an *answer* to Mrs. Spottiswoode's asseverations, backed up as they were by documentary proof? An answer, in my judgment, must be a genuine reply, a counter-statement both logical and coherent, not a bald denunciation of an opponent's claims."

"Well, my dear, you are young yet, and you will probably soon learn that professional men are as a rule very resentful of any encroachment upon their territory. My nephew's education cost many thousand pounds, and you can hardly expect a hot-headed young enthusiast who *worships* exact science to be very lenient with a woman who, as he would phrase it, puts on airs and sets herself up to know as much, and positively more, than he does. I love Mrs. Spottiswoode myself and I know her to be a good woman," continued her ladyship, "but I must admit she is a little arrogant in manner sometimes, and she certainly did call my nephew a puppy to his face one afternoon in my drawing-room, and that was certainly going a little too far; don't *you* think so?"

Miss Merton slightly bowed her assent.

"I immediately suggested a sedative for both of them; but my nephew significantly tapped his finger on his forehead, pointed in the direction of my guest, and whispering in my ear, 'Crazy as the Count himself, but not such a humbug wilfully,' prepared to accomplish his exit. But Mrs. Spottiswoode was more than he reckoned upon; I confess I was almost terrified,— dear Miss Poyntz told me afterwards she trembled for my fluttering heart; well, Mrs. Spottiswoode placed herself against the door and drawing herself up to her full height, — and she is five feet ten inches, I am confident; he is only five feet seven inches,— she lectured him for twenty minutes in one steady tide of burning eloquence; she literally lashed him, and then without a word of conciliation she fired her parting shot in these identical words: 'Now, young sir, you know better; and if you ever again in my hearing repeat the libel you have uttered to-day, I shall hold you responsible for criminal defamation of character, and you will have to answer to the charge as best you can.' Imagine that on a Thursday afternoon in my drawing-room; and I actually took Mrs. Spottiswoode out driving in my carriage half an hour later and dropped her at the Oratory for Benediction, picked her up when the service ended, brought her home to dinner with Madame Discalcelis, and fell asleep after dessert listening to the two ladies sizing up my nephew to the accompaniment of silvery peals of merry laughter. It didn't hurt my heart a bit; I was better for it. And now, my dear Miss Merton, I do want to see how your theory will get along under the fire of my nephew's artillery. You are so much gentler than Mrs. Spottiswoode, and so many years younger, that I really do think — especially as he dotes on beautiful girls — that you will not find him so very disagreeable, and he really is a learned fellow."

"I am so confident that my position is a sound one," quietly remarked Miss Merton, "that I am willing to state it clearly to any one, but I do not *seek* arguments with self-satisfied physicians. What little missionary work I can do will be, I trust, among those who are seeking a better way in diet, and when I think that I may be the means of helping to release at least a few poor sufferers from chronic ailments, I do feel that my work is not unimportant, though I am yet but a beginner in this great undertaking. The Food Question must be considered, and I think *settled*, before there can be much progress made even in morality; for, as Dr. Moresden said the other day, when controverting the assertions of a prominent leader in vegetarian circles: 'To my apprehension there is no greater duty than that of keeping ourselves in the best condition of health. I believe it is highly immoral to be ill. I think it can be clearly shown that all illness is the result of some disobedience to natural law; and when such transgressions are knowingly undertaken, the immorality is not less in the case of wrong feeding than in any other instance.' "

The result of this evening's discussion was that Miss Mozier enlisted fifteen members for a reading-club, and set tongues wagging in every direction on the *new* diet movement: that word *new* was the sugar on an otherwise bitter pill, and because of the sweet, the bitter was at least tolerated. People were set to thinking, and to induce people to think for themselves on any subject is always profitable.

CHAPTER X.

THE GOSPEL OF VIBRATION.

It is a week later, and again it is Monday evening; the season is dying, for the date is now July 17, and there will be only two more *soirées* at Lady Porchester's before the house closes for the summer and its frequenters are scattered far and wide,—wider this season than usual; for many are going to Chicago to witness the great Columbian Exposition.

On this occasion food is not the topic of discussion, and the essayist is not a young lady. By dint of much persuasion the renowned mystic Aldebaran has consented to write a paper on the "Amplitude of Force," and trust the reading of it to Mr. Fitzcraven, at a time when *vibration* was vibrating in the ears of every one, and Mrs. Margaret Peeke's *Zenia the Vestal* was on everybody's reading-table.

Aldebaran never appeared in public in any capacity whatsoever; one might meet him at dinner at Lady Tomlinson's, and occasionally he was seen at a theatre; but though possessed of a veritable mine of occult information, and willing, moreover, to impart instruction to any whom he felt might profit by the teaching, he could never be induced to become a "lion," or to "star," either on the platform or in a drawing-room.

Clarence Fitzcraven was a good reader, and one who enjoyed "dress parade" immensely, and was never more in his element than when in faultless evening attire, — his glossy raven hair parted exactly in the middle and brushed to the extremest point of silkiness, and his handsome mustache curved in the very latest bend,— he stood up to read a paper some one else had written. The essay lost nothing of its distinctiveness by being entrusted to his care; and as it was a fashionable occasion, the decidedly tailor-made appearance of the reader served in a certain way, to accommodate by dint of appropriate framing, the transcendental picture to the realistic room. Mr. Fitzcraven was far above the average of *critical* journalists; he would never have stooped to one in ten of their ordinary meannesses, still he was in a degree supercilious, and though not by any means a scoffer, he affected a mild *fin de siècle* cynicism, which agreed very well with his slightly conceited manner, and was the one point upon which his transparently straightforward sister always twitted him. The few extempore sentences in which he introduced the paper were timely and well-chosen; he modestly repudiated all knowledge of the subject-matter of his "esteemed friend's able contribution to the literature of the occult," and then raising his voice to an agreeable pitch, in a leisurely, forcible manner gave utterance to the following essay, which bore the title —

Amplitude of Force.

The amplitude of vibrations is directly increased or diminished by increasing or diminishing the size or number of creative aggregates.

The human EGO, subject to the forces of love or hate, kindness or cruelty, forgiveness or revenge, is according to circumstances ruled or dominated by these forces in proportion to their intensity.

The intensity of a force is precisely proportionate to the number of units vibrating at that particular pitch. For instance, let fear assail one man, and according to its intensity will be the effect; but let a crowd of men experience fear, see the result in the augmentation of fear, though its source be relatively insignificant. A curtain in a theatre, for example, takes fire; one or two persons, cowardly at heart, become afraid through the dominance of the purely animal instinct of bodily preservation; there is actually no real danger, but these two or three persons are sufficient to arouse the unreasoning dread which lies latent in every breast, with perhaps a very few remarkable exceptions. The fire burns nobody; but blind fear, which is extremely contagious among people mutually sympathetic, by reason of the rapidity with which etheric waves transmit all feeling, occasions a terrible panic, during which many severe accidents and many instances of fierce cruelty occur, all because of this sympathetic transfer of feeling starting from one or two augmented or intensified fear-centres, each person being a centre emanating the feeling of fear. Were there no counteracting centres of influence in an audience, radiating contrary feelings, the result of a panic would be the total bodily extinction of a very large percentage of the assembled multitude.

Thus the human race is immersed in forces whose intensity is vast in proportion to the number of EGOS adding each its quota to the already intense vibration, tending either to love or hate, kindness or cruelty, timidity or bravery. Those who intensify the force of cruelty in the place where they reside, may be strengthening a murderer's hand to strike the deadly blow in a distant land. This result is brought about through the agency of etheric waves, which transmit forces with undiminished intensity even to uncalculated distances. This phenomenon may be termed *transympathetic*.

They who feel that force called love, which on higher planes is known as sympathy, thrill with waves of force which are already strong, augmenting them or increasing their intensity. They who indulge such sentiments and encourage such forces may stop the falling hand on evil sped.

In order to protect ourselves effectually from becoming the dispensers or propagators of deadly force, we must consciously and deliberately relate ourselves by resolute determination, to awaken within us such centres only as are concordantly sympathetic with all force radiating in the interest of universal goodwill, thereby aiding the establishment of universal brotherhood.

All ye who feel a longing for a better life or nobler existence draw to yourselves streams of force which they alone feel who have attuned their bodies to the higher harmonies. For a moment you feel as they who dwell perpetually in communion with higher harmonies, living immersed in that higher force; they are the true hierophants, and you, O neophytes, struggling to attain the goal which they have reached, do not despair though at present you find yourselves unable to maintain this high altitude for long together. Though you fall many times, be not discouraged, for as yet your organisms and all their centres of resonation are not yet concordant to the focalized vibrations of the higher harmonies; being still related to the mass, you are drawn again and again into the whirlpool of the vibrations which affect the mass, for these you cannot yet resist. But know that you can change all this rapidly or slowly as your purpose is steadily intense or vacillating.

With the cessation of your lower desires comes the cessation of the action upon you of the lower forces; the resonating centres which formerly distributed this force, no longer active, become latent and are absorbed back to an embryonic condition.

Every man contains, developed or embryonic, all conditions of the Infinite; therefore no height is too great to reach. Impossibility is a meaningless word to the man who apprehends the fathomless contents of his own nature. Thou comest here, O man, with the instrument thou hast graduated in thy many past existences; how few of thy chord-settings, if thou art numbered with the many, respond to the higher harmonies! Universal unity or fraternity has been absorbed to almost embryonic conditions by the prevalence of material self-regard. Charity has been rendered almost latent, that beautiful chord-setting found even in the lowest forms of creation — LOVE, the dominant chord of the cycles. Love has an amplitude of action in the brute which may well make the selfish man ashamed, but until the crust of selfishness is broken through, the beauty of love is obscured, and though it exists all about him, the poor blind egotist has no eye to discern it. The centres of love, brotherhood, charity, voice their music loud and clear, yet the masses will not listen. I do not mean the immortal EGO when I say man will not listen; I refer to the personality which is the resultant of all the ages of action in this, now rapidly closing, cycle.

You who exist to-day, to-morrow would exist no longer in your present personalities did you but dare to yield to these higher harmonies. I say YIELD because it is a *yielding* process for this personality. In a moment your outer life would end, and you, the warrior, would enter peace.

The immortal EGO is an entity of which man can become thoroughly conscious while here on earth, but to arrive at this consciousness necessitates the entire abandonment of all the petty considerations involved in the transient and subordinate EGO, which is the only self of which the unenlightened man is conscious. Let him who desires to reach this inner consciousness enter his inner sanctuary, wherever that sanctuary may be; it matters not whether it be his own chamber, the open field, the mountain top, the seashore, the stately cathedral, or the humble village chapel. Let him realize fully the transient character of his own personality and contrast therewith his eager longing to know the immortal. Let him concentrate his whole consciousness upon his personality, fully arousing all his personal conditions as a distinct individual; then with all the aspiration of which this personality is capable, let him beseech of the immortal EGO — which is eternal and does not incarnate, but overshadows all incarnations, waiting until one is formed capable of illumination, to whom it may reveal itself — to consider him worthy of illumination, and according to his preparedness to receive illumination will it then be granted. He who asks this, knows not what he asks; for were the prayer answered, life henceforth for such an one would be a weary round, as Hamlet says: " to-morrow and to-morrow and to-morrow brings in this weary round of life "; for, having seen the glory of this immortal EGO, all else seems so base, so commonplace and mean, so inglorious, that oftentimes the personality has utterly collapsed when thrown back from the radiant vision of this glorious immortal entity possessed by all alike, though scarcely dreamed of by any save the very few who, discontented with the ignorance and emptiness of terrene existence, aspire to know the great reality of the supernal. As the incarnations of every entity, passing through certain orders of experience through numerous lives, inevitably culminate in this moment of conscious realization of the immortal entity; the Buddha says: " All shall reach the sunlit snows."

You who through your daily life move on unthinking, not caring, inactive, you shall hear when your supplications reach this high entity, "Lo! thou didst not even try, knowing that even thy failures were acceptable to me."

The speaker, whose voice had become almost tender at the close, ceased as it seemed abruptly, and a profound silence reigned unbroken. Professor Monteith, who was present, was utterly lost in reverie, and a subdued hush was over all.

CHAPTER XI.

THE FLIGHT OF THE VULTURES.

MRS. EASTLAKE-GORE and her son Arthur had departed for Scotland, to spend three weeks on their estate in Perthshire before taking ship for America. Madame Discalcelis, having some business with her publishers, which required her presence in London till about the eighth of August, had accepted Lady Porchester's invitation to be her guest from the time the Gores departed till she also should sail for America. Mr. and Mrs. Bromleykite were also *honored* if not *honorable* sharers of her ladyship's unstinted bounty; and though Madame Discalcelis and Mrs. Bromleykite could scarcely be said to love each other in a very particular sense, Miss Poyntz had from the first impressed the rather fastidious Visalia as a really nice woman, despite the fact of her individuality being to some extent painfully contracted in the corsets of conventionalism. A lady who wears dresses of almost Grecian type, perfectly comfortable and always graceful,— one, moreover, whose beautiful natural hair curls all over her head at its own sweet pleasure,— cannot fail to be a little sobered at the sight of very tight-fitting garments, whose ponderosity is everlastingly obtruding itself, and stiff braids of foreign hair piled severely upon an evidently burdened cranium. But such superficial differences could never destroy friendship between two such women as Madame Discalcelis and Miss Poyntz, who were both thoroughly true at heart, though the one was decidedly a braver and stronger character than the other.

The Bromleykites had "dwelt in clover" under Lady Porchester's hospitable roof; her ladyship — despite their vulgarities, which occasionally grated upon her raspingly — really admired them, and what was more, believed in them. Miss Poyntz did not approve of their persistent attempts to keep Lady Porchester under hypnotic influence, and she told them so. As a result of this outspokenness on her part they began to manœuvre against her in every dastardly, deceitful way their perverted ingenuity could devise, till one day there was actually a scene between Lady Porchester and her faithful, doting companion. Madame Discalcelis divined the situation immediately on her arrival, and it can hardly be said that she treated the Bromleykites civilly or uncivilly; she simply ignored their presence, and never permitted herself to be drawn into any conversation with or concerning them.

When Miss Poyntz, bathed in tears on account of the petulance of her ladyship, — who had just promised them another thousand pounds, — rushed into Madame Discalcelis' presence to condole her wretchedness, that lady only condescended to remark: —

"It is largely your own fault, my dear; you are second mistress in this establishment, and had you been as firm as I would have been in your place, this house would never have been polluted with their presence; you are honest, but you are weak, and moral cowardice is surely as out of place in a modern drawing-room as it ever was in days of old, when rack or stake may have loomed before the uncompromising."

"Oh, I know it!" sighed the desolate Katherine between her sobs; "I have never had your bravery. If I had, I should never have permitted thousands of things I have winked at for fear of offending her ladyship's satellites; but we are not at all as strong as you are, Madame, and the strong must bear gently with the infirmities of the weak."

"Am I strong, dear?" responded Visalia, now entirely melted; "do you think because I can subdue emotion that I feel nothing?" and then, lifting her beautiful clear, blue eyes, and gazing steadily into the hazel depths of her companion's orbs with a boundless wealth of sisterly tenderness, she put her arms round the quivering frame of the elder woman and comforted her as a mother might soothe her wounded infant. There and then between these widely differing natures a compact of friendship was sealed, never to be broken.

The butterfly touched the star above and the cross below its wings, on the beautiful brooch which was the only ornament Visalia really valued. This exquisite decoration had been presented to her by the Queen of Italy, and she attached to it an almost mystical importance; for it seemed to her whenever that diamond butterfly kissed first the golden cross and then the seven-pointed star between which it was poised, it symbolized victory through conquered sorrow, and true it was that at that instant the germ of true nobility was stimulated in Katherine's soul far beyond its ordinary wont. A strange Nemesis-like power seemed embodied in Visalia; wherever she went wrongs were righted, injustice was rebuked, the innocent were extricated from the meshes of a seeming adverse destiny; and, as the two ladies sat hour after hour that quiet summer afternoon, talking confidentially of life, its meaning, and its outlook, it seemed to both as though they were being prepared to battle against an insidious enemy and to conquer in some strange encounter with impalpable shapes of darkness.

The day had been sultry, and as evening approached the sky grew overcast; there was an uncanny feeling about the house, and Lady Porchester, far from well, was locked in her bedroom with Mrs. Bromleykite as sole attendant. Mr. Bromleykite was writing prescriptions, on the basis of a geocentric system of astrology, which included all the witcheries and vagaries of sixteenth century superstition, and which he claimed had been miraculously revealed to him by "T.H.E.M."

Suddenly a storm broke over London, with almost unexampled fury; the rain fell in sheets from the overburdened clouds, which seemed to have suddenly come from nowhere; hail, wind, thunder, all combined to make the weird occasion terrible to all whose nerves were in the least shattered, or whose consciences at all upbraided them. The servants were terrified, and after the manner of timid souls they huddled together in the housekeeper's room, telling each other bloodcurdling tales, presumably to keep their fainting hearts from utterly refusing to beat longer.

Not knowing that Madame Discalcelis and Miss Poyntz were in Lady Porchester's boudoir, preparing and drinking chocolate unattended by domestics and enjoying a lengthy *tête-a-tête* confab, Mr. Bromleykite deemed it a favorable opportunity for abstracting from Lady Porchester's jewel case, which was in her dressing-room, all that remained of the family heirlooms which she had, even though hypnotized, steadily refused to let go out of her possession. Mrs. Bromleykite had by stealth acquired the key, and while her ladyship was sleeping it was an easy task for her faithful spouse to empty the casket of its entire contents. This he had no hesitation in doing, as, if the robbery were detected, "occult agency" would explain the disappearance of the gems. But as must often, if not ever, be the case, these wily tricksters had not reckoned with their host. A slight tremor passed through the sensitive frame of Madame Discalcelis who, closing her eyes for an instant, soon startled her companion by exclaiming:—

"There is a robbery now going on upstairs in this house; you and I must see to it that it is rendered unsuccessful." Then darting forward with the agility of a fawn, she bounded up the broad stairway, closely followed by Miss Poyntz, till she paused outside Lady Porchester's chamber.

After a few moments the door opened, and Mrs. Bromleykite appeared, casting furtive glances about her in the dim twilight and treading with cat-like stealth upon the heavily carpeted landing. Quick as the lightning flash which revealed in a sudden moment her livid features she felt her wrists grasped by a firm though delicate pair of hands, and the voice of a woman who hated deception sounded warningly in her ears.

"I give you one minute to deliver up those jewels, or I will have you immediately arrested."

Mrs. Bromleykite's expression, when thus brought to bay, defies description; wrath, fear, venom, cowardice, hatred, bitter disappointment, all struggled for the mastery. At last fear conquered, and throwing herself at her just accuser's feet she grovelled, crawled, whined, whimpered, begged for mercy, then throwing herself flat on her face across the landing, she fawned spaniel-like at the feet of the woman into whose eyes she dared not gaze, and cringed for forgiveness, maudlin tears coursing down her sunken, painted cheeks till the melting rouge appeared ghastly as a trickling stream of blood.

"Oh, my dearest lady, I implore you not to expose us; we did it all for 'T.H.E.M.' 'T.H.E.Y.' counselled everything; we are only their servants; oh, be merciful, be merciful! we are but poor stranded vultures, far from our ancestral nests; the world is cruel, cold, pitiless; we are 'T.H.E.I.R.' messengers, and what can we do but obey orders, though what appears like theft must land us in an English dungeon?"

"Speak no more of an infernal or fictitious 'THEY'," rang out in vibrating though low-toned accents the voice of the righteously indignant exposer of such vile artifice; "confess your own atrocious crime, acknowledge your inexcusable, unpardonable perfidy, and leave this house with your guilty accomplice, never to disturb its atmosphere again."

Mortified, chagrined beyond words, the guilty groveller, so unmistakably detected in the very act of robbery, now turned a terrified, imploring glance upon the noble woman whose electric radiation was by this time beginning to tell seriously upon the wretched impostor, whose sole desire in this plight was to accomplish undetected flight, for like all base and cowardly natures in which generosity and mercy are at the lowest ebb, she could not conceive it possible that Madame Discalcelis would do other than openly expose her, and even gloat publicly over her downfall.

Such, however, was remoter than pole from pole to the thought of a thoroughly noble-hearted lady, who never crushed even an insect that was in her power, though she would never permit a wrong to go unrighted were it in her power to set the crooked straight, no matter at what cost of personal self-sacrifice.

Hearing the lamenting tones of his agonized wife on the landing, Mr. Bromleykite — who was watching like a sentinel at the foot of Lady Porchester's bed, to see that she did not wake too soon from the hypnotic trance into which he had plunged her — quickly, but noiselessly, glided from the room, just in time to see his partner in guilt yield into the hand of Madame Discalcelis, with Miss Poyntz as witness, all the priceless necklaces, bracelets, rings, brooches, and other valuable family jewels which she had so recently abstracted from her hostess's jewel case.

"Are you mad, Sanskrita?" hissed Sanskritikus in the ear of his crouching, trembling spouse.

"Alas! we have both been mad," groaned the convulsed victim of her own unrighteous deed, as she turned her frightened, blood-shot eyes to the frenzied, quivering countenance of her livid mate; "we are both arrested now, our game is played out, we are defeated; even 'T.H.E.Y.' have deserted us in our extremity."

"If we are not rescued in this our hour of peril from the enemy, I shall renounce, and even denounce the Nameless Ones," and with an imprecation, too horrible to be reported, the frenzied, gasping biped — who seemed to have lost for the time the form of man and to have been transfigured into a hideous ape — attempted an attack of sheer violence upon Madame Discalcelis, who now held the jewels.

Once he lifted his arm to seize them from her grasp, but as he touched the firm white delicate flesh of her exquisitely moulded hand a shock went through his body conveying the biting, stinging sensation of a scorching living flame, and he lay prostrate at her feet, the muscles of his mouth twisted into execrable contortions and quivering as though with nameless blasphemies. Was it the lightning flash which felled him to the floor, — just as he fell a tremendous peal of thunder shook the house, — or was it the wondrous inner force which, unbeknown to all save very few, had been for several years slowly but surely ripening for action in the pure, healthy organism of the noble woman he so venturesomely dared to molest?

Seeing her husband fall, the now almost demented

Mrs. Bromleykite piteously wailed for mercy, and as she poured out a tale of such harrowing anguish that words fail utterly to do it justice, Madame Discalcelis, now perfectly calm and serenely majestic, stood like an angel above two imps of darkness, and reverently said:

"My poor sister, go and sin no more."

"What! are you not going to have us arrested?" fairly screamed the distracted wretch, who in fancy was already behind prison bars awaiting some awful sentence of doom; "can we after this go back to India and no one know that we have been exposed? Oh, if you grant us this reprieve, you are more than mortal, you are a divine being, even like unto one of 'T.H.E.M.'"

At the sound of the last sentence Visalia's face somewhat darkened, for she saw plainly that the terrified creature before her was still as much a hypocrite as ever, still trotting out allusions to mythical concoctions which furnished her with the stock in trade of her nefarious traffic, and only alive to the personal distress and bitter humiliation of arrest and imprisonment for theft.

"You deserve no clemency, but I am not your judge; give back all the articles you have stolen under pretext of their miraculous transit to the East, and leave London to-night never to return, unless some day you should walk its streets a lowly penitent, seeking to atone by blessed acts of virtue for foul deeds of crime. I shall restore before another five minutes have passed all that you have taken from my hostess this afternoon. I shall tell her nothing; I have now the key of her jewel case, wherein Miss Poyntz and I will instantly replace the gems. Go now to your room, pack your trunks, put an address on them where they may be forwarded, leave no word or line behind you, and depart; be to this house as though you had never entered it. I will keep your secret unless you cross my path again and I detect you in fresh perfidy. May God turn your heart, and may you live to bless mankind wherein you have formerly cursed society. This is all I can or will say to you or do for you. You have the opportunity to lead a new and honorable life if you so desire, but your destiny is entirely in your own hands. God willeth not the doom of any sinner, but moral suicide is possible to those who deliberately commit it."

These were the last syllables from the lips of Madame Discalcelis which fell on the aching ears of her rightful prisoner, as Mrs. Bromleykite slowly rose from her reptilian attitude to comply with what she doubtless called "the inevitability of her wretched karma."

Mr. Bromleykite was in a heavy swoon; but as Madame Discalcelis knew he was in no danger she restrained the anxious Katherine, who had been the silent spectator of the whole scene, from calling servants or creating the least disturbance. Entering Lady Porchester's chamber, the two ladies found her still asleep, resting placidly, and breathing at regular intervals, though not very vigorously. The first thing to do was to restore all the trinkets to their positions in the jewel box,—a work not difficult to accomplish and not involving the expenditure of more than five minutes' space. Miss Poyntz took charge of the key, — for she was the appointed key-bearer, — and the ladies quietly descended to the drawing-room, rang for the footman, and gave orders for a cab to take Mr. and Mrs. Bromleykite to the station.

Mr. Bromleykite was not long in awaking from the stupor into which electric force, human or other, had thrown him, and when he awoke he was only dazed and not sufficiently bewildered to express astonishment when, entering his chamber, he found his wife throwing all their belongings into boxes and bags as quickly as her palsied fingers could be made to move. In less than an hour the guilty couple had turned their backs on Grosvenor Square and were speeding to Euston Station, where they took the earliest express for Liverpool, from which port they intended embarking for America, as they had no intention whatever of missing the Columbian Exposition. They had left one large trunk behind them at Lady Porchester's and had labelled it "Mr. and Mrs. Lupus Geeseplucker, Adjutant Hotel, Liverpool." Their intention was to spend a week in that city and in Manchester before sailing on the *Umbria* for New York. Mr. and Mrs. Bromleykite had disappeared; their very name had vanished, and though they had been forced to restore the jewels, they had three thousand pounds (fifteen thousand dollars) with them as a "gift" from Lady Porchester, who had fulfilled three promises, made on three distinct occasions while in a hypnotic condition, to give to these "holy probationers" one thousand pounds to be used by them for the establishment of theosophical headquarters. It is needless to say the Theosophical Society knew nothing of the bequest and never saw a fraction of the money.

* * * * * * * *

Seven o'clock arrived, and dinner was announced as usual. As the house-party, now reduced to three, sat down to it, Lady Porchester said in a rather anxious tone:—

"Where are the dear Bromleykites; are they going to deprive us of their company this evening?"

"I believe they have left London; they had good reason evidently for their departure; may they not have been summoned elsewhere by the unmentionable ones?" suggested Madame Discalcelis.

"Oh dear, how very tiresome! but I daresay they have been; dear hearts, their life is *so* self-abnegating, they are so truly altruistic; they almost hinted to me the other day that 'T.H.E.Y.' might send for them."

"Well, at any rate, we must console ourselves in their absence; and as Mrs. Spottiswoode is to spend this evening with us, I do not think we need be desolate," chimed in Miss Poyntz, who felt as though a crushing weight had just been lifted from her shoulders.

"We must bear our loss with resignation; though, sweet souls! I should like to have kissed them good-bye, they were so good to me, and I have learned so much from them," articulated Lady Porchester, almost sobbingly.

Though the virtues of two barefaced scoundrels

were sounded in trumpet-tones by her ladyship all through dinner and dessert, neither Madame Discalcelis nor Miss Poyntz showed the slightest sign of knowing anything; and though Mrs. Spottiswoode arrived at half-past eight and remained chatting till nearly eleven, not a syllable did either of them whisper to even suggest that they knew anything of *why* the Bromleykites had so suddenly and mysteriously departed.

That evening, however, the diamond earrings and bracelets which on a former occasion had been "transported to India to be blessed by 'T.H.E.M.'" seemingly made or completed the return voyage, for they were found, when the cloth was removed, close to Lady Porchester's plate on the dining-table. This incident in itself was enough to keep the conversation lively for one evening, at any rate. Lady Porchester's ingenious speculative theories with frequent interjectory interruptions of, "but what do *you* think about it?" first to one and then to another of her listeners, provoked decided merriment within, though no one laughed openly at the dear, credulous old dame, who was herself the very incarnation of sincerity, though her gullible disposition had often made her the easy prey of designing adventurers. Mrs. Spottiswoode spoke freely on the subject from her own standpoint, which, however, was far from "occult"; but though she did not agree with Lady Porchester's conclusions, she was so truly polite and graciously considerate of her feelings that the worthy dame retired peacefully to rest when her visitor departed, to dream contentedly of "the dis- and reintegration of matter."

CHAPTER XII.

ARE THERE MARRIAGES IN HEAVEN?

WHEN at length it could no longer be concealed from Lady Porchester that the Bromleykites had been detected in deliberate fraud and theft, and that by her own honored guest in presence of her devoted companion, the kindly old lady heaved a sigh or two of patient resignation to what she deemed a pitiful inevitable, and then consoled herself with the quieting assurance that the experience was a necessity and the consequence of her *Karma.*

Karma is a very wonderful institution. As interpreted, or misinterpreted, by Occidental aspirants to Oriental wisdom, it is both mutable and immutable, and can be so peculiarly adjusted to the favorite conceits of individual theorists that though it is *per se* unchangeable, it can be decidedly "interfered with" by presumptuous "mental healers," who by their "hypnotic" action can cause this unchanging though changeable equation to vary in a way disastrous to the soul-growth of the impertinent ones and to the even greater detriment of the victims of the "hypnotic" art.

Madame Discalcelis had pretty thoroughly investigated "theosophy"; she had attended many meetings at the headquarters of the Theosophical Society, had enjoyed a lengthy conversation with Mrs. Besant, and had read quite extensively the voluminous literature of the "movement." As a result of these investigations she was convinced, as people say, that "there is something in it," but that "something" she found far from unadulterated truth.

Too much stress is laid by theosophists on *Oriental* doctrines, and their views of "Masters" are decidedly restricted and hazy, with but few exceptions. Starting out with the profound desire "to establish the nucleus of a universal brotherhood," they overlook the fact that to do this even in theory requires that all religions and scriptures be *impartially* examined, and that Lucretia Mott's noble motto, TRUTH FOR AUTHORITY, NOT AUTHORITY FOR TRUTH, be adopted in principle and practice alike. Theosophists, being only ordinary human entities, fall quite naturally into the errors of other denominations; they have their prejudices, idols, bugbears, scarecrows, and all the rest of the paraphernalia — including skeletons, sometimes closeted, but not infrequently paraded — which constitute the *débris* of other organizations; they preach *altruism*, and yet they practise no more philanthropy than the rest of mankind. In a word, they are just about as human, or as inhuman, as their neighbors, whichever way one likes to phrase the fact.

Madame Discalcelis was possessed with so extremely high an ideal of what theosophy should be, that she rather shrank from it as she found it, particularly as its claim for superiority to other systems was based on nothing less than the stupendous assumption that it was engineered and sustained by no less a power than that of Adepts, whose control over all earthly passions and whose knowledge of universal law is so complete that there is practically no limit to their wisdom and possible achievements.

Lady Porchester had been for many years a Spiritualist, and — though Miss Poyntz would never let it be publicly known — she was in private an excellent clairvoyante, and frequent indeed had been the messages from the unseen state that had been given through her pliant instrumentality. After the departure of the Bromleykites, Lady Porchester began to reflect a little upon the curious doctrines concerning "babbling shells," "discarded astrals," and many other concoctions of orientalized hysteria, which had been frequent topics of conversation of late; she now decided that though Spiritualism had its drawbacks, and clairvoyant predictions of coming events were not always fulfilled, there was — notwithstanding these imperfections — a solid basis of consolation and instruction in the faith of the earnest Spiritualist which nothing could successfully overturn.

TELEPATHY greatly interested many of Lady Porchester's friends, to whom the *name* rather than the *idea* of Spiritualism was offensive; these were loyal members of the English Church, who interpreted its doctrines in a peculiarly elastic manner, and found nothing in the three creeds and thirty-nine articles to interfere with their study of psychical science as members of the highly reputable body known as the Psychical Research Society of Great Britain.

In presence of strangers Miss Poyntz was usually reticent as to her "mediumistic" gifts, so much so that she always seemed pained and embarrassed if any one ventured to call attention to her possessing any such; but since the Bromleykite exposure and the constant strength derived from association with her new friend, she opened like a flower in the sunshine under the genial influence of true friendly appreciation.

It was a beautiful evening in August, after the season was entirely over, and only a very few of the *élite* were left in town, that the Eastlake-Gores, having returned from Scotland for a flying visit to London previous to their visit to the United States, called with Professor Monteith, who by this time was quite intimate in the family, to pay a farewell visit at Lady Porchester's. Madame Discalcelis was to start for Liverpool with Mrs. Gore the next morning; her trunks were already packed, and a feeling of soberness which invariably precedes parting hung over the little party, as they chatted reminiscently and then turned their conversation to the great Columbian Exposition which some of them were about to visit. More than three months of the great Fair's short but brilliant existence had already passed, and those who were bent on seeing its numberless wonders felt they must lose no time in speeding to the scene of so much human ingenuity and activity.

Professor Monteith had derived great strength and much light from his interviews with the mystical Aldebaran; but though he regarded that marvellous young *savant* as peerless in his way, he was still far from satisfied that there was, after all, any direct proof of man's individual immortality forthcoming through devotion to a study of even such profound science as Aldebaran had introduced to him. There was, in spite of all, a yearning wistfulness coupled with a corroding scepticism in his entire nature. Sometimes the angel of faith seemed to triumph for a span, then again would the demon of doubt whisper in his aching ears the old word *hallucination*, till he often felt as though the reeling of his tormented brain must land him sooner or later in the madhouse. But though occasionally his case seemed to himself desperate, whenever a climax was reached, the crisis was safely passed; for in the moment of direst extremity the voice and often the form of his beloved one would come before him in all the serene beauty of angelic loveliness, and it seemed at such times as though the aromatic breath from Sicilian lemon groves was close to his very nostrils as the presence of his unseen guardian was so palpably at hand.

Quite a discussion was carried on between the professor and Madame Discalcelis on the question of soul mates or spiritual affinities. The professor longed to believe with the lady that sex is eternal and that there are marriages in heaven, but he had of late been so much accustomed to the cold, self-satisfied theory of some occultists, that every individuality must look within itself and find completeness in its own duality, that he could scarcely do more than politely smile, shake his head, and sigh dissidently as the fair exponent of a brighter creed assured him that the theory was all a fallacy to which he had listened, and that there was no sweetness or light, to use Matthew Arnold's favorite adjectives, in a doctrine which makes introspection instead of extrospection the high road to the heights of sanctity.

"Every soul is dual," said Madame Discalcelis, warming to the subject as she proceeded, till her beautiful, expressive countenance gleamed with more than earthly radiance; "your own undying love for the companion of your youth, the heroine of your holiest dreams, the central figure in all your visions, attests the truth of my asseveration. Let your heart speak, crush no longer the dictates of your spirit, and you will know, as I know, that whatever affection ennobles us on earth will, when purified from the last iota of sensuous dross, shine forth in immortal splendor in the realm of eternal joy."

"But," remonstrated the other, "you profess to accept the Gospels; to you the teachings of the Christ are divine. How do you reconcile your assertions with the gospel words attributed to this Christ, 'In the resurrection they neither marry nor are given in marriage, but are as the angels of God'?"

"I know that passage is a stumbling-block to many," Visalia responded frankly, "but to me it surely means that the atrocious farce of re-marriage several times on the plea of widowhood could not be for an instant compared with the glorious reality of marriage in the celestial state among the beatified. One woman may become the wife of seven men in turn, if six successive husbands drop the mortal coil. Are such repeated unions heavenly? Do such marriages as those compare with angelic bliss?"

"I readily follow you so far as your detestation of several marriage unions is concerned, but do not the evangelists distinctly declare that marriage of any kind is impossible in the celestial spheres? What always appears incomprehensible to me is that women like yourself, who are evidently sincere and who entertain and freely express ideas of your own on religious subjects which, so far as I can see, no church indorses, should so persistently cling to the teachings of a prophet, many of whose recorded utterances are plainly at variance with your own convictions, and whose professed followers unsparingly denounce your views as awfully heretical if not downright blasphemous."

"My dear professor," retorted Madame Discalcelis, in her characteristically mild but penetrating way, "I care nothing for the barren say-so of any man, woman, or company of men and women, who seek to foist their mere opinions on the world as gospel truth. I do, however, behold in the evangels, as you rightly judge, a record — not unmutilated — of the supremest truth ever revealed to the family of mankind. There are no teachings extant — I care not whether you con the pages of the Vedas, Zend-Avesta, or any other collection of ancient documents venerated by millions of the human race — which contain anything like so clear and succinct a statement of the way of life as can be found in the four Gospels of the New Testament; and as to the views on marriage outlined therein, I must become familiar with the idea of angels entertained by contemporaries before an interpretation of the phrase 'they are as the angels' can be accurately or rationally offered. Originality is by no means the distinguishing mark of all the sayings of Him who declared when on trial before Pilate, 'I came to bear witness to the truth; whosoever loveth the truth heareth my voice.' Mark you, witness to the *truth*, not to *new doctrine;* truth is ancient as God, unchanging as the law of the Eternal; therefore, when the Great Teacher says that he witnesses to truth, he does not thereby deny aught that is true in any earlier revelation. 'In my father's house are many mansions; *if it were not so, I would have told you,*' is a sentence the obvious construction of which points definitely to an indorsement of a previous revelation; so do I take it that the sublime Grecian idea of the soul's duality embodied in the classics of Plato receives indorsement at the hand of the Light of the World. You remember, of course, what this distinguished Grecian sage said concerning the source of the world-wide attraction between the sexes. His theory was that one soul was divided into two parts during terrestrial expression, and that one portion of the soul was ever seeking to reunite itself with its *alter ego.* I believe in the inviolable sanctity of true marriage, I indorse the good old saying, 'marriages are made in heaven'; but by true marriages I mean such unions as stand the test of all time and all trial, and which are not 'until death parts,' but beyond the grave, even into eternity."

While she was speaking, the face of the calm but impassioned pleader for spiritual realities became so exquisitely illuminated that all eyes were riveted upon her. There seemed a subtle, all-pervasive spell which hung about her words and glorified her presence, and as she ceased speaking, it seemed as though some fairy angel had visited the spot and inspired the gifted authoress to speak, as she often wrote, under the magic spell of some divine entrancement which lifted her to supernormal heights of quite unusual eloquence.

Lady Porchester, who loved pathetic ballads and always wanted at least three songs in succession, literally implored Visalia to sing for them. As it was her last evening in London, she readily complied, and in a soft, clear, expressive voice, to her own exquisite accompaniment, she gave, at her hostess's urgent request, "Darby and Joan," "Gretna Green," and "Some Day." Between her second and third numbers she played an accompaniment to "My Queen," which Mr. Gore rendered superbly, reminding those who had heard Sims Reeves in his best days of that wonderful tenor's unequalled rendering of that gem of Blumenthal's. As song followed song, each expressing similar pure sentiment, — though each in a different way, — Mrs. Gore whispered to Lady Porchester: —

"If my son should find *his* queen in that good woman, I should be more than satisfied. She is the only person I have ever met whom I could welcome as a daughter without a single pang or shadow of reluctance."

They formed a magnificent couple. One contrasted with the other in appearance as perfectly as their splendid voices reflected glory each on the other; and when at length they sang a duet, — Gounod's "Maying," —

there seemed so complete a blending of soul as well as tone in the subtle harmony of the great French composer so recently called to swell the ranks of the great majority, that Lady Porchester herself felt that, after all, the charming Visalia was better adapted to the noble Arthur than even her own priceless Katherine, and then, the dear old lady seemed to reflect, with perhaps the slightest shade of self-thoughtfulness, which even the most benevolent among us have not *entirely* overcome, "if Katherine were to marry, what should I do without her?"

It had always been a matter of comment and wonder that Madame Discalcelis (properly Signorina) always adopted the mature Madame in preference to the more appropriate Mademoiselle, and it was known that when certain gentlemen of her acquaintance had discovered that she was both single and unpledged, and they had in rapid succession offered her their hearts and fortunes, — several were very wealthy and distinguished, — she had invariably made but one answer: "If ever I marry, it will be in answer to the call of Heaven, and that call comes not when you address me." People thought her odd, lacking in affection, devoted to curious theories of mysticism, etc., etc.; they talked about her with bated breath, as though her refusal of matrimonial offers from men she could not truly love was an evidence of partial insanity or that it suggested some uncanny witchcraft connected with her. But she cared little, if at all, for impertinent comments, and went on the even tenor of her way without so much as a thought bestowed upon the gossips who sought to attribute what would be in their eyes a sufficient reason for "her most extraordinary conduct."

On one occasion Mrs. Florence Nimblecat — a young widow, obliged to earn her living by interviewing celebrities for the *Westminster Codfisher* — declared it was positively wicked of any woman to refuse such eligible men; had any one of them proposed to *her*, *she* would have literally sprung to him and sealed the compact there and then with tears and kisses. Mrs. Nimblecat owed Madame Discalcelis a decided grudge, and in some stealthy manner she hoped some day to be able to pay it off with compound interest. Interviewers are usually vulgar and always intrusive; not content with seeking to elicit facts concerning one's *public* efforts, they pry conscioncelessly into the most private matters of a human life. Veiled skeletons are their greatest perquisites, and to reveal a carefully guarded secret, especially if it be of a delicate or painful character, they will sail through seas of scandal, and gloat over the suffering they cause to natures more sensitive than their own. The private life of the fair Visalia was *sans peur et sans reproche*, but that mattered not to Mrs. Nimblecat; if she could not sensationalize innocently, then she must — to butter her bread of course — *invent* scandal, and on one occasion, after having called sixteen times and been refused, she crept into the drawing-room one Monday afternoon unannounced, at the heels of Mrs. Montley Moorhouse, — a portly dowager with flowing skirts, — and sidling up to her intended victim, said in a stage whisper: —

"As a friend I have come to warn you, madame, that

Askalon will be utterly annihilated by Mr. Sneakswell Pfhule, the eminent critic for the Belgravia *Tattler*, unless you give me within the next twenty-four hours a personal sketch of your private life, accompanied by your portrait"; then in wheedling tone and with an assumed mirthfulness, "You may tell me all the *lies* you please; that makes no difference whatever: we get paid as much, and it sells the paper just as readily; and as to your portrait, you may give me anybody else's if you prefer, so long as I can *say* that it is the very latest of yourself. And, by the way, as to the book review, you may write it yourself, and Mr. Pfhule will sign his name to it for ten pounds if it is a long article; if you write only a short notice, he will put you through for half that amount; and as for myself, I leave it to your generosity."

"Tell Mr. Pfhule," replied the authoress, unmoved by this brazen, dishonest effrontery, "that his *condemnation* of my book might be a compliment; a liar's indorsement of anything is a deliberate insult." With which retort she turned away from Mrs. Nimblecat abruptly and entered into animated conversation with a young debutante who had been cruelly and grossly insulted by the notorious Pfhule in the latest *Tattler*, because she would not purchase criticisms from a man who received twenty pounds a week to report the proceedings at the places whither his employer sent him.

Mr. Gore, hearing of the incident, had straightway fallen truly and deeply in love with the one literary woman whom he had found utterly fearless and entirely conscientious, and she had almost reciprocated his emotion when she discovered that he alone of all the reviewers of her acquaintance would never accept a bribe, never say a heartless word of or to a struggling aspirant to fame, and never bid for mediocrity's approval.

A soft spell, as though the wings of the legendary Peace Angel were outspread over the company, seemed to brood in silence over all. Lady Porchester softly murmured as she saw the old, familiar, far-away, dreamy look in Katherine's eyes, "We may now expect a word of counsel." Then gently and quietly, but with intense earnestness, there came from the lips of the partially entranced sensitive the words: —

"Marriages are made in heaven; when they are made is a divine secret pertaining to a cycle in eternity to which our feeble recollection while embodied here may not revert. Here or elsewhere, every spirit will find and be blissfully united with its counterpart; many a time in the lives of those who pass their days unmated here, there comes a sweet conviction that in the happy *Elsewhere* they are already one with the other. Conscious at times of such true union, even when in their ordinary waking state, are keenly sensitive lives on earth, and when such consciousness infills and pervades the nature of any man or woman, then does selfishness yield to selflessness, as the divine passion of spiritual affection causes the whole being to dilate with love to all humanity. Wrapped in the mantle of self-satisfaction, centred in one's own immediate affairs, given to incessant introspection only, the spirit of man or woman fails to expand. God has ordained the dual state; spiritual unions are eternal, and happy indeed are they in any state, in any period, who discover this truth and whose lives are consequently illumined with a bliss and satisfaction otherwise impossible of realization."

As the inspired speaker ceased, there was a gentle rustle as of pinions of light, a soft murmur as of sweet, distant music floating mystically across the air, and suddenly, yet without the slightest shock or start, Professor Monteith exclaimed, a smile of rapture illumining his ordinarily depressed countenance: —

"Yes, it is true; this is now the third time within two months that I have actually seen her."

An hour or more glided by in sweet, restful silence; the professor occasionally ejaculated an expression such as, "Yes, it *is* true; I *cannot* be mistaken." No one wished to talk or seemed disposed to move, till the clock broke the stillness by sounding the hour of eleven. Then, guided by the unspoken thought of some one seen or unseen, Madame Discalcelis and Mr. Eastlake-Gore went together to the piano and sang, as only exquisitely natural singers can sing, duets from the Italian composers, those rare masters of melody who more than the musicians of any other clime know how to express in perfect musical forms the profoundest emotions of the human heart. The last song was by Visalia alone. A copy of *Love Letters of a Violinist* by Eric Mackay — a very favorite book of poems in the Porchester household — was lying near the piano, and the fair songstress taking it up, as it appeared thoughtlessly, improvised an air which exactly suited the tender, graceful sentiment of one of the Italian gems in that beautiful collection of poems — nearly all in the English language — which lend themselves instantly to the most exalted feelings of a refined and sympathetic spirit. As the singer ceased her singing, the book fell to the floor. Arthur stooped to pick it up and replace it on the piano; as he bent to reach the volume his hair lightly touched the lady's hand. In that momentary contact the infallible indicator within her unusually unfolded being told her as words could never have told that the noble, knightly gentleman, whose irreproachable honor was greater than all his other charms of character and person, was the one in all the earth to whom she could link her life and destiny without one thought of misgiving or fear. The recognition though silent was instant and complete.

Professor Monteith was positively merry over chocolate; the iron which had for so long dwelt in his soul seemed now to have been extracted, and for once he was bright and happy as a healthy boy home for holidays after his examinations have been passed with honor.

There is always a tinge of sadness at a parting hour when some are going across the briny deep; but so full of spiritual light and consolation was the very apartment, that good-bye only implied God bless you, and farewell signified only, May you ever fare on the best that Heaven affords.

CHAPTER XIII.

LADY HUNTLEY'S REMINISCENCES AND A TELEPATHIC INCIDENT.

WITH much genuine regret at parting from so true and amiable a friend, Lady Porchester and Miss Poyntz bade a tearful farewell to Madame Discalcelis at Euston Station the day following, at which terminus she joined the Eastlake-Gores and Professor Monteith, who were on their way to the Columbian Exposition in company.

Returning home after bidding adieu to their beloved guest, the two ladies were not sorry to find a visitor from Brighton, Lady Clementina Huntley, ready to regale them in her always entertaining manner with some of her most recent spiritual experiences.

Lady Huntley was a queenly woman in style and bearing, and one, moreover, who had been accustomed to command a regiment of domestics before her marriage to Lord Colin Huntley, at her father's beautiful castle in Scotland, where her youth had been most happily spent. Since their marriage Lord and Lady Huntley had travelled three quarters over the world; they had been in Egypt, India, Syria, Turkey, and no one knew how many more historic lands, and had returned to England with mental as well as physical trophies of their extended voyagings by sea and land in quest of health, pleasure, and information. During the last two or three years Lady Huntley had been the recipient of some very striking evidences of the action upon or within herself of a power which impelled her to write poems and hymns of great force and rare beauty, and as Lady Porchester was always eager for the latest and the fullest tidings which could be brought to her of all phases of psychical experience, Lady Huntley knew she could always find in her old friend and confidante an appreciative listener.

Lunch was scarcely over when, opening her reticule and taking out a roll of manuscripts, Lady Huntley commenced reading poem after poem which had "come to her," she declared, in the most unexpected manner.

"The following," she said, "I consider a remarkable experience, not only from the way in which I received it, but also that it points to the purest theism, as the religion taught by the most advanced spirits. Two years ago, in Chicago, while attending Sunday spiritual services there, a hymn, little above doggerel, was sung to the tune 'America.' (In fact, except the national anthems of England and America, which I do not presume to criticise, I have rarely seen hymns to that metre, worthy of the tune.) On leaving the church, I made this remark to my husband, and said, 'I wish I could be influenced to write a suitable hymn for that tune.' I do not think I gave the subject any further thought, but a few days after, while otherwise occupied, I asked my husband to write from my dictation the following hymn: —

"Thou love ineffable,
Father unchangeable,
Ruler o'er all;
Of light, infinite source;
Of life, eternal force;
Of worlds who mark'st the course,
On thee we call.

"Thee, sun and stars adore.
As they all space explore
They worship thee.
Thou author of our days,
While seraphs hymn thy praise,
We chant our noblest lays,
Thine offspring we.

"Almighty parent thou,
We at thy footstool bow,
We thee adore;
Enthroned in light who art
New life to every heart,
Of thy free grace impart,
We thee implore.

"As angels, who thy will,
All thy behests fulfil
With willing feet;
Thy spirit us inspire,
Baptize with sacred fire,
Be it our soul's desire
Thy will to meet.

"Omnipotence Divine!
All power and glory thine.
May every soul
Receive thy gracious word,
Thy Kingdom come, O Lord,
Thy spirit be outpoured
To make earth whole.

"When finished, I said: 'I believe that is an adaptation from the Sanscrit, and was sung in ancient Atlantis.' Judge, then, of our surprise, the following Sunday evening to hear, as the inspired speaker's invocation, the hymn of the previous week, not in exactly the same metre, but line by line in blank verse, or poetical prose.

"On leaving the church, a clairvoyante said to me: 'Are you aware your guide was on the platform tonight influencing the lecturer?' I think this accounts for the hymn and invocation being almost identical; and I have reasons to believe, which to us are conclusive, that this guide whom the lady saw was Yermah, the Atlantian."

The conversation changing after this to the topic of spiritual marriage, the discussion of the previous evening having considerably exercised Lady Porchester, so much so that she was eager to talk it over with Lady Huntley, whom she regarded as quite an authority on all questions somewhat beyond the ordinary — that ever-reminiscent lady gave the following singular narration, which she declared to be correct in every detail:

"It was in the winter of 1878 that our kind friends Mr. and Mrs. Gordon were residing at Bournemouth, in the home of Mr. and Mrs. Thaw, 18 West Cliff Street, who had long been so interested in psychic phenomena, that almost every inmate of their house, whether relative or servant, became decidedly mediumistic; a fact we can only explain in accordance with our very decided conviction that psychic gifts are dormant in the great majority of the people we meet on our daily path in life, whatever that path may be, only needing a stimulating influence from their neighbors, if not from their own desires, to fan the lambent spark into a flame. A girl about fifteen years of age, quite illiterate, and with no previous knowledge of aught pertaining to Spiritualism, entered the Thaw household as a kitchen-maid. About three months later, this untutored child, whose humble occupation, like Dickens' 'Marchioness,' filled all her time and employed all her energy, was the subject of the following amazing experience. Mrs. Thaw's sister had passed out of the body shortly before her intended marriage to a young man who followed her to spirit-life soon after. One evening when this little maid was called upon to prepare the evening meal as usual, it was found impossible to awaken her; she had retired to her chamber and locked herself in; she appeared between eight and nine o'clock, to inform Mrs. Thaw that she had been present at a marriage ceremony in the spiritual world, the contracting parties being Mrs. Thaw's sister and the young man to whom she was engaged on earth. The escort was 'Pietro,' the familiar spirit-guide of a famous London medium. She gave a full account of the marriage, which was performed by a clergyman of the Anglican Church and in the words of the book of Common Prayer. She gave the names of many of the persons present, who included many notable individuals known to Mr. and Mrs. Thaw, prominent among whom was the celebrated American, Judge Edmonds. The temple was beautifully decorated with flowers. 'Pietro' having to return to earth to be present at a *séance* given in London that evening, told Margerie that if she would lock her door on retiring for the night, he would accompany her to the festivities in honor of the nuptials. On again arriving in the spiritual world she was magnificently attired as became a wedding guest; the dressing-rooms were all bowers of flowers. A splendid ball was given in a spacious hall luxuriously adorned, at which she danced from midnight till six in the morning, except during the interval for refreshments, when she was treated to viands of so *recherché* a character, consisting principally of marvellous fruits, that when she returned to her earthly consciousness and her duties in the kitchen, she could not eat the food presented to her for days, and regretted bitterly that 'Pietro' had not acceded to her request, which was a piteous appeal to be permitted to remain permanently in the spiritual state. The food she had partaken of in her exalted condition was evidently of so sustaining a character that the forty-eight hours' fast which followed its consumption in no way reduced her strength or disqualified her from the performance of her monotonous labor, distasteful and gross though it appeared. To show that this girl (Margerie) had become a wonderful medium whose clairvoyance was susceptible of verification, we append the following interesting narrative: While 'Pietro' was absent in London at Mr. Eglantine's *séance*, a private circle was being held at Mr. Thaw's, at which Mr. and Mrs. Thaw, Miss Emeline Thaw, Mr. and Mrs. Gordon, and Margerie were present. Margerie and Emeline were seated side by side. Shortly after singing and when conversation had subsided, Emeline exclaimed, 'Don't you hear guns firing?' Margerie answered, 'Don't you see ships?' Emeline replied, 'No, I do not'; when Margerie continued, 'Come up here where I am and you will see them plainly.' (The two girls, it must be remembered, were seated close together at a table.) Emeline, after a moment's silence, said, 'Yes, I see them now, and the firing is from these ships into a city, but no one seems to be hurt and the people are moving about.' Mr. Thaw asked, 'Can you give the name of the city?' The answer came hesitatingly: 'B-A-T-O,' and then stopped. Next day the London journals gave an account of a false attack made on Batoum the night before, to see whether the garrison was watchful. This is but one out of many instances going far to prove the genuineness of the psychic discernment of these remarkable girls, the elder of which was only sixteen. Later the same evening Margerie passed into a trance and appeared terror-struck, shouting '*Fire*, FIRE; *murder*, MURDER; the soldiers are killing all the people and burning the houses.' Others in the room saw the reflection of the fire, but heard nothing; next morning the same London papers reported that during the previous night Russian soldiers had attacked a village among the mountains of Asia Minor, massacred the inhabitants, and set fire to the village — a pretty strong corroboration of Margerie's clairvoyance. Many similar incidents are to my positive knowledge quite frequent in the experiences of thoroughly well-balanced people, positively confirming the existence of seerships in the present generation."

Had Lady Huntley not been obliged to meet a pressing engagement at four o'clock, she could doubtless have continued her psychical narrations indefinitely; but being a very punctual woman, hating to be kept waiting herself or to keep others waiting, she could not be induced to stay a moment longer when the clock warned her she had only just time to meet her engagement, and the footman announced that her carriage was in waiting.

Shortly after Lady Huntley's departure, Miss Poyntz experienced a tingling sensation in her right hand, which always made her feel that some friend was desirous of conveying a message to or through her telepathically. Taking pencil in hand and letting it rest gently on a large sheet of white paper spread out on the table before her, quite automatically the pencil wrote in a clear, fine hand, quite unlike her own: —

"We had a delightful journey to Liverpool, where we have just arrived. We like our rooms at the Queen's Hotel very much, and wish you were both with us. The steamer sails to-morrow at four in the afternoon. We are going to a grand concert in St. George's Hall this evening, and hope you will realize where we are and how we are drinking in the harmonies. Your faithful friend, VISALIA."

Only very seldom did Miss Poyntz receive such distinctly definite messages, and as she was something of a novice in telepathy, they interested her intensely, while they occasioned rapture in the breast of Lady Porchester. An hour later a telegram arrived containing those identical words in precisely the same order but with the omission of the sentence "your faithful friend," and the signature "Eastlake-Gore," instead of "Visalia." The perfect accuracy of the message and the reason for the discrepancy in the dispatch was fully explained the day following, when a letter for both ladies came from Madame Discalcelis, in which she related the fact of her dictating the telegram and asking Mr. Gore to send it, and at the same time *willing* that Miss Poyntz should receive a telepathic message.

Telepathy is still only in its infancy and but very imperfectly understood even by those who most fully accept it as a reality. For the enlightenment of all who are really interested in it as a science, we will say that three conditions are imperatively necessary for its successful demonstration.

1st. Perfect easy confidence on the part of the sender.

2d. Passivity and freedom from all interference with what is being written on the part of the receiver.

3d. Sympathy in thought between sender and receiver, amounting to concordance of mutual vibrations.

When these three indispensable requisites are furnished, telepathy is as exactly demonstrable as ordinary electric telegraphy.

CHAPTER XIV.

'TWIXT SHORE AND SHORE. — A GLIMPSE OF MARS.

THOUGH the *City of Alexandria* was more crowded than it usually is on an outgoing passage in August, in consequence of the great concourse of tourists *en route* to the Fair, Mr. Gore had exercised such admirable discretion in booking passage six weeks ahead of sailing date that his mother and her guest, as well as himself and Professor Monteith, were provided with the very choicest rooms that magnificent vessel contains.

Madame Discalcelis was never ill at sea — indeed, she was rarely unwell anywhere; for though of an unusually sensitive organization, her constitution was so phenomenally sound and her general health so excellent, that she astonished every one who met her with the apparent contradiction between a very delicately organized body and an amazing amount of vitality. To her the trip to America had all the charm of complete novelty, for hitherto she had never sailed on other waters than the North Sea, the Bay of Biscay, and the Mediterranean. Though a very young woman, she had travelled largely in Europe, having visited within the last five years Spain, Italy, France, Norway, and Austria, in all of which countries she had enjoyed perfect health and entered sympathetically as well as intelligently into the life and manners of the people among whom she resided, not as an alien, but as a friend. With all the merry joyousness of a girl, this woman — whom many people in "society" thought cold and heartless, because her depth of character was beyond their power to fathom — paced lightly as a bird up and down the steamer deck in even the roughest weather, and never once absented herself from table on plea of *mal de mer*. The free bounding ocean suited her temperament far better than the gas-illumined salons of the English nobility, and it was a rare and real delight to her to feel that there was no roof over her head but the star-gemmed vault of azure, as on the upper deck of the steamer she sat or stood hour after hour — when most of the passengers had retired to their cabins or were afraid to leave them — gazing into the peerless wonders of the celestial canopy.

There were times when the glory of the night inspired her to sing, again it would move her to fervent prayer, and yet again to tears; but her tears were sweet, not bitter, for they were tears of faith and gratitude, not even touched by complaining or despair. Sometimes Mrs. Gore would sit by her and endeavor to read her face, but she could never penetrate the meaning of the mystic light in those expressive orbs, which were sometimes blue as sapphires and then would change till they appeared almost hazel. A truly mystical face, when it is a perfectly healthy and open countenance, is a wonderful and glorious study. The play of light and shade is so exquisitely fine, the glimpses gained of the soul behind are so vivid, yet so incomprehensible, that the face of one who is truly inspired is a living mirror in which are reflected forms of beauty, conceptions of grace and perfectness, far beyond all mortal designation.

Visalia was not satisfied with *Askalon*, though it had sold to the extent of 350,000 copies and had netted her seven thousand pounds; she knew it was a success artistically and financially, but it did not embody half she desired to reveal to the few among the masses who would eagerly read all she wrote, who could really appreciate the best she had to disclose to them. She was asking the stars to tell her about themselves, and as fiery Mars rode high in the heavens, it seemed to her that she could see within its atmosphere the life of its inhabitants. Astronomers are forever speculating as to whether Mars is or is not inhabited, but so far their painstaking researches have availed little to settle this disputed point, and perhaps, after all, it may be reserved for spiritual insight or psychic perception to actually pierce the earthly veil and discern the true condition of the earth's brother planet.

To the eyes of the fair seeress, as she reclined one lovely evening in her steamer chair, after the moon had risen and the calm of night spread like a gracious protecting pall over the sleeping passengers (she was utterly alone on deck and it was near midnight), it seemed to her that the body of Mars shone out through a silvery drapery of cloud like the exquisite form of a glorious statue through the filmiest veil of lace drapery. As the planet revealed itself, it exhibited a state far in advance of the condition of this semi-benighted star; and as the panorama of its wonders appeared slowly to unroll, the buildings in the cities disclosed themselves as such perfect specimens of architectural design that the builders of earth might seek to cultivate the higher clairvoyance, if by its means they could catch glimpses of the supernal splendor of those majestic habitations. The air seemed very clear, bracing, intellectually stimulating to the highest degree, and so rarefied that the range of perspective was at least three times greater than on earth. As to natural scenery, it was bold and impressive in outline and general features, but nothing appeared large. The Martians are almost a Lilliputian race, but they are exquisitely modelled and their forms are moulded into the most enchanting symmetry.

To the vision of the ecstatically entranced Visalia the forms which floated before her superconscious vision seemed like stately forms of mind, wherein the passions were so entirely governed that though Mars was worshipped by ancient Greeks and Romans as the god of war, the very idea of anything so senseless and barbaric as a sanguinary conflict seemed impossible on the part of those superbly wise creatures, whose mellow mien suggested such ripened intelligence as bespeaks the impulse to warfare completely surpassed by understanding of the true science of equitable government.

In a hall of legislation there appeared a tribunal, where on twelve raised seats sat twenty-four rulers of the twelve provinces of the special territory to the sight of which Madame Discalcelis was intromitted;

these twenty-four rulers or representatives-in-chief of the twelve districts were married couples whose thoughts flowed so perfectly in harmony that one might well believe they represented the twelve signs of the zodiac, and therefore in their complementary deliberations each pair perceived and suggested something essential to the general good not beheld by any or all of the other eleven couples. There was no strife, no harsh contradictory arguments, no endeavor on the part of any to antagonize the others, but sweetly, rhythmically, like the cadence of a perfectly rendered song, the united thought of the twelve senatorial couples flowed forth into the splendid council chamber, which in shape was a perfect duo-decimon. When any one proposed any measure or made any suggestion all the others listened quietly and with the utmost attention, and though immediate acquiescence was not always forthcoming, it never appeared necessary to *fight* for an issue when cool deliberation always in due time resulted in the adoption of every desirable proposition.

The social condition on Mars has been for many centuries far more perfect than the most zealous enthusiasts for socialism and nationalism have ever hoped would prevail on earth by the opening of the twenty-first century; for, owing to the superiority of the Martians to such sordid mercenariness and such vulgar plutocracy as prevails on earth, it is not difficult to persuade the multitude to co-operate for the common good. Business on Mars is conducted on strictly scientific principles, and as to Art, it receives that untrammelled expression which is only possible where the vulgar necessity of sacrificing genius to mediocre taste, for physical maintenance, does not in even the smallest measure prevail. On Mars religion seems to consist in such faithful discharge of every obligation, in such fealty to conviction, and such perfect loyalty to duty, that there is no gulf or barrier separating the creed *professed* on one day of a week to the life *lived* on six other days. Religion there is, for though the Martians are giants in intellect and have made scientific discoveries and applications far in advance of the most romantic dreams of the *savans* of Earth, they are no doubters, nor do they think *agnosticism* scientific, when the GNOSTIC (knowing one) is and can be the only true scientist. To the dwellers on Mars GOD *is a reality;* if they have ever passed through the materialistic stage they have happily left it far behind them, and as they study the marvellous *phenomena* of the universe they plainly discern the majestic working of the infinite NOUMENON, without whom there could be no phenomena.

* * * * * * * * * *

Softly as the footfall of a cat, a quiet step gently vibrated on the deck, and the vacant chair a few feet from where Madame Discalcelis was reclining was occupied by Professor Monteith, who, drawn partly by the beauty of the night, but far more by his own restless spirit, had wandered to the upper deck in search of he knew not what. He had that very day been reading in the *Popular Science Monthly* of an Italian astronomer's recent theories of the possible inhabitation of other worlds than ours, and as he read the thought occurred to him over and over again with haunting persistency, "Why, oh why, is there so much speculation and seemingly no certainty whatever even among our greatest scientific lights? If, indeed, there be such a thing as science, which means knowledge, if it is not a ridiculous farce and ironical misnomer, why should there be no *definite knowledge* concerning something, even though our knowledge necessarily is limited to a mere fragment of the universe? But surely concerning the fragment which we can explore we ought to be able to find out something." Whenever he ruminated thus, and such ruminations were becoming very frequent with him, his thoughts turned partly to Aldebaran, who was beyond his reach, and partly to Madame Discalcelis, between whom and himself there was growing up a steady bond of genuine sympathy, begotten of his wondrous visions of the *inamorata* of his youth, whose gentle, searching, spiritual presence always seemed more real to him after he had spent an hour in Visalia's presence; for, though she was not what the world usually calls a spiritualist, he knew of no one who was so ever-ready to indorse and encourage that kind of spiritual communion which is expressed by sincere desire to become conscious of union with the higher life through a lifting of our own consciousness, not seeking to attract the dwellers in a brighter state to the dark shadows and sordid miseries of ordinary mortal undertakings.

When Visalia was in "one of her trances," as many people styled her periods of superconscious activity, she appeared singularly beautiful; no trace of catalepsy or hysteria marred the loveliness of her exalted condition, and no rigidity of muscle or death-like swoon rendered her state alarming to the physiologist. Perfect health was indicated in her pose, in her regular breathing, in the gentle movements of her chest, and in the perfect regularity of her heart-beats and her pulse, while her countenance was irradiated with an expression of intense delight, indicating her absolute concentration upon an object presented to her inner gaze.

When Professor Monteith approached within her atmosphere, she was just returning to her ordinary waking condition, and according to her invariable experience at such a time, was feeling not only ready but anxious to tell to some appreciative listener the tale of her recent vision. Professor Monteith seemed to divine the nature of her "dream," as he called it, for his first words to her were: —

"I have been studying to-day, and you have been dreaming to-night on the same subject, but while I have gained nothing satisfactory from my perusal of recent scientific writings, you, I venture to presume, have been favored with what to you is conclusive evidence on the score of Mars and its interesting population. I wish I could believe as you do in this inner sense. I joined the Society for Psychical Research two years ago, and I have listened attentively to testimony, but nothing, not even my own occasional blissful visions of my beloved one, can silence finally my doubts."

"If you are going to speak in that strain, I have nothing to say to you: we have already gone over that ground too often; you know that I affirm that no one need doubt, — faith and doubt alike are voluntary. I choose the former as being far nobler and more soul-satisfying; as the latter brings you no joy or sweet contentment, I advise you to abandon it. If you let evidence appeal to you, and you are impartial in your attitude toward it, you can be as sure as I am that the *unseen* realm is not *invisible* and that the *unknown* truth is not *unknowable*. But if you are here to ask me about Mars, I will tell you what I have witnessed; take it as a fancy sketch if you prefer, though to me it is reality."

Seeing the professor really interested and in no mood for idle carping, the gifted seeress related all she had seen and heard within the past two hours. As she finished her narration the professor, deeply interested, plied her with question after question, and as she answered them it seemed for the first time clear to him that, whatever might be the source of her instruction, she was unmistakably inspired; for here was a young woman devoid of what he and his school would call all scientific education, able to answer profoundly, learnedly, explicitly, questions touching upon the technical points of exact science, and beyond being equal to the task of answering, she anticipated and raised inquiries which none but an accomplished expert could possibly devise or handle. Mystification is certainly not conviction, but to be mystified as Professor Monteith that night was mystified was to be almost, if not entirely, persuaded to accept Visalia's cherished theory that the book of universal knowledge is an unsealed volume to all who are determined to bravely launch upon its occult waters and ascend into its currents of superterrestrial air.

"But, my dear Madame, what do *you* understand by inspiration when you say we may all become inspired? You do not evidently mean that you are in direct communion with the Infinite, nor are you *under* any influence, as spiritualist mediums claim to be; there is, for example, an appreciable difference between your condition and that of Miss Poyntz, though she strikes me as far above the plane of ordinary mediums or clairvoyants. You say you do not leave your body, you do not travel through space in an 'astral form,' as certain theosophists claim they do; how, then, do you account for your own experiences? Can you explain the *modus operandi* of your superior states so that I may at least be able to consider them on the basis of an intelligible working hypothesis?"

"To answer you as you and the subject deserve would require knowledge far greater than mine, and I hope some day you will meet the teacher who taught me first how to relate myself at will to the unseen circles; I can give you his theory, which I fully accept, as he gave it to me in Genoa when we were waiting for a steamer to carry us to Naples. 'There are,' he said, 'circles of souls who are in such complete unison that they constitute, to use the expressive Gospel phrase, "a mansion in the Father's house"; to one or other of these circles all of us belong, whether we are aware of it or not. When we become conscious of this relationship and claim our privilege of working within our confraternity, the knowledge possessed by the entire society — by its incarnate and excarnate members equally — is open to us for our use to the extent we can absorb or comprehend it. When we acknowledge this relationship and claim the privileges springing from it we feel ourselves intromitted to the spiritual state, and when this is our experience we see, hear, taste, touch, and smell on another and higher plane of consciousness than the highest of which we are at other times aware.' This night I felt myself in vibratory unison with those members of the circle to which I belong who are familiar with the state of Mars, because they are capable of seeing it. But it is now near one o'clock, and we must postpone further conversation till to-morrow."

Madame Discalcelis never said more than what she deemed sufficient on any occasion, and when she had spoken she quietly but firmly ended an interview; her interlocutors might wish to keep it up indefinitely, but she would wish them a graceful *au revoir* and trip lightly away to her retirement where none could follow her.

CHAPTER XV.

CAN WE REGULATE OUR DREAMS?

THE experiences of Madame Discalcelis and of Professor Monteith, though supposed to be of a strictly private nature, could not be kept entirely secret from the more inquisitive or inquiring among the passengers, and there were several among them who professed far more than superficial interest in matters pertaining to the occult.

One lady in particular, who was fascinated with *Peter Ibbetson*, and wanted everybody to read it, had tried for several nights in succession to acquire the delightful faculty of DREAMING TRUE, by following as closely as possible the directions given in that extraordinary book for attaining this much-to-be-desired result; but though Mrs. Emily Guy Throgmorton had tried hard to go to sleep at will in a most unnatural and uncomfortable position, she still declared there was a missing link somewhere in the chain of her knowledge of how to proceed.

Mrs. Throgmorton being a decidedly voluble woman, very fond of conversing at all times and in all places with anybody who sympathized in the least with her theories and aspirations, very soon succeeded in identifying Mrs. Felina Wolf-Katzenheimer, who was going to the World's Fair as a delegate to nine congresses as well as to the Parliament of Religions, but who, despite her prominent position on the lecture platform, had no desire to be lionized or quizzed while making the passage from Liverpool to New York.

To avoid recognition, if possible, Mrs. Katzenheimer had registered her maiden name, and passed therefore as plain Miss Wolf, an appellation which excited no curiosity. As four days out of the eight required for the trip were now over, and no one had ferreted out her identity, the delegate to so many congresses felt herself pretty secure from molestation; but she knew not that Mrs. Throgmorton was on board, a fit of sea-sickness having confined that usually over-active personage to her stateroom from within two hours of leaving the dock at Liverpool.

Mrs. Throgmorton had by this time recovered, and the day being singularly bright and welcoming, she basked in the sunshine on deck, comfortably pillowed and shawled in a luxurious reclining-chair, watching with eager interest all the passers-by and striving as far as possible to catch the drift of floating conversation, that she might, if possible, discover who on the ship was interested in psychical research, to which she was herself supremely and passionately devoted. Her observations soon resulted in her discovery of Mrs. Katzenheimer, whom she recognized instantly as the well-known teacher and writer on mental science whom she had invited on several occasions to speak to select coteries of her bosom friends in her own stately house in Kensington Mall.

Mrs. Katzenheimer was engrossed in conversation with an English clergyman on one side, and the wife of an American Unitarian preacher on the other, both of whom she was entertaining with an account of some of her own decidedly noteworthy psychical experiences. As her voice was clear and penetrating, every syllable being distinctly enunciated, though with a slight German accent, Mrs. Throgmorton, whose hearing was very acute, heard every iota of the conversation and it interested her immensely, the subject being closely allied to the narrative of *Peter Ibbetson.*

"I often dream true myself," declared Mrs. Katzenheimer; "and many of my dreams are prophetic," she continued, as the Rev. Percival Saint George regarded her with mild wonder, and Mrs. Geoffrey Arlington ejaculated:—

"You don't mean to tell us so!"

To the Teutonic intellect many Americanisms are slightly embarrassing, and when one says by way of displaying interest in what another is relating, "You *don't* say so," the German mind is apt to become a little confused if not resentful, and exclaim, "But I *do* mean to say it"; then follow mutual explanations, ending with perfect comprehension of each other's intentions.

What a pity it is, however, that language is not so simplified in its usage that words are employed in harmony with their obvious significance and in accord with their derivations; were this the case, how much fewer would be the perplexities and misunderstandings which at present needlessly and afflictingly perplex all who are strangers by birth to some special forms of the English tongue.

Mrs. Throgmorton, hearing distinctly Mrs. Arlington's proposal that Mrs. Katzenheimer should deliver an address on "The Science of Dreaming True, and how we may receive an Education while Asleep," took her earliest opportunity to mention the fact to every man, woman, and child who passed her chair while promenading the deck. When she met the lecturer face to face, she at once engaged her in a confab which lasted till the bell for the second dinner warned the loquacious enthusiasts that, were they to converse much longer, they would lose their principal repast, and as they were both hungry they agreed to let *psychical research* and *mental healing* remain in abeyance till the meal had ended.

That very evening at half-past eight, permission having been easily obtained from the captain, Mrs. Katzenheimer held forth to a crowded *salon*. She was a woman of rather striking appearance, about middle height, and not portly, but very well built; her hair was a decided yellow and her eyes were pure Saxon blue; her voice was clear and at times loud, but never harsh or grating, and though her delivery was often rapid, she enunciated so distinctly that not a word was lost. Knowing that many on the ship besides Mrs. Throgmorton had been reading *Peter Ibbetson* during the voyage, she led off with a little review of that extraordinary autobiography, and then gave, as was her usual wont, philosophical arguments, among which were interweaved many singular personal experiences. Unbeknown to Mrs. Katzenheimer, there was a stenographer almost at her elbow, a young man who was desirous of seeing how an "inspirational" address would read if reported *verbatim in extenso*. The following is Mrs. Katzenheimer's speech just as she delivered it, according to the testimony of Mr. Charles Mountford Collins, special correspondent to one of the largest New York dailies.

Dreaming True.

Among the many psychic stories with which the book market has recently been flooded we know of none so full of thrilling, intense, sustained interest as *Peter Ibbetson*, published by Harpers, a work which, while professedly a series of autobiographical sketches given to the world subsequent to the demise of their author, has from first to last all the characteristics of a fascinating, and we must add somewhat improbable, though not impossible, romance. An English lady of title, who writes under the assumed name of "Madge Plunkett," declares in her introductory statement that a distant relative of her own actually passed through experiences almost, if not entirely, identical with those related of the hero in the narrative, and as the work itself, whether considered as prose or poetry, fact or fiction, possesses many features of intense interest to the student of psychology or psychic science, we will briefly review and comment upon the particularly salient portions of the tale, which may be summarized thus: Many years ago in France two children grew up with many kindred tastes and much warm, mutual affection, though this boy and girl were exceeding dissimilar in all physical and other outward respects. The boy was strong and healthy, while the girl was delicate and diffident; but as vivid contrasts blend in the most perfect harmonies, so this couple of children grew to think the same thoughts, enjoy the same pleasures, and take the tenderest interest in each other's welfare. Just as they arrived at an age when mutual companionship was growing intensely profitable, and one seemed a positive necessity to the other, fate separated them, and for several years they neither saw nor heard anything of each other. During these years the boy had grown to be a studious, intelligent young man, but one upon whom Fortune bestowed but very few of her always fickle smiles, while the somewhat unpromising little maid had been transformed into a magnificent woman, an almost perfect type of moral, mental, and bodily grace and symmetry. The young man and woman meet, as it seems, by chance at a ball where he was an invited guest, through the kindness of a distinguished friend who appreciated worth rather than wealth or social standing — but she had become the "Duchess of Towers." From the instant they encountered each other at the ball to the end of their earthly lives they were psychically unseparated, no matter what distances by land or sea, or even prison walls, might divide their bodies. Fate, in the persons of British administrators of "*justice*," behaved very harshly to the young man, who is represented as anything but an undesirable character; he was, however, unfortunately involved in a quarrel, and for unintentionally causing the death of a ruffian who wore the livery of a gentleman he was condemned to life-long imprisonment. The sentence was neither repealed nor modified, but during a period of from twenty-five to thirty years he was sustained and blest in lonely and unjust captivity through the agency of such a marvellous, but by no means incredible, faculty of *dreaming true*, that on an average, he enjoyed for eight hours out of every twenty-four, uninterrupted communion with the lovely widow, between whom and himself there existed the purest and most faithful bond of sincerest affection. We dwell briefly on these incidents because they serve to illustrate the conditions under which the highest and most perfect manifestations of telepathy, or thought transference, may be secured. Two persons devotedly attached to each other, so much so that they may be said to be literally wrapped up in each other, can secure satisfactory mental inter-communion practically impossible under other circumstances; the closest sympathy between donor and receiver is ever necessary to the demonstration of a perfect telepathic test, particularly one that can be repeated at will. This faculty of *dreaming true* is, however, so advanced a stage of telepathy that it far transcends the most successful hypnotic experiments of Charcôt, Bernheim, and other illustrious professors of the hypnotic art; it really amounts to absolute interblending of psychic spheres to the extent of virtually annihilating space and becoming capable of projecting mental emanations at will to a chosen spot ordained to receive them. The most singular feature of all in the experiences of "Peter Ibbetson" and the "Duchess of Towers" is that they selected a place in France — the site of their childhood's home — as the scene of their nightly psychic *rendezvous*, and while both of them went to sleep, and awoke duly refreshed the following morning, they had spent the hours of their bodily repose together in a palace of their own construction, in which they reviewed at will all their experiences gained in waking hours. To the man confined in prison the woman who was at large in the world, and travelling frequently from place to place gathering up rich stores of knowledge, and seeing much of the finest natural beauty as well as art treasure which Europe affords, gave glowing descriptions of all the beauty amid which she freely roamed; and not only could they meet and talk it over, they could behold it vividly reproduced in their enchanted mansion which they built as a model home, one where they always met. If it be once admitted that thought is substantial, and therefore we can build palaces of thought, the unlikeliness of such an experience quickly diminishes and, at length, totally departs. In this day of widespread scepticism there is rapidly growing up as an all-sufficient cure for weary doubt a glorious PSYCHIC SCIENCE which is rapidly dispelling the materialistic gloom which hung like a sable pall over the thought of the entire Western Hemisphere till within the past very few years; this new science is partially represented by several varieties of inquirers into the region of the physically unseen, but so far as we have made their acquaintance we have found no body of people undertaking to address themselves practically to the solution of the vast psychic problem in its entirety.

Perhaps the subject is too vast to admit of universal scrutiny, but our opinion is that even when prejudice is absent, the culture of the psychic sense which is common to all mankind — though it is undoubtedly more active in a minority than in the majority of persons — involves more thorough-going devotion of time and attention than superficially interested people are disposed to give to it. There are not many persons who would fill the rôle of "Peter Ibbetson," or "Duchess of Towers"; thus while directions for psychic development are often given in outline by persons who have some genuine acquaintance with *psychometry*, or an *inner* sense often called a *sixth*, but very few individuals profit largely by reading even such a story as *From the Old World to the New*, by the justly renowned Mr. W. T. Stead, editor of the *Review of Reviews*, or by perusing such really scientific treatises as *The Soul of Things*, by William Denton, or *The Manual of Psychometry*, by Dr. J. R. Buchanan, in which a history is given of a large number of cases, where this subtle sense of *soul measurement* has been abundantly and accurately displayed. The first requisite for the culture of this hidden — though singularly useful, and, when developed, amazingly powerful — faculty is *absolute concentration on a given point;* but whenever concentration is mentioned, people are all too apt to exclaim, "Oh! I cannot concentrate." Concentration is a habit and can be acquired, or — to speak more correctly — developed like any other habit, the germ of which we all possess, but which needs earnest regular exercise to bring to actual perfection, or even to a useful degree of prominence or proficiency. The great mistake usually made is in thinking that it is so extremely difficult to concentrate attention, that we might almost as well abandon the exercise at the start. Concentration on a *beloved* object is not difficult; thus, after all, it appears that lack of *interest* more than of *ability* lies at the root of the prevailing deficiency in this respect. What is concentration, but fixed attention centred on a special occupation? and do not children frequently concentrate so thoroughly upon their play that you may call them many times before they hear you, so engrossed are they in what is to them of absorbing interest, while, to their elders, it might seem tedious and tiresome in the extreme? When people are in love with each other, they do not find it irksome or a strain to think of one another, but they would find it very hard, indeed, to put each other out of mind; and this experience of lovers is not confined to love between persons, for science, art, business, or whatever has enlisted profound affection and appears of paramount importance to its devotee, engages and holds the attention of its pursuer to the exclusion of all beside. Our attention was called some years ago to this fact in the most striking manner. A young artist, studying in Paris, went one morning to the Louvre in company with several friends, with whom he continued moving to and fro, chatting freely the while, till suddenly his countenance became completely altered, almost transfigured, one might say, as he stood gazing, with whole-souled rapture, *into*, we cannot say *upon*, a singularly beautiful painting by one of the famous old masters of the Roman school; for more than thirty minutes he stood motionless before that wonderfully beautiful and singularly expressive canvas, and then, heaving a deep sigh, he reluctantly withdrew his gaze and said to an artist friend, who was one of the party, " I *must* and *will* get permission to copy that picture, and it shall be copied *faithfully*." During a meal at a restaurant and the walk home, which followed, he would either talk of this only picture for which he had any thought, or lapse into complete taciturnity. Permission was easily obtained for this enthusiastic young landscape painter to copy a sublime work of the most elaborate character introducing a number of highly finished human portraits, and he had never painted a human face or form before. His friends, though not displeased at his ambition, were of the united opinion that he had undertaken a task far beyond his power to execute; what, then, must have been their surprise, when, on the occasion of his next visit to the famous gallery for the express purpose of beginning the work of copying this wonderful *chef d'œuvre*, he spent over three hours in a motionless attitude, gazing, as he afterwards declared, into the very soul of the canvas, and then rushed to his studio, locked himself in, and never appeared among his friends till he could bring with him, for their amazed and delighted inspection, a perfect facsimile of that marvellous production, which had so perfectly called into expression *his artistic soul*. The experience of the young man, while gazing steadfastly into the picture, gathered from his own words, was substantially as follows: "I stood no longer on earth; I was no more confined to my outer frame; I was a free spirit at liberty to roam as I pleased, amid the indescribable glories of an artist's heaven; I saw the real scenes which the great master, when on earth, had portrayed with so dexterous a hand; I was in the very midst of the group of immortals, of whom this painter (Correggio) appeared as chief; he himself was telling me that in conjunction with his spirit, I should reproduce his earthly masterpiece. As he spoke and I listened with reverential awe, mingled with unspeakable gladness, I felt as though an inner chamber of my consciousness had suddenly unclosed, and I saw reflected there the image of the scene, which I knew would never again desert me and which I could speedily and effectively reproduce. I learned, on my return to ordinary waking consciousness, that I had been entranced for three full hours, but as it often happens that we dream in a few seconds what seems to occupy a lengthened period, it seemed to me that my exquisite experience in the artist's heaven was but of a very few moments' duration, but it evidently lasted long enough to so relate me to it thenceforward, that I now feel as though whenever I need inspiration for my work, I have but to deliberately shut out all intrusive worldly cares and commune with invisible states alone."

The subsequent career of this remarkable young man has thoroughly justified the claim that by perfect concentration upon a given subject, when one's entire affection is enlisted, the most complete result can be obtained in harmony with most adventurous desire.

During sleep we are practically dead to all external sights and sounds; when our slumber is profound and we have passed beyond what nurses have called a child's *third sigh*, we are as truly in the spiritual world as we should be were we to become finally divested of our material habiliment. Certain Methodists have presented young people with cards headed, " Where would you go, were you to die to-night?" and if an answer were given strictly in accordance with the spiritual law of attraction which is universal, the reply would be: " Exactly where I am sure to go, provided I sleep profoundly." The Bible and, indeed, all sacred literature and many scientific works as well, contains numberless instances of counsel and instruction, received in sleep, which could never be obtained in a waking state. And why is it thus? Surely the answer is evident. During sixteen hours out of every twenty-four on an average, we are concerned with external forms of things; even if we attend religious exercises, hymns, prayers, sermons, etc., are all addressed to the outer ear, and we think we must keep wide awake to listen, or take part in them; therefore, people ignorant of psychic science, think they lose everything if they fall asleep during a service, and if they are deaf, it does them no good to attend religious exercises. Such purblind externality is all of a kind with the gross materialism of the period, which estimates everything in dollars and cramps utility within the narrow limit of ministration to the physical body. Various serious diseases and certainly chronic nervous prostration accompanied by abject physical debility, can be easily traced to this utter lack of interior perception. Hypnotism is a great blessing to this age, as it is helping materialists to recognize the power of thought silently conveyed, while true hypnosis is not putting people to sleep without, much less against, their will, but helping them to obtain relief from *insomnia*, which is one of the most wearing of ailments, and more than that, assisting them to reach a higher or deeper state of consciousness than that acknowledged by the majority during waking hours. Every third part of our time should be devoted to rest, but rest and idleness are widely distinct. Man's organism is a perpetual-motion machine, and were the machinery to stop running, death of the body would ensue; nature shows us plainly enough that rest and recreation, but not inactivity, are what we need. The beautiful text, "God giveth his beloved sleep," may be correctly translated, "He giveth to his beloved while sleeping," and this rendering harmonizes with the experience of the seers of the ages. It is strange that Bible students and people who found all their belief upon the Bible, should overlook the patent teaching concerning illumination gained in sleep, which is so abundant throughout the sacred canon. Joseph, the foster-father of Jesus, was about to put Mary away from him, till an angel appeared to him in sleep and told him to accept her as his honored wife; then again the flight of the holy child with his parents into Egypt and their return to Palestine was all directed by the experiences of a dreamer, who conversed with angels in the night. Modern agnosticism is only reactionary; it is a protest against superstition and comes like a bracing wind to clear away fogs and disperse vapors, but its work is nearly finished, and we are now entering upon an age of scientific spiritualism, in which all psychic experiences will be discussed, in relation to unchanging law; the *supernatural* element may be eliminated, even the *supernormal* idea may pass away, but, however thoroughly they are accounted for on a scientific base, they will be accepted and encouraged. Nightmare and bad dreams are quite unnecessary, and though hygienists may attempt to account for them as the result of heavy late suppers, what occasions them when a very light supper, or no supper at all, has been eaten? Metaphysics can alone account for dreaming, either false or true, and as false dreaming is the rule and true dreaming the exception, we seek to suggest a practical, efficient antidote to much prevailing misery. "Peter Ibbetson" and the "Duchess of Towers" are only extreme illustrations of what can be universally demonstrated, just as the young artist referred to was only exceptional in degree of concentration. Before we can rely upon having our own way and going where we please in sleep, we must control our thoughts, while awake, and the difficulty in so doing is not permanent; habit makes it easy, but persistence is necessary to success. We have a right to our own thoughts, and to keep what company we please at any time, and if we take a strong attitude of independence, no one can long continue to molest us, unless there is a just claim upon us, — for example, an unsettled bill; in that case, the creditor has a right to demand from the debtor a settlement of the account, and if he is a proficient telepathist, he can present his claim mentally, if he chooses.

Settle all your debts; owe no man anything but the common debt of universal love, and take delight in paying that continually. Before permitting yourself to fall asleep, fix your thought attentively on the sphere whence you desire enlightenment. Compose yourself to the extent of perfect tranquillity; then allow sleep to come to you as you are affirming with quiet, but strong expectancy that your desire will be fulfilled. As everything takes time to grow, we do not say you will get supreme results instantly, but you will draw ever nearer to a stupendous revelation of your own psychic possibilities as you persistently follow this practice night after night. If you have any misunderstanding with anybody, settle it before you retire, if possible; if you cannot reach the person outwardly, send him a mental telegram wherever he may be; whether you know his whereabouts or not, call his name distinctly in silence, and cable: " You and I are at peace." Having thus removed what might prove a cause of serious disturbance, you are ready to fix your thought entirely upon the subject of your search. If you wish to become proficient in any art or science, or become familiar with the contents of a literature, or the details of a business, you can serve an apprenticeship in sleep by putting yourself *en rapport* with whatever you desire to become familiar with, and, though for some time you may remember nothing definite in the morning, you will from the start experience both mental and physical improvement, as you will feel refreshed on awaking as never before. If you become sleepy anywhere through lack of interest or laziness, then it is well to arouse yourself by a determined mental effort;

but if when you are deeply interested you fall asleep, or even feel sleepy, never resist the approach of slumber, and if you have believed that no instruction reaches us in sleep, make the affirmation decidedly: " I shall learn whatever it is best for me to know and hold all it is useful for me to keep"; then let sleep come and you will absorb into your inner nature far more than you could ordinarily retain if you heard it outwardly. When you have gone anywhere with a definite intention and a positive expectation, you lose nothing by sleeping, provided you fall asleep when most interested; it is, therefore, only necessary to guard against sleep induced by distraction, for when we are distracted by unwelcome thoughts, falling asleep under such a condition can lead to no profitable outcome. Not only is it possible to be educated in sleep; we can travel in sleep. In hot weather, if business confines us in city offices, we can picture out the country or seashore directly we are in bed, and spend the night in direct relation to salt breezes or mountain air. If any students find it difficult at first to rely entirely upon fixity of thought, let them employ suggestive outward aids; for instance, a picture, or a book, or a newspaper article bearing directly upon something they wish to know more about, or become psychically related with, may prove of great help. If pictures in a chamber where you have to sleep are objectionable, take them down or cover them; never talk late at night on anything you would object to dream about; read in bed as much as you like, but carefully select such literature as through force of suggestion leads you where you would like to go. Never take an unwelcome room-mate to save expense, and never at any time allow yourself to be led into disagreeable conversation just before retiring. These hints are necessary for beginners, but old hands who have had long experience in DREAMING TRUE can sleep equally well anywhere, and can afford to be careless of their outer surroundings.

It is needless to add that so extraordinary a discourse was listened to with rapt attention by the entire audience, and provoked considerable inquiry.

CHAPTER XVI.

SOME EXPERIMENTS IN TELEPATHY.

Mrs. Katzenheimer's address opened the way for an all-round discussion of psychic matters of every description; the proposition was hailed with universal delight that some experiments in telepathy should be conducted the following evening, and the unanimous vote was, that Mr. Collins and Mrs. Katzenheimer should, if possible, take prominent part in the demonstrations.

Mr. Collins had the great advantage over many, of being able to concentrate his mental gaze steadily on any object he chose to place before his mental vision; he was also a young gentleman of considerable will power, and one who, when he determined to accomplish anything, was rarely baffled by adverse circumstances.

Mrs. Katzenheimer was quite favorably impressed with his intelligence and serenity, as she expressed it, and as she could never be driven to do anything unwelcome to her, but was quite easily persuaded to accommodate and interest her neighbors when she was in the right mood, or, as she would say, *condition*, it was agreed that, on the following evening at half-past eight precisely, all who were really interested in thought transference, and desired to remain quite quiet during the experiments, should assemble in the *salon*.

So many persons desired to witness these projected experiments in what most of them called mind-reading, that it was with great difficulty a circle was at length arranged to the satisfaction of Mrs. Katzenheimer, who showed decided repugnance to close proximity with her audience, and insisted that no one ·but those she individually selected and permitted should be allowed to approach her during the *séance*.

After a committee of six (three ladies and three gentlemen) had been chosen from the nearly two hundred who were present in the dining-room, Mr. Collins was requested to commit to memory a sentence dictated to him extemporaneously by Dr. Gustavus Ferguson, a prominent physician, unanimously chosen as the best man for the office. Not desiring to unnecessarily complicate matters, but still being anxious to prevent any likelihood of guessing on the part of Mrs. Katzenheimer, whom he designated "a shrewd, smart woman, with eyes like a hawk's, and unusually quick hearing," Dr. Ferguson, after locking her in her stateroom and pocketing the key, returned to the *salon* and repeated to Mr. Collins, until he could feel sure he knew every syllable thoroughly, the following extraordinary combination of irrelevant words: —

"When the hare runs a race, then my hair grows thin; when the bear hibernates, to bear burdens I begin; when the monk dons his cowl, then the monkey hunts for fowl; when the horse ceases neighing, I am hoarse, my friend is saying."

The comicality as well as ingenious alliteration of the above ridiculous but rather clever sentence provoked peals of laughter, and thereby served a useful end by inducing merriment throughout the room, which, when it is not too loud, boisterous, or unseemly, is far more conducive to the successful conduct of psychical experiments than strained excitement or funereal gloom.

Mr. Collins, who was an apt scholar, soon learned the funny doggerel and repeated it three times in succession, to firmly impress it on his memory and to make it seem to him like an old, familiar rhyme. After he had satisfied himself and his auditors that he was sufficiently coached, Dr. Ferguson released Mrs. Katzenheimer and personally conducted her to the *salon*, in company with Dr. Amelia Poodlehurst, another member of the committee and an eminent specialist in cases of nervous peculiarity.

Mrs. Katzenheimer took the seat provided for her near the piano quite leisurely and composedly, and after singing a song to her own accompaniment, turned to the committee, who formed a group in her immediate neighborhood, and asked them to seat Mr. Collins exactly opposite to her in a comfortable chair, while she retained possession of the music stool. After Mr. Collins declared himself *comfortably* seated, she requested him to hand her some article belonging exclusively to himself, as she desired to hold it in her hand as a link with him to facilitate the experiment. In attempted compliance with her request, he proffered the use of his pocket-knife, but this she declared was embarrassing, because he had that very evening lent it to another gentleman who wished to sharpen a pencil; the knife had therefore "contracted an aura" from this other person. The next proposition was that she should hold his pocket-book, but this she also refused, stating that it was a diary and memorandum-book in which he had permitted other people to write their names and addresses. At length, after several reflections, she finally accepted his necktie, which he declared was not a new one and had never been worn by anybody but himself. No sooner had she "got acquainted with the cravat," to use her own words, than she closed her eyes and slightly shuddered, then began to articulate very slowly: —

"When the hare runs a race, then my hair grows thin," and so on, word for word, till she reached the end of the long sentence. When she reached the last word, "saying," she was greeted with a tempestuous salvo of applause.

"How *did* she do it? How could she know it?" was uttered on all sides.

Mr. Collins had not touched her, but she had looked steadily into his eyes and he had returned her gaze throughout her recitation. His statement was simply to the effect that he had held the sentence firmly in mind, repeating it very deliberately, though silently, and had felt himself literally generating and throwing out a current of human electricity direct to Mrs. Katzenheimer, who was voluntarily receptive to his influence; her statement fully corroborated his, for her declaration was that she had felt his psychic emanation enter her eyeballs and thence travel to her brain, and that instantly it reached the sensorium, she became aware of the exact words which this electric current carried.

Having proved the fact of thought transfer so thoroughly in this instance, it was proposed that Mrs. Katzenheimer should read some one else's mind, if she would consent to do so, but this she steadily declined to attempt, saying that to change the influence would only confuse her and nullify results; she was, however, quite willing to try other experiments suggested by the committee, provided Mr. Collins continued to serve as active transmitter of intelligence to her *via* the psychic current.

The next experiment was a far more ambitious one, as it involved no less than the transmission of the entire contents of a recent letter addressed to Dr. Ferguson by one of his patients, and which he never permitted to leave his own hand. To accomplish this test, it was decided that Dr. Ferguson and Mr. Collins should retire together behind a screen over which no one in the room could peer, Dr. Ferguson holding his letter immediately under the eyes of Mr. Collins, but retaining possession of it in his own hands. At first it appeared as though no results would follow, as Mrs. Katzenheimer became apparently entranced, or she might have only fallen asleep, but she held the necktie very firmly and breathed heavily, as though she were not quite at ease. After fully fifteen minutes had elapsed, and the silence was beginning to grow oppressive, she suddenly started to her feet and, with her eyes tightly closed, began in a loud staccato voice: —

"My dear Doctor,—I wish to express my sincerest gratitude to you for all your kindness to me and my family during our recent bereavement, and to tell you that the advice given to Alfred has been the saving of my dear nephew's life. May Heaven shower its blessings on you now and ever, is the fervent prayer of your devoted friend."

No name could she pronounce, though she evidently tried hard to grasp it; then, finding all her efforts useless, she proceeded: —

"P.S. I shall hope to see you, as soon as you return to England, at my country house in —"

Again she could get no name, and after striving for a moment to finish the sentence, she sank back on her stool, exclaiming: —

"Well, I got it, but it was a hard struggle; don't ask me to do any more this evening: I've reached my limit."

Dr. Ferguson bounced from behind the screen, letter in hand, ready to let every person in the room examine it; and as he held it up, that all might see it as quickly as possible, it was soon discovered, to everybody's unbounded satisfaction, that every word which had met Mr. Collins' eyes had been exactly repeated by Mrs. Katzenheimer, and in order not to betray a patient's confidence, Dr. Ferguson had completely erased from the paper the name of his correspondent, and also the location of her country residence.

It is needless to say that this additional proof of perfect telepathy overwhelmed any lingering vestiges of scepticism which might have outlived the former evidence, convincing though that was; and as Dr. Ferguson was a reputable, regular, somewhat conservative physician, of the highest standing professionally and socially, and well known to many of the most distinguished persons in the audience, no question was raised as to even a possibility of collusion. But while no one appeared to doubt the genuineness of the phenomenon, many were the inquiries made into its origin, and particularly concerning the part played by Mr. Collins. It was Mrs. Throgmorton, whose delight knew no bounds, who became the mouthpiece of the company in propounding the following inquiry: —

"My dear Mrs. Katzenheimer, do please enlighten us on this one point, which seems a little obscure to most of us: how did you get a mental message of such length and with such perfect accuracy from a gentleman who is almost a stranger to you, and between whom and yourself I understand there is nothing but a slight acquaintanceship, and not even that till yesterday? Why would not some other person in the room have answered just as well? And do tell us of what special benefit the necktie was to you?"

"To answer such questions fully," responded Mrs. Katzenheimer, "would require far more knowledge than I possess, but so far as I can, I will gladly enlighten you. Mr. Collins possesses two distinguishing traits which render him particularly well adapted to fill the rôle he has so ably filled this evening. In the first place, he is unusually self-centred, and can withstand the temptation to mental distraction far better than most people; in the second place, he can project his thought clearly and decisively, I may say that his mental articulation is singularly distinct. Then as to myself, his electro-magnetic effluence does not irritate me, as he is not in the least hysterical, and most men are, as well as women, though our sex is usually accredited with a monopoly of hysterical tendencies."

At this decided opinion on hysteria there was much laughter, many of the gentlemen present being twitted by their wives or sisters with their decidedly hysterical conduct on many occasions, while good-natured banter on all sides kept alive the mirthful element which had reigned so conspicuously when the proceedings opened.

The hour having grown much later than any of the company supposed it had, and early hours being the rule on shipboard, a most edifying as well as entertaining evening was suddenly brought to a close by the captain good-naturedly reminding his passengers that lights must be lowered and further conversation reserved for the deck on the morrow.

CHAPTER XVII.

A GLIMPSE OF THE COLUMBIAN EXPOSITION.

THE *City of Alexandria*, after a delightful passage, reached the New York landing-stage on the evening of the eighth day after leaving Liverpool, and quickly deposited its three hundred cabin passengers, two-thirds at least of whom were desirous of proceeding to Chicago as quickly as the fastest express trains could carry them. The trip from New York to Chicago occupies from twenty-four to thirty-six hours, according to the route selected. The Niagara Falls route is the one most frequently chosen by English tourists, as it affords special opportunity to view the magnificent cataract without losing any time or involving any extra expense.

Mrs. Eastlake-Gore, with Madame Discalcelis, Mr. Eastlake-Gore, and Professor Monteith, went immediately on arrival to the Hotel Martin in University Place, where they found the finest accommodations at reasonable prices, comparing favorably with a good Parisian hostelry. The Martin is a thoroughly French house and provides as good a *table d'hôte* as one is likely to find even in Paris; the rooms are light and sunny, and the service is in all respects admirable.

New York presented so many attractions that, had it not been for the urgent desire of every member of the party to reach the Fair grounds as soon as possible, two weeks, rather than two days, would have been the probable limit of their stay in the great metropolis of the United States. In many respects New York compares favorably with European capitals; all it lacks is the sense of age and repose which can only be developed in conditions remote from the life of this period and among people who are untouched with the burning fever for rapid change which is so singularly characteristic of these last strange years of the eventful nineteenth century.

The trip to Chicago was delightful. The perfectly appointed Pullman vestibuled trains make travelling a genuine luxury for all who can afford to purchase first-class tickets; but the second-class accommodation to and from all parts of the country to Chicago was so wretchedly inadequate, that in almost every instance it necessitated tourists sitting bolt upright in ordinary day coaches during the whole of one or two nights, as well as throughout the long and tedious days of their cramped, fatiguing journey.

Never in the history of European travel has aristocracy, or, more correctly, plutocracy, been more efficiently and steadily catered for than in democratic America during the term of the great Columbian Exposition. In almost every instance the golden calf was most pompously adored, and with what result? No sooner had the Fair closed, than a period of unprecedented distress commenced in the immediate vicinity of Jackson Park, where, had another and nobler policy been pursued, unexampled prosperity might have been inaugurated to reign supreme. Financial depression is quite unnecessary; it is only the miserable result of stupid blundering. But so long as selfishness is permitted to hold control, and false distinctions between classes and masses are permitted, there can be no panacea applied; so palliation is the best expedient resorted to, and benefactors of their less fortunate brethren must, we suppose, be encouraged to fatten their own self-esteem at the dire expense of the beneficiaries' self-respect. The policy pursued by the American railroads during the first three months of the Exposition was simply idiotic. Had the directors of the various lines been hopeless imbeciles, their conduct could not have been more unreasoning, and no higher compliment can honestly be paid to the great army of householders, boarding-table keepers, restaurateurs, and others, all of whom conspired to adopt so ruinous and senseless a line of proceeding that their united efforts certainly succeeded in keeping millions from the Fair, while the interest of everybody was only to be served by attracting the multitude, who, instead of receiving inducements to attend, were successfully scared into keeping away till the original policy was rescinded; then, though the crowds came and the gate receipts doubled, trebled, and quadrupled, the remaining term of the Exposition's brief but brilliant life was far too short to undo all the mischief which had previously been accomplished.

But whatever may be said in censure of the follies

indulged in by citizens and transportation companies, no one who ever saw the Fair can forget, no matter how long he lives or what he sees after it, the magnificence of the White City on the border of Lake Michigan, when viewed from the lake itself. The Fair was all and more than all that any who visited it had right or reason to expect,— a veritable poem in architecture, a dream materialized, it stood out as an embodied fulfilment of some marvellous vision granted to a seer whose eyes must have gazed upon fairer human workmanship than this planet in its present stage can boast.

As all our party preferred to go by water to the grounds on the occasion of their first visit, that they might catch a glimpse of the exquisite beauty of the scene gradually as they approached it, when they actually landed in the Park in the very midst of its thousand activities, they were at once familiar with the lay of the land, and felt quite at home among its almost bewildering maze and labyrinth of palaces and walks.

It was the *tout ensemble* which impressed every intelligent observer at first. The wonderful congruity evolved from strangely diverse shapes and substances appealed instantly to the artistic sense; the eye was delighted, but not wearied with the view, for there was resemblance enough between the larger buildings to make them appear at home as members of the same family circle, and diversity enough to give each structure a characteristic individuality peculiarly its own. And then, the smaller buildings containing the special exhibits of different nations were so picturesque and representative that, though they were in many instances of strange, irregular design, not one of them jarred upon the common sense of unity which was the keynote to the whole. Descriptions and views of the various edifices and their contents have been so widely distributed that it is scarcely possible to add anything of interest to such an oft-told tale; still, there are special features which strongly appeal to one tourist, which another passes by with scarce a word or thought. For this reason every historian of the Exposition has done something peculiarly his own to help the White City to live perennially in the minds of all who, if not privileged to have seen, have not missed an opportunity to read, of its glory and its doom.

As Mrs. Eastlake-Gore hated unseemly bustle, and had always been accustomed to live quietly and elegantly in her own home, and as she had the wisdom to make a home to her liking wherever she went, she avoided all noisy hotels and rickety World's Fair lodging and boarding houses, preferring to rent a comfortable cottage in the most retired part of Englewood, where she and Madame Discalcelis could enjoy home privacy and freedom, and yet be within easy access of the Exposition whenever they chose to attend it.

Three days after reaching Chicago, the two ladies, with one servant, were as much at home in their quiet cottage on the outskirts of Chicago as they had been in their beautiful suburban villa in the British metropolis; but for the privilege of this furnished retreat, with service of the maid attached to the premises included, they paid five hundred dollars for little more than two months, commencing with August 23 and ending with

October 31, when the great Fair closed, and rents immediately fell to zero, or families returned to reoccupy their own accustomed habitations.

Professor Monteith and Mr. Eastlake-Gore, who were both deeply interested and also well versed in the practical workings of electricity, spent days at a time in the Electrical Exhibit, and then when they desired a change, they betook themselves to the Palace of Fine Arts, or strolled up and down the boulevard facing the ocean-like lake, — whose waves in windy weather were like the billows of the tempestuous sea, — discussing each new problem as it presented itself to the fertile fancy of the younger man, who was always the first to see a possibility, while his elder and far graver companion could work out better than he the mechanical details necessary to its final ultimation.

Madame Discalcelis was not so much interested in mechanical achievements as the gentlemen were, nor did she express any longing to rise early and retire late, day after day, week in and week out, as many ladies did, for the sake of seeing *everything* and probably remembering next to nothing. Her method was to rise at a reasonable hour in the morning, breakfast alone in her private apartment on rolls and chocolate, spend the morning in any way which appeared on that particular morning most pleasant and desirable, lunch with Mrs. Gore about half-past one or two o'clock, then proceed to the Fair grounds with her kind hostess, provided they both desired to go there, which was by no means daily. The Woman's Building attracted them greatly; so did the Convent of *La Rabida*, containing, as it did, so many priceless relics of Columbus and his period; but the Fine Arts Building was ever the Mecca toward which their steps were finally turned.

To describe the wealth of artistic treasures in that sumptuous palatial structure, designed after the model of a vast Athenian palace, would be indeed well-nigh impossible; suffice it therefore to say, that no finer collection of paintings and statuary could well be imagined. Artists of all schools and of all nations were liberally and quite impartially represented, and no one who could in any measure respond to the appeal of the sublimely beautiful could leave those glorious precincts without carrying away with him the truly salutary, elevating, ennobling effect of a baptism in the limpid waters of the river of pure beauty which, though but feebly reflected in terrestrial moulds, is in its essence and ministry the most perfect link between earth and heaven, the human and the divine.

Madame Discalcelis was a prophetess in the Temple of Beauty; she believed in its hallowing, uplifting power, as did the Greeks of old in the palmiest days of Grecian thought and culture prior to the demoralization which succeeded; and though she freely admitted that, when depraved by becoming purely sensuous and devoted to base ends, even the greatest outward loveliness might be ensnaring and calculated to lead the soul of man downward instead of upward, she was far too wise a woman, as well as too gifted a seeress, to give the smallest place in her creed to the benighted theories of those ascetic pessimists who consider it essential to moral attainment to crush out the love of beauty and make bare and loveless the external world which, when in order it fulfils its Creator's beneficent design, reflects the transcendent glory of the spiritual realm — which is altogether symmetrical in its celestial inmost — as a clear, pellucid stream shadows forth in perfect outline, true at every point, the forms of grace and stateliness which mirror their majestic faces in its crystal depths.

After visiting the Fair about a dozen times, and meeting there occasionally some very interesting people, Mrs. Gore discovered a pretty nook in the Wooded Island where, except on evenings when there were special illuminations, a party of congenial friends could spend a quiet hour entirely to themselves. On one of the occasions when a little group of sympathizing friends had collected in this delightful sylvan retreat, so near and yet so far from the constant bustle of the throngs of sight-seers, several of the ladies, all of whom had felt that Madame Discalcelis was no ordinary person, requested her to give them her idea of what particular exhibits at the Fair were most beautiful and instructive, and also to favor them, if she would, with some impressions of her own. To this request, as they were quite a private party, she consented without reluctance, and in a quiet, easy manner expressed herself as follows: —

"The World's Fair is not something which can be easily described or 'written up' in a few terse paragraphs. It grows upon the thoughtful visitor day by day, as all great creations grow, so that, after many visits, the explorer feels more deeply impressed with its colossal magnificence than after few. The Fair suggests to me in some faint, far-off, dreamy manner a new and nobler state of society than any condition we have yet realized. I cannot say that it strikes me as in any degree perfect; there is far too much noise, confusion, and bustling to convey anything like the idea of a *perfected* social condition. Still, when one's eyes feast upon the glory of the scene at eventide, all the imposing structures and the banks of the canals lit up with thousands of electric lamps, the music of the bands reaching the contemplative listener from a distance of, say, half a mile, the garishness of the day scene is entirely absent, the strife of tongues and clatter of hurrying feet are forgotten, and only the ideal beauty of the vision remains with the spectator. Those of you who *know* me to any extent, are too well acquainted with my theory of rest to be surprised when I pronounce the conduct of most sight-seers completely idiotic. Many there are who daily rush frantically from building to building, from early morning till late at night, and see almost nothing, while the few who behave sensibly and *enjoy* their visits to the great Fair are never exhausted, and they see nearly everything, and what is still more to the point, they carry away with them graphic memory pictures of what they have beheld. I am not a convert to Buddhism, though it is so fashionable at present in America, nor am I any sort of an Oriental enthusiast. I do not worship at any of the shrines of Arya, but for all that, I would far rather resemble the calm Asiatic who mildly tells the excited Westerner that *rest* is more important than bustle, than be numbered among the restless, peaceless throng who rise early and retire late to gratify nothing but hysteria, and pay for their dissipation with aching heads and weary limbs. To me the dream-side of the Fair is its beauty-side. We can see canned fruits on Oxford Street in London, and if we desire a shopping tour, Regent Street is nearer by four thousand miles than Chicago; but I may search London in vain for a picture like that upon which I have already gazed times without number, when I have taken my favorite seat fronting the lagoon an hour or so after sunset, and watched the electric glow deepen and brighten, till from a few faint jets of promise there arises, to glorify the wondrous scene, a burst of illumination which defies description."

"But my dear poetess," broke in the staccato tones of Mrs. Lumley Calhoun (a distinguished writer for one of the New York dailies), "I suppose even you admire the Electrical Exhibit; you, who are so enthusiastic on the subject of electricity, surely could not fail to admire *that* exhibit."

"Yes," answered the *unimpassioned dreamer*, as her friends often styled her, "I admire it, but more for what it betokens than for anything it now reveals. It is certainly very wonderful and very beautiful, but it is not by any means the ideal *attained*, and scarcely is it an ideal *suggested*. To me the prospective triumphs of electrical science are so infinitely beyond the meagre exhibitions presented by ordinary mechanics, that while I hail with intense delight even this poor prelude to the electrical anthem of the future, I cannot cheat myself, when I know that I am only standing in a vestibule, into the belief that I am already within the most sacred enclosure of a splendid temple. The Electrical Exhibit is no doubt educational beyond all the others for the masses, but to an ambitious explorer in the electrical field, it is in many respects quite sadly disappointing. The one ever-recurring, unanswered question in my mind is, If you can do thus much, why not immeasurably more? I agree with Count Mattei and his intelligent disciples, that with electricity all things are possible, but where are the electricians to demonstrate the higher possibilities? Verily do we all receive that for which we ask; we find only what we seek, and no other door opens for us than the one upon which we knock; consequently, if commercial advantage is the measure of desired attainment, the richer and more truly beneficent demonstrations of electric force cannot be forthcoming. Enterprise and ingenuity have done much; purely philanthropic exertion will do far more."

As the quiet, earnest words of this almost sphinx-like, though singularly earnest woman died away, there seemed a quiet hush in the grove, as though a subtle unseen presence had been recently manifesting and just retired. Such a sequence was not uncommon when Madame Discalcelis had been drawn into an important conversation and had expressed her views freely on a vital question. This sense of a *presence* was rather perplexing to the sceptical and worldly disposed members of the gathering, but to those who longed for something deeper than *soirées* and dinners, it came as an almost tantalizing hint of something vaguely desired but certainly unattained, and which for them might be practically unattainable.

CHAPTER XVIII.

ARE WE NOT ALL BRETHREN? HATH NOT ONE GOD CREATED US?

"THE shadows of a lovely early autumn evening were slowly gathering over the White City, whose days, I regret to feel, are now rapidly drawing to a close, when before my enraptured eyes a vision of almost more than earthly glory transfigured the entire scene, rendering the beautiful structures all the more fascinating because of the veil of mystery which the approaching darkness cast over them all. I was alone by the lake, yes, perfectly alone so far as mortal companionship is concerned, though there were many thousands of my fellows within the gates, but I saw them not nor did I hear them. I was, however, in no trance; I knew exactly what I was doing, and I had a definite purpose in all my movements, but I was beyond the reach of contact with my entimed and enspaced companions. Slowly the last rays of the setting sun sank into the waters of the lake, and then I was no more alone, for there stood beside me a form of such exquisite and indescribable loveliness that to say more than that she was divinely, perfectly human would be to utter sacrilege. I shall not seek to describe a form that is beyond description, nor attempt to reduce to cold words the thrill of ecstasy which filled me till I felt lifted above all things. Softly, caressingly, as a mother might fondle her first-born, a hand was laid upon my eyes, and a voice, liquid and sweet as the music of a fairy fountain, said to me, 'BEHOLD.' I turned my eyes to the waters, where but a moment before the sun had lingeringly kissed the far horizon ere he departed out of sight, and I beheld another sun whose rays emitted cadences of song as well as iris-hued shafts of light. Into the centre of that mildly refulgent orb I gazed even till I peered into the precincts of the Great White City of the Central Sphere, whence all that is fair, pure, and beautiful in its feeble earthly satellite derives its impetus of thought, to be made manifest in beauty. Here I saw the actual reality of what had seemed to me before only a magnificent probability; here I saw the embodied beauty of the stupendous idea suggested in the creedal phrase One Holy Catholic Church. From my childhood I had been dazed, bewildered, with the blind assumptions of those unknowing prelates who would narrow the church of God to an organization whose members could be counted, and outside of whose visible pale there is no safety and possibly no salvation. I had visited the Mosque on the Midway Plaisance that very afternoon but two hours earlier, and had wondered in a dim way what would be the fate hereafter of those who embrace the crescent but reject the cross. What, think you, was my surprise to see in that celestial territory a company of Arabs in the posture of prayer, surrounded with light which took crescent form as it encircled their persons? In the midst of this City in the heavens, and over these Arabs as over all others whom I saw there, the light which shed a mellow radiance everywhere was in shape both cross and crown. I saw what seemed to me to be a stairway of electric light connecting this group of transfigured Arabs with the great mosque of St. Sophia in Constantinople and with other temples devoted to Islam throughout the world; and as the light reached the truly faithful among those who call the Eternal by the name of Allah, the light spoke to them, and it breathed into their hearts the words: ALL-HOLY AND ALL-MERCIFUL. I gazed again, and among the Bedouins of the desert I beheld many who had received it, and they heard the words: ALL-POWERFUL BUT ALL-MERCIFUL; and wherever I turned, gazing toward any quarter of the earth, I saw there were those in all and outside of all systems of religion who heeded the sacred intonation. To those who listened to obey among the Moslems, he who was once known as Mahomet was sent with the message: 'Allah alone is great, and Mahomet was one of His messengers, but God's messengers are numberless and they are everywhere;' and as the sacred light descended on these receptive ones, they said one to the other, — I know not that they spake save in thought, — 'We too will be merciful, for mercy endureth forever.' My unspoken question, 'Are these Arabs redeemed who know not Christ?' was answered, oh! so sweetly and so convincingly by the radiant presence at my side, 'He who loveth his brother whom he hath seen loveth, even though he knoweth him not, the

God whom he hath not seen, and *whosoever* loveth is born of God.' But what of belief? I queried. Then the presence answered me, 'Love is greater than knowledge and containeth faith which obtaineth salvation.' The vision faded. I stood alone, but yet not alone; for humanity was with me, and I felt the touch of universal kinship as never before."

So spake Madame Discalcelis in answer to the question of an earnest but tired-looking little woman who lingered after the group had scattered, to implore a personal response from Visalia to the deep questioning which had been tormenting her sensitive spirit for the past three weeks by reason of the blind, blasphemous teaching of a narrow-minded, impudent ecclesiastic, who, while officiating in the church she regularly attended, had taken occasion to villify the Parliament of Religions then in session in Chicago, and declare from the pulpit to his simple-minded, easily befooled, because unthinking congregation, that it was a heinous offence in the sight of the Almighty to even listen to the arguments of men who knew not Christianity and dared to affirm that God had spoken to the human race in any other way than through one or other of the sixty-six documents which "orthodoxy" in England and America regard as constituting the sum-total of "God's most holy word."

Mrs. Phœbe Blessing Oyster was a pious New England Congregationalist, who from her youth had taken active part in the work of foreign missions, though she could never quite understand how it turned out that, Christian "orthodoxy" being absolutely necessary to the eternal salvation of immortal souls, those who declared it to be so quite complacently deposited one dollar annually in the box or plate, for saving the heathen from sempiternal torment, and then coolly invested two hundred and fifty dollars in a sealskin sacque to adorn a "perishable house of clay,"—an epithet they always humbly and piously applied to their own physical organisms. Of late Mrs. Oyster had been sorely puzzled, and since she had been in Chicago visiting the Fair, mingling with Orientals, sitting down with Jews to dinner at her boarding-place, and hearing Mahometanism discussed as one of the "inspired" religions, she felt dazed and sick at heart. She knew not where to turn for advice or consolation; modern books perplexed her, and her worried brain utterly refused to unravel the tangled skein of difficulties in which she felt herself hopelessly enmeshed. But though till the moment of her interview with Madame Discalcelis she had felt herself in a *cul de sac*, no sooner had the gifted authoress recited her own sweet, true visionary experience than poor Mrs. Oyster burst into tears of relief and gratitude.

"Ah," she exclaimed, "I see now I have distrusted God while I have idolized those self-appointed blind ones who teach us contrary to all our instinctive faith as well as reason, that creed is greater than deed and that salvation depends upon belief in Christ in so horrible a way that in order to believe in him we are compelled to dissent from all that is most beautiful in his recorded utterance. My dear friend and helpful sister,— I know I may call you such, — the record of your vision has opened up to me forever those grand impressive words of heavenly teaching from the lips of our Divine Lord, 'Other sheep I have which are not of *this* fold; them also I will bring; and there shall be one fold and one shepherd.'"

"There *shall* be, there is not now; now there are many folds and many shepherds on earth, but there is only one in heaven, and as the *pater noster* teaches us to pray that God's will may yet be done on earth as it is already done in heaven, so do I feel convinced that our Saviour teaches us that every human heart which yearns for truth is in one of the many divisions of his illimitable fold. Christ is no mere man; he is the eternal Word, truly begotten Son of the Infinite; and this glorious truth will yet be revealed to all men. But his followers are all who love humanity; they may never have heard of him, they may even question his existence, but they are spiritually conjoined with him if they are in the love of truth and neighbor."

As the fair seeress uttered these parting words to her grateful companion, who had now quite emerged from darkness into sunshine of spirit, her features were illumined with a superterrestrial radiance which imparted to her words the living glow of genuine prophetic fire. As she finished speaking, the butterfly in her valued brooch lightly touched first the cross beneath and then the star above its wings.

Mrs. Oyster smiled understandingly as she watched the expressive action of a piece of jewelry, which seemed to have so far imbibed its wearer's psychic emanation that it acted as a living creature responsive to her moods.

"First the cross, then the star,— and that a seven-pointed one, — and we are to be butterflies; I think I understand it," brightly exclaimed Mrs. Oyster, as she tripped away lightly as a girl (and her age was over sixty). "I shall do some true missionary work tomorrow on the basis of what you have taught me; may God help you to bless others as you have this day blessed me." And she had vanished, leaving Visalia, as she thought, alone.

Professor Monteith had, however, seen and heard everything from a quiet nook where he had been reading. Stepping forward and apologizing for being unintentionally an eavesdropper, he said fervently:—

"If Christianity were what you teach and believe, I would this instant implore its Founder on my bended knees to accept me as a disciple; but, alas! in the world and the churches one finds it vastly otherwise. But I thank you, madam; you have taught me another lesson in kindliness, and I as well as your recent pupil am grateful." And he also quickly departed.

After such an episode the heart of the noble lady who had been privileged through perfect frankness to give true help to a weary, toilworn spirit, and to strengthen the good work already begun in an honest but doubting scientific explorer, felt deep peace and thankfulness of spirit; she was never self-elated, but very grateful when she had been of use to others.

When a few minutes later Mrs. Gore and Arthur met her in the Menier Building, where she was taking her favorite food and beverage, she appeared merry as a kitten; her eyes were sparkling, and the natural exuberance of her healthy youthful spirits asserted itself to the utmost. True spirituality is always bright as summer sunshine, but deep as a well whose depth no plummet can sound. Only when healthy happiness characterizes a life have we unmistakable evidence that real regeneration is in process. Sad, sallow, pucker-faced religion is either pathology or hypocrisy caricaturing piety. Dr. Watts spoke truly indeed, in spite of all his errors, when he sang: —

> "Religion never was designed
> To make our pleasures less."

CHAPTER XIX.

FOOTSTEPS OF ANGELS.

> "When the hours of day are numbered
> And the voices of the night
> Wake the better soul that slumbered
> To a holy, calm delight,
>
> * * * * * * * *
>
> Then the forms of the departed
> Enter at the open door;
> The beloved ones, the true-hearted,
> Come to visit us once more."

It was nearing six o'clock on the evening of the day following when Professor Monteith, engaged in diligent perusal of the latest scientific news from Europe, heard the sweet, clear voice of Madame Discalcelis singing in an adjoining apartment the above beautiful words from the pen of the truly gifted and inspired Henry Wadsworth Longfellow. As she sang, a holy hush seemed to pervade the library where he was sitting, as though the tone vibrations from the neighboring drawing-room had penetrated the walls, and made the other room a portion of the sanctum wherein the music was actually produced. * * * Was it sleep or was it a trance into which he fell? Whichever it may have been, — or perchance some state which is neither sleep nor trance, but superior to both or either, — Professor Monteith realized that the fair singer, in company with her hostess and her hostess' son, entered the apartment where he was sitting, smiled kindly upon him, greeted him politely and cheerily; still he could not respond to their greetings nor return their glances. * * * The book he was reading fell from his hands on to the floor, but he could not stoop to pick it up nor thank Mr. Gore for replacing it on the centre-table; he was in the room, conscious of the presence of its other inmates, aware of their kindly interest in himself and their solicitude for his welfare, but he was also elsewhere. Elsewhere, but where? How came Sicily to be in Chicago? How came lemon groves into the library of an Englewood villa? How came he, Regulus Monteith, an English professor of natural sciences, to be attired in the costume of a knight of old, with helmet, cuirass, and sword? * * * Who is that taking him by the hand, and pressing her lips to his brow? Surely, not one of the ladies in the library with him! No, indeed; they are sitting near each other at the other end of the apartment, one of them reading, the other embroidering. Who, then, can the third lady be? Her form is graceful, supple as a willow; she is all white, — clear, beautiful, dazzling, spotless white, calling to mind the glorious imagery which the evangelists employ to describe the transfiguration of the Divine Man. Is it possible that this fair, slender, fleecy form of light is a human shape? It has no solidity, it is well-nigh transparent; and yet the flesh, if flesh it be, has a consistency. * * * The lips move; he feels the breath issuing through those parted lips upon his cheek; and then the piano in the drawing-room begins to play, and Madame Discalcelis cannot now be its manipulator, for she is reading at Mrs. Gore's side. * * * Is she reading? What is that fleecy, slender column of light that rises from her head? What is that marvellous, white, tremulous flame which is playing about her golden curls, and literally dancing on her snowy forehead? and what has that to do with the lily-crowned maiden at his side, whose hands are full of lilies-of-the-valley, and whose vesture is a sheen of light, darting forth opalescent streams of radiance as from a diamond robe? * * * Chicago is not; America is not discovered; the nineteenth century is not born, no, nor the eighteenth, nor the seventeenth, nor the sixteenth, nor the fifteenth. What century is it? Who shall answer? Professor Monteith is not, he has never been born; but Claudius Regulus Monaldini is alive, and so is Lavinia Marghuerita di Balesco, and they are walking arm in arm, as lovers walk, through spicy lemon groves at dewy eve; and the knight in armor presses his bearded lips upon the snowy hand of the maiden, and swears by all the saints and angels, yea, and by all the stars that stud the azure canopy, that to her and to her only will he be faithful even unto death. * * * The scene has changed. Who is that dark-eyed, raven-locked, Neapolitan beauty, who bids him forget his vows, scatter honor to the winds, and flee with her to Corsica, where they may live, she tells him, in an enchanted bower laden with every conceivable delight, a life that even gods might envy? * * * It is night: the evil compact has been sealed, vows to truth and honor have been broken, the very name of God has been blasphemed, and saints and angels have been invoked to witness to a bond with hell. Brave, bold oaths of lawless defiance of God and man have been mingled with passionate kisses and protestations of undying love, and against it all, yet above it all, as stars shine brightly and serenely through the otherwise dark midnight over a guilty city, — self-doomed to foulest degradation and uttermost damnation, — there hovers a gentle angel-presence. The air is stirred mysteriously, the companions in guilt shiver, and above the rustle of the leaves and the murmur of the breeze, the notes ring out mournfully but sweetly, solemnly but not despairingly, "*Semper credo in vitam æternam.*" "Oh! not that; anything but that," shrieks the plumed knight, so brave but an instant before. For a moment he staggers, falls, reels blind, senseless, at the feet of the syren who has taught him the arts of sin, and whose diabolical witcheries have wrested from him his slender stock of real manliness and trust in Heaven. Even she, the perfidious Pythonia, trembles; for her companion's lips are ashen, his cheeks are livid, his brow is wet with what resembles the sweat of death, while out of the silvery silence there echoes a voice, not loud, but penetrating to the very marrow of her bones, whose words ring in her ears and she cannot shut them out, though they madden her. "Earth at length must claim his body; you for a few short years may anticipate the worms, but I, as God's ambassador, am commissioned to keep watch for his soul." The voice is so mysterious, the words are so ominous, — and Pythonia's black soul, like that of any fiend, *believes* and *trembles*, — that she rushes from the grove and leaves the senseless partner of her sin to recover as best he may, and, waking, find his *inamorata* fled. * * * He wakes, alone, deserted, mocked, cheated by the viper to whom he would have sold his spirit, — but yet not alone; for the evening star seems to bear him company, and from one of its many shafts of scintillating radiance comes the old refrain, which carries him back to the memory of a love, outraged and scorned, but ever true and ever patient. "Credo *semper* in vitam *æternam*." * * * For nine long years he hears that voice no more; Pythonia never returns to him; he wins the Malta cross; he dies at length, untended, on the battle-field; but as his lips close and his eyes grow heavy, a gentle hand is pressed upon his brow, and a sweet song sounds in his ears ere his naked spirit doffs its coil of lacerated flesh. "After five hundred years you will again behold me; I shall ever be your guardian, but your path and mine must appear diverse till then. *Ego sum semper fidelis.*" * * * A deep, dark, dismal blank, — years, generations, centuries of time, are not marked off in purgatory as they are on earth. Once in a while a faint ray of glory pierced the gloom, as a vision of the uplifted Host raised during Mass in a little Sicilian chapel amid the hills cheered for a brief space the utter gloom of his long tarrying in Limbo; that was when a requiem Mass was being offered, at which he, poor soul, was being remembered in prayer; but these glimpses of light, revealing a far-off paradise, were so infrequent and so brief that they served only as milestones to mark off the weary waiting in the strange, exterior darkness, into which all earthbound souls must enter when they drop the robe of flesh. No fire, no torment, no companionship of any sort, only the sense of driest, dreariest loneliness, awaits the sensual and false in the interval between their death and resurrection. * * * Five hundred years have sped their course; it is now 1869, but the place is again Sicily, and the scene is again a lemon grove. This time a young English subaltern is walking arm in arm, but very slowly, with a fragile but lovely maiden, to whom he plights his honest troth, but feels, alas! all too plainly, that not on earth can he hope to realize his dearly expected joy. Suddenly she falls prone on the earth beside him; her face lights up with more than earthly radiance, she smiles, speaks, sings, and then breathes her last of earth and first of paradise, while there rings in his ear, as though a company of heavenly choristers were chanting in majestic harmony, led by one resonating, triumphal voice, "*Credo semper, semper credo, in vitam, vitam, vitam æternam.*" The music is a concluding harmony from the *Gloria* of Haydn's Imperial Mass. * * * Twenty-four years have sped their changeful course; the young subaltern has given up the army and devoted himself to science. Cheerless, atheistic, hopeless, but never vile, has he been through all those years of lonely struggle and determined effort to solve, if may be, the speechless riddle of the universal sphinx; and now, in another land, in company with new-found friends, the same sweet song reverberates in his ears, while a heavenly vision floats before his eyes, and with a triumphant shout, " Yes, it is she, she in all her beauty, in the deathlessness of her quenchless love; she, my true bride, my everlasting mate, through the cycles of eternity," he wakes, starts, gazes about him, while Visalia Discalcelis, her face almost as bright as that of the departing angel, says gently, to quiet his agitation, and, if possible, to fully reassure him, — for he is now trembling, agitated, and beginning to doubt, —

"I also have seen her and heard her. You have seen this day what your faithfulness has won for you."

No words can answer the deepest questions of the world. No speculative treatises on re-embodiment can make plain to the unrealizing what must be *felt* to be *known*. Regulus Monteith had peered behind the mystic curtain which shrouded his present from a former existence, and he *knew* then, even though he may have often doubted it afterward, that his old dead self had been shown to him in that hour, and a disclosure made to him, the patient, toiling seeker after knowledge, which is vouchsafed to few. Madame Discalcelis had furnished the conditions into which the lovely spirit could enter, who showed herself thus plainly to the professor's extended senses of hearing, sight, and recollection.

Whether a series of tableaux were presented to his mental gaze, whether the interstellar, etheric volume in which all events are recorded, was opened to his view, or whether memory alone served him, let those who *can*, decide. Facts are facts, explain, deny, question, deride, accept them, as we may; and in this age of startling psychical phenomena, we may well expect cases to multiply, and that so rapidly on every hand, that the unseen will *make* itself felt, even by those whose empty boast it long has been, that nothing whatever can be known by any one save through the evidence presented to one or more of the five bodily senses. Five bodily senses, indeed! as though these were man's only way of grasping ideas or arriving at knowledge, when every scientific theory now put forward is itself a perfect refutation of any such absurd pretence. The five senses are the veriest bond-servants of imagination, as well as intellect, and until they are relegated to their proper position as subordinates, and held there, science will be given over to vapid vaporings, which are the stock in trade of agnostic platitudinizers.

It is the search for truth, the eager quest for knowledge, which makes science glorious, or even possible; and those among distinguished scientists, who are to-day investigating spiritual phenomena, are the only real ornaments of their professions. The science of the future will be so great and majestic a thing, that while it encompasses earth, it will also seek to fathom the Great Beyond; and though there will ever be mysteries, untrodden paths, up which the feet of finite reason may never climb, such glimpses will come, yea, are now coming, from the mountain summits of spiritual attainment, that soon it will be only possible to willingly accept or wilfully deny the evidence of life immortal, which will be on every hand forthcoming.

In some such spirit Professor Monteith was forced to

ruminate upon the wondrous demonstration of spiritual power which had just been granted him; but so strong is bias oftentimes, so obstinate is habit, that prejudice asserts itself again, and yet again, when it would seem to all but angels, that whoever still persists in doubt must be indeed a voluntary infidel. Not so always; the pressure of material belief is intensely strong, and when once the mind has become encased in an armor of Materialism, the rhinoceros-like hide yields but slowly, even to the pressure of celestial light.

While Professor Monteith recovered slowly from the dazed estate into which he had been thrown by his late experience, Madame Discalcelis returned to the drawing-room, and continuing her musical recitation of the gem of Longfellow she had commenced an hour earlier, she sang on till dinner was announced.

> " Uttered not, yet comprehended,
>   Is the spirit's voiceless prayer.
> Soft rebukes in blessings ended,
>   Breaking from those lips of air."

At dinner the spirits of all the party regained their ordinary equilibrium; conversation flowed freely, and no one who had suddenly popped in upon the quiet, well-conducted quartet at the table, could have imagined, scarcely could have been made to believe, that to at least two out of the four, only a few minutes earlier, the heavens had opened and music had floated through the pearly gates from the lips of angelic choristers.

CHAPTER XX.

A GLIMPSE OF TWO WHITE CITIES.

AFTER the thrilling experiences of a purely mental and subjective character to which Professor Monteith had so recently been intromitted, it was with something akin to a sense of relief from such high tension of feeling that he responded to Mrs. Gore's cordial invitation to make one of their party the same evening to visit the White City in all the splendor of its electric illumination.

Ever beautiful and deeply impressive by day, this fairy city was a materialized dream of glory at eventide. In the garish light of day imperfections were often discernible; the too conspicuous evidences of economical lunches, eaten in State buildings or out of doors, were unpleasantly intrusive, and whatever of vulgar realism was contained in the plan and conduct of the Exposition, stood out in harsh and grating contrast to the silent splendor of the exquisite, though not extremely substantial, Exhibition buildings. After sunset all this was changed, save when an occasional search-light of unusual power revealed for a moment the crudities, while it heightened the glories, of the majestic *tout ensemble* of the scene.

This was a lovely evening; though near the close of September, the air was soft and balmy as in a poet's dream of a perfect night in June; myriads of electric lights, in all the wonder of their incandescent mystery, illuminated the short-lived palaces of this fair dream-city, veiling in bright yet mellow radiance all that could suggest fragility or impending doom. The waters of the great Lake Michigan — often lashed to fury, like waves of the tempestuous ocean, by violence of fierce winds — now rested tranquilly as a sea of glass, ordained to mirror forth in its crystalline depths the opaline splendors of the dazzling scene. It was an hour of rest, and yet of joyful activity; for the wonder-seekers on that evening were not boisterous, nor were they too numerous. There was no anticipation of pyrotechnics, and no "special attractions" of any kind, and on a quiet night the White City always appeared at its best.

As soon as he could speak — for the scene at first utterly silenced him — Professor Monteith exclaimed: —

"Is this fair work of man, think you, a feeble hint of what the New Jerusalem must be? Has the spiritual realm its domes, its minarets, its tapering spires, its varied, gorgeous forms of decorative art, as well as its electric fountains, brilliant search-lights, and happy moving throngs; or is this superb panorama merely an illusion of our senses, a dream of a moment, a false conception, an empty mirage in the desert of our mortal pilgrimage? I cannot think these questions out; they are far too high for me; my brain reels, intellect totters, reason is baffled utterly. I must abhor this lovely scene if it is but a mocking syren, taunting us with hopes of what may never be; but since I have been among you, and heard your wonderful interpretations of the universal whole, I venture fondly, though still very feebly, to hope that there may be a reality behind this beautiful ephemera, even a Divine Breath, which blows these bubbles into space and will only recall the symbols when His little ones are prepared to stand face to face with the substance which casts this fair reflection."

"What! agnostic still, yet only *hoping?*" broke in the kindly tones of Arthur Gore — between whom and the laboring professor a ripening friendship was daily increasing — "honest questioning is indeed the road to knowledge; but since you were *convinced* this afternoon, how can you be but vaguely *hoping* now? Does *conviction* also dwell in the shadowy region of baseless ephemera? Wake up, my good friend, collect your scattered forces, and DARE (you love boldness, you claim) to declare once for all, in the presence of this dazzling semblance of the real — for the IDEAL is the only REAL — 'I KNOW that my Redeemer liveth.'"

Very faintly, and withal tremulously, Professor Monteith uttered the syllables after his young preceptor, whose ringing accents betrayed never a shade of doubt; and then he sank to slumber, his eyes closed, his breath came quickly but evenly, his countenance seemed to have caught something of the glow of the entrancing scene around, and as though partly in prayer and partly in exultation, his lips moved slightly, and he murmured again and yet again, as in a tranceful dream: —

"I *know* it, yes, now verily, I KNOW it."

For two full hours he sat, or rather reclined thus, on a settee facing the lagoon; the Venetian gondolas, manned by Italian gondoliers in the picturesque costume of their native land, glided swiftly by; the hum of conversation from adjacent benches broke the quiet of the evening, the bands in the near distance lent enchantment to the hour while they discoursed sweet music; but the professor slumbered on, and yet slumbered not, for though his outer orbs were hidden behind the fallen lids, the eyes of his spirit were open to something of the beauties of a WORLD'S FAIR in HEAVEN.

Mrs. Gore and Madame Discalcelis wandered together up and down the walks, and occasionally peeped into an open building, but Arthur never left the professor's side for a single instant; he seemed almost like a tender father to the man who was twenty years his senior, and it was, if truth be told, the electric current from the young man's healthy, well-ordered frame flowing gently and continuously into the world-worn brain of the older man, which kept the latter so peacefully at rest in body while his soul for the time was almost free from the shackles of the flesh, almost, but not *entirely* free.

Just as the hour of ten was striking, and most of the visitors were scampering to the stairways leading to the elevated cars or to the depots of the Illinois Central trains, Professor Monteith awoke suddenly, but without the slightest start, and looking steadily into the eyes of his faithful companion, said in a clear, confident voice, as though he were uttering but a commonplace: —

"Yes, there are two of them, for I have seen the other."

"Two of what, my good sir?" said Madame Discalcelis, who, with Mrs. Gore, had just returned to the seat.

"Why, two Expositions, most noble madam," responded Professor Monteith; "and oh! how much fairer is the second than the first, though perhaps I ought to correct myself and say the first than the second, for now I KNOW that all this vast agglomeration of material, resplendent though it is, is naught but a poor effect of a spiritual cause whose sublimity defies all description."

"So you do not wonder and *hope* any longer, do you? At last you *know*; but take care that the little demon Doubt doesn't gain another entrance. Mr. Gore has helped you this time to overcome the demon, and we have all co-operated with him in his happily successful endeavor, but none can continue to *see*, much less to *dwell within*, the glorious White City of the skies, until without another's aid a soul will cling directly to the All-Glorious."

A soft wind arose from the lake, the stars came out in greater numbers, the moon rose higher toward the zenith, the butterfly kissed the star on the fair speaker's corsage, and then the professor knew no more than that he was happy with his friends and contentedly sipping chocolate in the Menier Building.

CHAPTER XXI.

WHAT OF PERPETUAL MOTION?

THE World's Fair is over; the World's Parliament of Religions has passed into history, preserved in two massive volumes of eight hundred pages each. Chicago is beginning to suffer a reaction from the strain of the past summer, and the many tourists and visitors to this great metropolis of the West have carried home with them varied memories and countless trophies from the scene of the recent Exposition.

Mrs. Eastlake-Gore, with her son and Madame Discalcelis, has returned to London; Professor Monteith has remained in America and gone to Philadelphia, with the express purpose of personally interviewing John Worrell Keely, the painstaking, tireless worker, who for thirty years or more has been steadily working out, almost alone, some of the most stupendous problems which the human intellect can ever seek to solve. Those wonderful documents entrusted to his charge by Aldebaran the mystic, in London, had induced Professor Monteith to seek in every possible way to utilize the marvellous information therein embodied, but hitherto he had found the statements, though probably scientifically sound in every detail, entirely beyond his grasp for purposes of practical experiment. His recent spiritual experiences had so greatly softened the previous asperity of his disposition, that, cynical no longer, he was now ready to calmly and hopefully investigate whatever promised to throw any light at all on the great question of how far man can dominate the forces of exterior nature. During his stay in Philadelphia, it was his good fortune to meet and become quite well acquainted with the Reverend Albert Plum, a Boston clergyman, who had spent much time and thought over Keely's remarkable discovery. Dr. Plum being always renowned for fearlessness of utterance as well as sincerity of purpose, it is not surprising that he has openly, through the columns of so widely circulating a newspaper as the *Boston Transcript*, espoused the cause of Keely's stupendous discovery, at a time when much undeserved contempt and derision have been cast upon the work of one of the loyalest truth-seekers of the nineteenth century.

In the reading-room of the Hotel Metropole, one blustering winter evening, when the cheery fireside was infinitely preferable to the gusty streets, Dr. Plum related to Professor Monteith, in the following words, the result of his long-continued, oft-repeated visits to Mr. Keely, whom he always found desirous of giving all information possible to honorable investigators.

"I have seen a spectacle I would have pronounced impossible according to all accepted theories of physics with which I am familiar. Without apparent exhibition of heat, electricity, or any other form of energy hitherto operated by man, I have seen a strong metallic wheel, weighing seventy-two pounds, in swift and steady revolution by the hour, and absolutely without cost. It is but a subsidiary engine, made and used simply to help equip with similar mysterious capacity of movement the large commercial engine by its side. And that is a most strange and complex mechanism, which perhaps no one but the inventor can even understand at present, and which, but for too frequent previous unauthorized fixing of dates, might be said to give promise of being itself in motion very soon. What is 'very soon' in such an undertaking? Another thirty years of patient, lonely plodding on this labyrinthine path would be nothing, if then this explorer could reach his goal. How long after Franklin's kite did the world wait, and how many hundred great experimenters, before a dynamo engine kindled our lamps and whirred our wheels? Yet this solitary pioneer, grown half blind by groping in these dim intricacies so long, again and again hurled aside, broken and almost dying by the terrific force with which he is seeking to cope, is met with the sneer, 'Why don't you do something?' He has done much, done it single-handed and alone, and amid storms of ignorant, senseless, and cruel abuse. His immortality, however, is sure. For the world at length honors an honorable purpose, persistently pursued in a high undertaking. And he has already so enlarged the domain of human knowledge, he has lifted man into such a new world of fact, the truths his experiments unveil are so novel, suggestive, and inspiring, that whether all this is ever turned to practical account or not, his name will never die. But if he should turn out to be a prophet, if he is a seer, and does really discern a promised land of lightened toil into which mankind will eventually enter, even though he may not live to lead them in, then the world will gratefully build his tomb.

"But the world asks, who is the witness that testifies so boldly to these surprising things? Is he competent and worthy of trust? The witness is not a capitalist, and he has no relations with investors, and is free to say that if Keely were to die to-morrow, it might be a hundred years before another mind would arise able to complete his work; if, indeed, it is capable of being completed at all, which no one at present knows. Impelled by a life-long interest in the wonders of natural science, and honored by the personal friendship of Keely and a few of his advisers, I have followed the course of this investigator for years with the intensest interest and sincerest admiration. I spent more of my vacation this season in the Philadelphia laboratory, and saw greater wonders there, than in the Chicago Fair.

"In whose judgment greater? Is a layman in physical science competent to judge in such matters? Confessedly not, on some questions. To most men the learned physicists speak an unknown tongue. Too profound for the common apprehension are the mathematical formulas, even, with which their works abound, though their theories and arguments are full of interest. And many would confess also that they can no more understand the ground of Keely's assertions concerning the number of millions of oscillations taking place in a given substance each second, nor his fluent discourse upon clustered thirds and introductory ninths, upon nodal transmitters and neutral centres, and upon streams and waves of polar and depolar influence. On these declarations this witness has no testimony to offer. In electrical science the world gladly accepts the terminology and the philosophy by which the specialists creditably seek to gain some practical apprehension of the elusive mystery with which they deal; elusive, for through all their technical terms and finespun theories, the futility of their endeavor to gain any exhaustive comprehension of it plainly appears. Experts have their field, but as Mr. Gladstone says of the Hebraist and the scientist in reference to the higher criticism and the scriptural cosmogony, 'their title to speak with authority is confined to their special province, nor are they inerrable there; and if we allow them to go beyond it, and still to claim their authority, when they are what is called at school "out of bounds," we are much to blame, and may suffer for our carelessness.' 'My contention is,' he says, 'that there is a ground which the specialist is not entitled to occupy in his character as a specialist, and on which he has no warrant for entering, except in so far as he is a just observer and reasoner in a much wider field.'

"It is into this wider field of fact, where any can go whose general training fits him to be in any wise 'a just observer and reasoner,' that this witness deems it not improper to enter, especially as he follows in the wake of not a few who rank high as experts in mechanical engineering, in chemistry, in electricity, and other departments of superior culture. For, not only has Keely's legal counsellor, Charles B. Collier, an experienced patent lawyer, acute, cultured, and discerning, given him from the first his sincere and hearty support, but numbers of other men of honorable character and position, many of them eminent for scientific attainments, have given their unqualified testimony that Keely is an original and able investigator in an interesting and promising, though wholly novel, field — a wonder-worker, whose work seems to overturn certain accepted theories, and has puzzled and baffled their learned advocates. Yet, partly, perhaps, because Keely is not in the fraternity of college bred men, but has educated himself (though his writings show a familiarity with scholarly works), partly because his claims are so astonishing and his methods so incomprehensible, and partly because of premature predictions of a practical issue of his labors, and because also of unfortunate differences reported in respect to the business side of his enterprise, there are comparatively few men of public prominence who seem to be willing to be known as believers in the importance of his investigations, or even in the integrity of the man. At any rate, ridicule and contempt continue to be thrown at him and at the faithful friends who have long and nobly stood by him. Only lately a prominent journal intimated that 'an interruption of Keely's personal freedom' ought to result from what it calls his 'gigantic jugglery.' It is these unworthy flings, together with a sense of the public importance of the whole matter, which have prompted my voluntary and unsolicited testimony in the interest of truth.

"For though scores of assemblies, comprising learned scientists, skilful engineers, and men of large success in the practical conduct of affairs, have witnessed various experiments by Keely during the past dozen years, and although their clear and positive statements of the interest and value of his researches have been repeatedly published in leading newspapers, with the names and professional titles of the witnesses given, yet the general public appears either to overlook or forget all these testimonies, and to be rudely impatient of every undertaking that does not immediately issue in commercial success. Seldom does any public journal refer to Keely in terms of appreciation and respect. As his labors have now reached some new results which only a few persons have witnessed, this further testimony is proffered as information upon a matter of scientific interest, certainly, and with a possible bearing upon industrial advance.

"What, then, is the testimony that the present witness has to give? After some ten years of acquaintance with Keely, and after personally seeing many of his experiments, 'witness deposeth and saith,' that Keely appears to him to be a man of sublime patience and persistence in his high purpose, modestly esteeming himself an agent of Divine Providence in the accomplishment of one of the most beneficent revolutions in the history of human progress; a man of wonderful insight and truly amazing fertility of inventive genius in overcoming obstacles and in contriving appliances for attaining his mechanical ends; that he is dealing with and trying to employ in practical mechanics a force absolutely new among all the forces hitherto handled by man, although its presence in nature is affirmed by the theories of scientists, and demonstrated by various observed phenomena; a force of mysterious and awful energy, boundless in extent, and literally costless as the air. Electricity is subtle and powerful and illimitable in supply, but it requires constant and costly expenditure of energy to call it into exercise and keep it at work. This new force, beyond the curious and complicated mechanism which this wonderful wizard has contrived for it to employ, the harness he has fashioned for it to wear, seems to require but a few slight musical sounds, the sonorous vibrations of certain metallic appliances, to set it in motion, and then it will keep in motion — for all that at present appears, in steady, noiseless, and almost resistless motion — till the solid metals of which it is composed wear out.

"What! one and all exclaim, is the absurdity of perpetual motion to be revived again? But the physicists tell us there is perpetual motion all around us in nature, intense and all-pervading, and always has been, since the hour 'when the morning stars sang together, and all the sons of God shouted for joy.' Here we touch the robe of the Infinite One, who 'upholdeth all things by the word of his power.' Of him the Unerring One declared, 'My Father worketh hitherto and I work.' Aye, works unceasingly now, in the incessant and intense molecular vibration all the time going on in all matter; in the solid oaken table by which we sit, in the firm granite of the building which encloses us. Action, motion in everything, by everything, everywhere, all the time, and swift, more nimble-footed sometimes than thought almost, but with such a soft and easy pace that no footfall is heard, no movement discerned save as we take observation by the distant heavenly orbs among which we all here on the earth are travelling, hurled along our pathway over a thousand miles a minute. Movement of everything from here to there, and movement in everything while here or there. And so harmonious is the movement, on such delicate anti-friction cushions do the bearings rest, that it is all inaudible, save to that One alone whose ear discerns the music of the spheres — the spheres immensely great and infinitesimally small —

"'Forever singing as they shine,
The hand that made us is divine.'

"And only now, after thousands of years of unheard song, this great magician arises and strikes the chord of sympathy to which this vibrating force responds, and lo! it comes forth from its secret chambers like the mighty Genius unloosed by the Arabian fishermen from the copper flask, and waits on man to do his bidding, bending its tough sinews and plying its facile fingers to perform his humblest tasks.

"And what proof can there be that this dream of poetry and fancy of story is in any degree an accomplished fact? Look and see. Here is a wooden table, sometimes covered by a heavy slab of glass. Standing on the glass or on the wood, and capable of being moved freely upon it, is a metal standard say a foot high, bearing a copper globe about a foot in diameter. Around the base of the standard project horizontally numbers of small metal rods a few inches long, of different sizes and lengths, vibrating like tuning-forks when twanged by the fingers. In the hollow globe is a Chladni plate and various metal tubes, the relation of which can be altered by turning a projection like a door-knob, on the outside of the globe, at the outer end of a small shaft, round and round to the right or left. This construction is called a 'sympathetic transmitter.' Some two or three feet distant on the table stands a movable metallic cylindrical case, some six inches by eight in size, composed of certain metal resonating tubes, and certain other metal fixtures. You take it all apart and see there is no magnet there. You place on top of this cylinder a small pocket compass, a brass cup two inches in diameter with its glass face. The needle points to the north. From the periphery of the globe of the 'sympathetic transmitter' extends a wire of the size of a common knitting-needle, made of gold and silver and of platinum. The free end of this wire is now attached to the cylinder. The needle is still true to the pole. Then the vibrating rods are twanged, the knob is turned, and on a rude harmonicon trumpet for a moment or two certain sounds are made, when lo! the needle is invisible, it is whirling on its pivot so fast. The operator talks of the variant length of waves and of a continuous stream, and in some instances it is half a minute, sometimes three minutes, before the needle comes to rest, and it has kept in swift revolution for many hours; but when it pauses it points no longer to the north, but to a particular part of the mechanism. You leave it there, and are busy with other wonders for an hour or so. Returning, you find the needle still points to its new master. You lift the compass off, and at once it resumes its normal position. You slowly lower it towards the silent cylinder, and when within an inch or two it obeys the new impulse again, and points as before. So also it veers from the north when you carry it near the knob of the copper globe. As Gladstone says, 'Our hands can lay hold of truths that our arms cannot embrace,' and though it takes a physicist to comprehend this miracle, any careful observer can apprehend it, and, after seeing it repeated many times, if he is measurably well read, is competent to testify that here is a new, subtle, silent, continuous influence, and that it is called into exercise in connection with certain brief musical sounds.

"Look again. On this rude harmonicon trumpet this magician blows through a small window into the next room towards a common zither some ten feet distant, held upright on a table by a small standard composed of a group of metal tubes. The two musical instruments have been carefully attuned to each other. Attached to the back of the zither is a common silk thread loosely hanging and extending some eight feet away, where it is tied to a movable framework of half-inch iron rods, supporting and bracing in position, on an isolated table of glass, a metal globe, fifteen inches in diameter, capable of turning freely in either direction, on its axis, which bears inside the globe certain resonant tubes and plates, the table standing at an angle of 45° from the face of the zither. Louder sounds the horn, till in a minute or two the metal globe begins to revolve. The horn stops, the globe stops. Again the horn resounds, again the globe turns, and the stronger and more continuous the blast, the more swiftly whirls the globe. You snip the thread apart with your scissors, and the ear of the globe has grown dull; no sound can awake it to motion again. Does a man need to be an expert in physics after he has seen that marvel repeated a few times, and has moved all the apparatus freely hither and thither, to testify that the rapid revolution of that metal globe was not caused by compressed air, coming in concealed tubes from a hidden reservoir, or that a silk thread is not the highway usually cast up for electricity to travel?

"But these are philosophical toys. What about an engine with power to help human toil?

"I have in my study a paper weight — a disc, said to be composed of an alloy of three metals. It looks like steel, measures two and a half inches by three-quarters of an inch, weighs about a pound, is enclosed in a brass ring, and exhibits no magnetic power. I am told that shut up in a glass chamber and connected with the wire which seemed to affect the compass, it absorbed some seven pints of hydrogen gas. The story runs that it was also rapidly whirled by a steam engine a certain number of hours, still in connection with the apparatus from which seemed to flow that subtle influence which the needle of the compass obeyed. Whatever may be thought of all this, it is a fact that the disc thus 'vitalized in its atomic or molecular constitution' adheres to the under side of a certain metallic resonant structure as if held there by magnetic attraction, and also supports a weight hung to itself of over two hundred and thirty pounds. Dissociated from the peculiar vibrating apparatus, it falls like any other heavy body, and though that apparatus attracts the disc, even with the attached weights, it is incapable of attracting anything else; it will not support the smallest iron filing. Here then is a strong pulling power in exercise in certain circumstances when two bodies are in contact. Can it pull bodies together which are not in contact?

"I see before me on a table a glass jar, ten inches in diameter and forty-eight inches high, filled with water. At the bottom lie three metal balls like one I hold in my hand, which weighs about two pounds. The jar has a metal cap to which is attached the gold and platinum wire reaching from the copper globe. I am told each ball, like every mass of matter, has its peculiar musical chord. I am reminded of well-known facts of sympathetic vibration; *e.g.*, a large mill trembling in response to the note of a neighboring waterfall, and only quieted and rendered safe by building on an addition, changing its musical chord. And now again the rods are twanged, the knob is turned, the trumpet sounds and keeps sounding till, in a moment or two, I see one ball begin to sway from right to left, then slowly leave the bottom of the jar and rise through the water till with a bump it strikes the metal cap, rebounds a few inches and comes to rest in contact with it on the surface of the water. Still the horn blows, and by this time the second ball responds in like manner, and then the third. Then the music ceases, and we turn to other experiments, but as long as I stayed in the shop that day something made that metal swim. My companion said he had often seen the weights brought slowly down, or held midway, as shown by photographs, by sounding other chords. On the top of the jar lay certain pieces of metal. Keely said, 'Do not remove those. I once did that, and crash went the balls through the bottom of my jar.' Now here was a pulling power acting at a distance of four feet, not capable of lifting the weights through the air, but before all eyes lifting them through water. Can this pulling power turn a wheel?

"Here is a wheel of stout metal weighing, as stated, seventy-two pounds, free to move either way on its stationary axis. Its hub is a cylinder containing certain resonant tubes parallel to the axis. It has eight spokes, each carrying one of the 'vitalized discs' at its outer end, the face of the disc at right angles with the spoke. There is no rim to the wheel, but there is a stationary metal rim some six inches wide and thirty-two inches in diameter, within which the wheel turns without touching it. This rim carries on its inner surface nine similar discs, and on the outside, attached to each disc, a resonating cylinder. The requisite amount of the metallic volume of this cylinder is obtained by inclosing in its tubes a few cambric needles, more or less as required, and curiously enough, some of these needles at length become magnetic. Attached to this engine is a gold and platinum wire, some ten feet in length, running through the small window to the copper globe in the other room, where sits the man who has fashioned all this. He twangs the rods of the sympathetic transmitter on the table at his side, he turns its knob, the musical instruments sound for a moment, and peering through the window along the line of the wire his face lights up with a smile of triumph. He settles back in his chair, and all is still. That wheel at the end of the wire is in rapid revolution before your eyes. You turn and look with amazement upon Orpheus returned to earth again and outdoing his fabled exploits of old. For by the enchantment of the subtle harmonies he evokes, too fine for human ear to catch, you see the untamed forces of nature obey his behest; that most constant of all things, the magnetic needle, you see charmed into fickleness by his magic spell; you see balls of iron swim; you see insensate matter — as you thought it, but sensitive now to his call — leap forward into instant rotation, continuous and swift. Long we stand around that flying wheel. The friend who photographed it at rest again levels his camera upon it. In vain; its spokes cannot tarry long enough to be caught by his snare. It is still as death, and almost as mysterious. We listen to long dissertations upon the reason for the relative position of the eight discs on the wheel and the nine on the stationary rim, and how the adjustment can be so altered that, instead of a revolution, there will be a violent oscillation back and forth. We are shown the corresponding wheel and the rim of the large engine close by, which is to bear the discs not singly, but in groups, the steel resonating drums with their circles of tubes inside, and thirty-five inch Chladni plate underneath the 'sympathetic transmitter' on top; the extra wheel bearing on its spokes cylindrical cases, each filled solid with a hundred thin-carved plates of steel, to get the utmost superficial area, we are told, and it is all so utterly beyond comprehension, that we can see no reason why it should have been made as it is, or how any one can be sure it will ever run. But we turn around and look again on that noiseless wheel, still running rapidly all alone, and confess we should have said the same thing about that. And we are inclined then to trust the word of the inventor when he says the running of the smaller insures the running of the larger; that the wheel you see spinning so fast cannot be stopped by any force except one that would tear it into fragments, unless with thumb and finger you loosen that golden wire along which 'the stream of sympathetic vibration' is said to flow, and that there is no reason why the wheel should not keep·in motion till the bearings wear out.

"I say nothing now of other wonders of which other witnesses can speak, and which are said to have appeared in the slow progress this incomprehensible man has been making all these years; of a pressure obtained from the disintegration of water by vibration of twenty thousand pounds to the square inch; of a slowly revolving drum which went no slower when winding tightly upon itself a stout inch and a half rope fastened to a beam, and no faster when the rope parted under the strain; of the disintegration of rock into impalpable powder; of raising heavy weights by aid of a 'vibratory lift,' recalling the 'negative gravity' of our modern story-teller.

"The engine you have been looking upon requires as part of itself for some mysterious purpose certain heavy tubular copper rings. Skilful artisans failed in various endeavors, by electrical deposit and otherwise, to make them right. The inventor contrived machinery for bending into semicircles sections of copper tube, one and a half inch bore, three-eighths of an inch thick, forcing a steel ball through them to keep the tube in shape. To make a ring, he placed two of those half-circles together and joined the ends in some way (without heat), by what he calls sympathetic attraction, so the resonant properties of the ring are satisfactory, and though you see the line of union, the two parts cannot be severed. You see one of these rings, some fifteen inches in diameter, hanging by block and tackle from the ceiling, and lashed to the lower half swings a big iron ball weighing five hundred and fifty pounds, and there it has swung for weeks. Has the man who has done simply that, and done it merely to furnish a subsidiary adjunct to his main contrivance, won no place among the great artificers? Is it worthy business to revile him as a swindling charlatan? The end is not yet. We shall see what we shall see, or some one will. One thing, however, we see clearly now, and that is that John Worrell Keely deserves the esteem and admiration of his fellow-men. Who does not hope that he has solid grounds for the persistent belief which has been his star of hope these many years; that a merciful Providence is about to confer a new boon upon the suffering industries of mankind; that the time at length has come when man is wise enough to fashion and strong enough to handle the beneficent gift of a costless motor to ease the burdens of human toil?

"Wise enough and strong enough, perhaps, some may say, but is man trusty? For the question has arisen whether a force of such fearful energy as some of these experiments disclose can safely be entrusted to such a being as man, who can destroy as well as build. But why should man have been set to discover and harness it? 'I take great comfort in God,' said James Russell Lowell, in one of his recently published letters, 'I think. . . . He would not let us get at the match-box as carelessly as he does unless he knew that the frame of his universe was fireproof.'"

As Dr. Plum finished his amazing recitation with the above apposite quotation from one of America's astutest philosophers, he declared his intention of writing to the *Boston Transcript* as fully and freely as he had spoken to Professor Monteith, remarking, "I am sure that excellent, liberal-minded journal will publish all I send as correspondence, though probably the editor will see fit to make some comment, to show that he is by no means responsible for my acceptance of what to many, I regret to say, appears a monstrous delusion, if not an imposition."

As Professor Monteith had very little time remaining at his disposal and his interviews with Keely were necessarily few, he saw nothing more remarkable than what is recorded in Dr. Plum's recital, but he did see the identical wonders therein described, causing him to return to England, pledged to exert whatever influence he could command to drum up recruits, and give the grand old worker at least the assurance of sympathy and good-will from some of the really earnest delvers into nature's mysteries on the other side of the Atlantic.

The *Boston Transcript* fully justified its excellent reputation as an instructive, progressive, family newspaper, by publishing without any curtailment the extremely valuable letter which the good clergyman prepared for its columns. The letter was issued Saturday, January 13, 1894.

Professor Monteith on his return to London sent an account of these astounding mysteries to many of the leading magazines and newspapers, several of which gladly published all he contributed; only a few were mediæval enough to decline to insert an honest communication. Those who declined to publish a true testimony were of course delighted to furnish their readers with ignorant, contemptuous ridicule.

CHAPTER XXII.

SPIRITUAL PHYSIOLOGY.

DETERMINED now to carefully and dispassionately investigate every phase of psychical phenomena which came under his notice, Professor Monteith, on his return to London, wended his way shortly after arriving in the metropolis, to the Bayswater Metaphysical University, where a course of lectures was being delivered on The Divine Science of Health, by Lady Copleigh, who had been cured by purely spiritual modes of treatment, of serious disorder, after the most distinguished physicians of different schools had pronounced her a helpless, lifelong invalid.

No sooner had Lady Copleigh recovered her own vigor, and more, — she had attained to a state of health utterly unknown to her in days gone by, — than she entered actively into the work of imparting to others a knowledge of the glorious truth which had been of such priceless value to herself. Though naturally of a retiring disposition, enjoying a life of elegant literary action, in a delightful villa in the most desirable part of Bayswater; at the call of what she felt to be her duty to humanity, she did not hesitate to take the platform and instruct miscellaneous audiences, as well as private classes, in the sublime principles of the esoteric science to which she owed so much, not only bodily but spiritually; for her whole nature had been enriched and sanctified, while her physical frame had also become invigorated, through her understanding and acceptance of the doctrine, that by perfect trust in the All-Good as the only Power in the universe we can become emancipated from mental errors and depression as well as from external ills.

Lady Francesca Copleigh, who was the president of the Bayswater Metaphysical University, was seconded in all things by her gifted niece, Lady Louise Huntington, who had given up an influential post in Germany, as lady-in-waiting to a princess very near the throne, for the sake of being with her aunt in London, to whom she was deeply attached, and working with her in the great work of usefulness to which Lady Copleigh had consecrated her life.

Professor Monteith was especially anxious to meet this philanthropic noblewoman, in consequence of his acquaintance with Mrs. Ajax Anad, an elderly New York lady, who had crossed the ocean on purpose to put herself under Lady Copleigh's treatment, and with such success that, though she had been bedridden for years and had to be carried on and off the steamer on the outward journey, she was so vigorous on the return trip that, though over eighty years of age, she was nimble as a girl, and able to resume her position as a public reader on her return to Brooklyn, much to the astonishment as well as delight of her many friends, most of whom feared she would never return alive to greet them when they saw her lifted on to the steamer to gratify her insatiable determination to visit the renowned healer, who had already been of inestimable service to many of her acquaintances.

As Lady Copleigh stepped upon the platform of the college lecture-room, in which nearly two hundred people were assembled on the Thursday afternoon when Professor Monteith was in the audience, she impressed all who saw her and felt her presence with a sense of *holy dignity*, which comported well with the quiet richness of her surroundings and the exquisite folds of her black satin dress, relieved with primrose flowers worked into the fabric by the deft fingers of Lady Huntington. As many of the attendants on that occasion were visitors new to the teachings, the teacher deemed it advisable to deliver an explanatory address of a general character. Speaking in distinct, well-modulated tones, earnestly but very quietly (she disapproved of *loud* utterances), she gave the following introductory discourse, intended for subsequent publication in *The Divine Science of Health*, a paper she was at that time editing. She took as the text for her remarks Spiritual Physiology and Mental Healing.

"In these days of advancement in all material science, it is uplifting to know that the spiritual is not discarded; therefore, in pursuance of the above-named subject, we will lay aside all negative or material thought and consider it from a purely spiritual standpoint, which is the positive or subjective, while the material is the negative or objective, though all is the manifestation of Infinite Spirit, whose thought is the only *real* or harmonious thought in the universe.

"We have no word that I know stronger than *real*, in the sense I am using it, by which to express the Infinite; therefore, that word which is strongest and expresses most power we give to God, for God is Real, Eternal, Unchangeable, Infinite Goodness.

"Physical man is the negative pole of life, changeable and finite.

"In proportion as we expand beyond the erroneous view of negative or limited conditions and contemplate the unlimited grandeur and positive condition of Omnipotent Mind, we disperse the negative condition of our material understanding that the body is our life, and more clearly see the *All Good* as our *real* and unlimited life. The existence of man is eternal because he is Mind. Thought is the product of mind. If we say we are sick, it is mind in its negative condition which first projects the thought of discord.

"If we have sore throat, we commence to doctor the throat, in place of seeking the cause of that which produced it. The same in rheumatism: if we complain of it, we rub the limb with liniment, to destroy the pain. So, generation after generation has been piling the imagination of disease upon disease in the system, error upon error, acting from the negative side of our nature, instead of seeking to learn of the positive, which is the understanding of God, or All Good.

"Thus are the Scriptures fulfilled: the sins of the fathers are visited upon the children; but we are not wholly responsible for that ignorance in which we have been educated; our responsibility lies in not seeking a better understanding of ourselves.

"If the material man is discordant, we consult the sensations of the body and trust much to medicine and little to God, thereby extolling the body and dethroning the kingdom of God within, apparently forgetting it is the life of God which permeates our organisms and gives us of his life: 'Who forgiveth all our sin and healeth all our infirmities.'

"None can tell until they study and take in this understanding what a power there is in thought, imbued with the law of the spiritual truth of the Science of Life, to heal the sick and raise us above the *imaginary* demands of the body.

"Let those who are deeply versed in *Materia Medica* speak for themselves of the error of the objective thought.

"Dr. John Mason Good, a learned professor of London, said: 'The science of medicine is an unintelligible jargon, and the effect of our drugging medicine on the human system is in the highest degree uncertain, except, indeed, that it has already destroyed more lives than has pestilence and famine combined.'

"Dr. Abercrombie, Fellow Royal College of Physicians, in Edinburgh, says: 'Medicine is the science of guessing.'

"Dr. James Johnson said: 'I declare my conscientious belief, founded on long observation and reflection, that if there was not a single physician, surgeon, apothecary, man midwife, chemist, druggist, or drug on the face of the earth, there would be less sickness and less mortality.'

"Voltaire said: 'The art of medicine consists in amusing the patient while nature cures the disease.'

"Dr. Abernethy, in his last days, said: 'I have studied the science of drugs all my life, and must die confessing I know nothing of them that I can demonstrate always the same, *so no result is sure.*'

"Oliver Wendell Holmes said: 'I firmly believe if the whole *Materia Medica* could be sunk to the bottom of the sea, it would be better for mankind, and the worse for the fishes.'

"Dr. J. H. Salisbury on 'The Relation of Alimentation and Disease,' says: 'The idle ramblings of an exaggerated fancy or the senseless worries of morbid anxieties weaken the mind; the automatic efforts of a listless body drain it of its life forces. This is especially manifest, and proven in handling disease. The drawbacks in a patient's restoration to health are as different in kind as there are individuals. Each and all of these peculiar drawbacks arise from the condition of the patient's mind, from something he has thought or done, when they are not caused by dietetic or other infringements of rule. Man acts upon man at every point, and we all radiate to our patient through every pore, in every gesture and tone, our life force. Our personal magnetisms are all in these, and if we are charged with peace and good-will, we radiate the same. Diseased states are established by complete absorption in mistaken habits of thought and living through a long period of years, therefore, time must be given the life forces to retrace our steps to health. Faith without works is dead. Faith in the physician alone can restore the diseased organs, therefore it is needful to seek the root of the cause. Imagination is a principal factor in the cause and cure of disease.'

"With such testimony as this from men of science and thought, whose characters, researches, and knowledge we must respect and be thankful for, does it not behoove us to search deeper for a cure for the ills that flesh is heir to, than pills, potions, etc.? For 'as we sow, we reap,' 'as we think, we are.'

"The law of God is the law of the universe, and throughout this universe there is no lack of vitality, for God expresses himself in ceaseless vitality, and it is man's privilege to be consciously a partaker of it. The mineral, vegetable, and animal kingdoms are partakers of it unconsciously, and thereby grow and are perfected according to their kind.

"Man is a compendium of his own beliefs; that which he holds positive in thought governs him.

"Mind is the active force or power of all that is, and the power of mind is what influences and constrains all creation.

"St. Paul accuses man of being so foolish as 'having begun in the Spirit' to think himself 'made perfect by the flesh.' Gal. iii. 3.

"The spirit is the life, the soul of which is the individual or real man; the body is the material garment or negative form through which the soul is made visible. All life is Spirit, but manifested in different degrees of density, positive and negative, man being the most positive of God's creation.

"Admitting this, shall we not look to Spirit, and see

that our creation endows us with a spiritual individuality which permeates the multiform individual parts of the physical system?

"Life comes to us from the ever-present God, our Father, and perfect health accompanies this life, for God holds no imperfection, such as sickness and disease, therefore can convey none to his children. In order to be receptive to this health and harmony, all thought of disease must be unrecognized.

"Our minds are laboratories for the gestation of thought, and as we think upon the law of Life, or growth in God, we realize that life is as active inside these bodies as outside of them. Man can only grow in this knowledge as he accepts the reality of life or God's power within him.

"If man lacks the recognition of this divine power within him, he lacks the recognition of the immensity of God's love, and is therefore negative to all discordant surroundings.

"Mind does not live in or from the body, but manifests its thought upon the body, therefore the condition of the body is the compendium of man's own thoughts. It is not something added to that which God has created, but is left to man in his free agency to govern, and when governed by material or negative thought it is under limitation. Thus when I say the spirit, which is the life-giving power, permeates the body, I do not imply that our minds are confined to the limits of our bodies, any more than music is confined to an instrument.

"The body is the visibility of the soul to ourselves and others, and being the temple of the Holy (whole)

Spirit, we ought to keep it pure and undefiled from sin, sickness, and disease.

"God lives, and in him we live and move and have our being; therefore our lives are linked with the Divine Infinite, and we are finite copies of the Divine, for we are created in his image and likeness.

"In like manner, as God manifests himself in the universe, so do we manifest our thoughts upon our bodies. Physiology, physiognomy, phrenology, etc., all tend to approve this assertion.

"All we know of sensation in the body is from the mind.

"The creations of the finite or limited thought, with all its deceptions and delusions, must be exterminated before we can realize the God power within, which is the kingdom of Christ, Emanuel, God with us.

"We are a spiritual creation, with a free will or agency which gives us the power to hold our lives perfect in God, free from sin, sickness, and disease; or to dwell in the negative or finite pole of life, which produces a changing, erring, sick, and dying inheritance.

"When we acknowledge our life, action, and entity to be from God, and *realize* it in every thought, we shall reason from God — cause — to — body — effect, and no more fear the food we eat, the weight of the clothes we wear, or the atmospheric changes, for we shall know, *i.e.* inwardly, consciously understand, that God is perfect life, and that we are in the image and likeness of that perfect life, and if we hold to that image and likeness, we are participators of the Divine reality of life, and thus eat of that Divine bread (love) and drink of that Divine blood (truth) which feeds our spiritual thoughts and gives us every day our daily bread (spiritual sustenance), enabling us to be ever ready to acknowledge the good and so lay aside the way of evil. To attain this positive attitude — the law of our life in God — we must constantly acknowledge it, then we shall demonstrate the true life which God has given us — a life free from error, sickness, disease, and suffering.

"The world's statement of man and God's creation of him differ widely. The world's idea of man attributes life to the body, whereas all life is from God.

"God being our power of action and source of entity, or real self, the kingdom within cannot be sick, diseased, or suffering; this truth is being constantly demonstrated in the practice of the Science of Spiritual Healing.

"As this positive truth submerges itself into our lives, it exerts its mastery over our negative bodies, and we do not permit sin, sickness, and suffering to hold us in their bondage. The Science of Spiritual Healing is not difficult to understand when we can once lay aside our old beliefs.

"We cannot serve two masters: one will war against the other; but we can scientifically govern the body by positive thought, and thereby learn more of the unchangeable infinite wisdom and love of God; because we learn by experience and demonstration, and consequently realize in our life the positive truth of our divine origin.

"Mortal laws of health are only mortal beliefs, and

beliefs are a force of thought producing corresponding results.

"The Science of Spiritual Healing challenges all material beliefs relative to man's life, and acknowledges God as the centrifugal force of all life, for we live and move and have our being in God; and how can we live in God when we are living a life of suffering? How can we move in God when we realize pain in our movements? How can we wish in God when our whole being is discordant in disease? These are questions which, when answered from our interior self, will make manifest life and vigor where we now behold sickness and inactivity. Joy and pleasure will dwell within the family circle where now reign despondency, sorrow, and suffering.

"When we are able truly to understand how the law of mind operates, through thought, upon the body, then will we understand *how* the law of harmony destroys and puts under foot all discord.

"Realizing the undeviating law of this science as fully as I do, by my personal experience in my own body, and that of my patients, I wish it were as broadly proclaimed as the anatomy of our physical structure, and thereby destroy suffering and crime; for the science is not only applicable to physical disease, but also to lack of moral rectitude.

"To those who are strong in their religious beliefs, it gives them the understanding of why they believe. It not only aids the unchaste to abstain from their errors, but it enhances a moral purity which thinks no evil, and introduces the Christ Spirit, which knows no condemnation.

"Where this truth is a mystery, it is from a non-understanding of the law of the Science of Being, which science is as a grain of mustard-seed: when sown, able to spring up and bring forth fruit a hundred-fold; the destroying of sin, disease, and suffering causes the material world to lose its hold on the thought of man, for those who know and practise its truth will be enabled to keep their bodies in subjection and govern them in harmony.

"Christ, our Master, sent out his disciples in twos, he understanding how easily we are overcome by surrounding negative conditions, and how apt to turn to the visible outward, instead of to the invisible inward, for help; and *I think* he thus designed to show us our need and ability to help one another.

"This Science of Spiritual Healing opens to us a mine of golden thought and practical truth; it gives us the law by which the stronger can assist the weaker; it unlocks the mystery of disease, and works from the harmonious standpoint of positive truth, to make health a conscious reality, a God-given birthright.

"Standing on this rock, we are enabled to guard our thoughts against the treacherous enemy, sickness, in the recognition of life from and in God.

"This science brings us into an available nearness to the true life, which will awaken and uplift mankind from a trust in matter to a higher and more ennobling realm of thought.

"You may all ask, Can I acquire this knowledge? I answer, You can if you so desire, for the laws of God are ever operating to aid us to the attainment of noble ends and God-given qualities.

"A knowledge of the exemplary teachings of Christ, that God and his creation are spiritual, that the whole universe is moved by spirit, that all life is evolved from the Divine Infinite Life, God,— Perfection,— from whom no imperfection or suffering can proceed, and with whom is no variableness or shadow of turning, is the truth and basis of mental healing.

"Those who have labored for the welfare of souls, those who have striven to bring souls into the fold of our Master, those who have strengthened by their might every good society for the propagation of the Gospel of Christ, had they taught that man's nature is intrinsically noble, that God is the loving, living centre of man's life, whereby he possesses a spiritual inheritance, in place of presenting his sinful condition and holding the fear of punishment over him, the work would have been shorn of great difficulties, many lives would have been spared to us here which have been sacrificed to false belief concerning fevers, climate, food, and discomforts, and the world would now well-nigh have approached the millennium; for, 'where the spirit of the Lord is, there is liberty.' 2 Cor. iii. 17.

"To illustrate the power of mind in thought,— for I hold this to be a truth, and truth is radical, it admits of no deviation, not even one straw one way or the other, — just as two and two make four, so can this truth be delineated; for example: retire at night when the weather is pleasant and the thermometer registering between forty-five and fifty-five degrees, arise in the morning and behold through your window the landscape clad in a pure white fleecy robe; you shiver, and say 'winter has come; we must clothe more warmly, for it is cold.'

"What says it is cold?

"It is mind, for you have not been out to realize it is cold, but on beholding the snow, you have the sense of cold and do not realize that within yourself is the life principle which can control all.

"When the viper fastened on St. Paul's hand he shook it off, when all eye-witnesses were ready to condemn him and expected to see him die (Acts xxviii.). Paul had a true knowledge of his life; he had been taught of Christ that all life is perfect in God, therefore no harm came to him. Mental healers understand that no sickness shall befall those who realize the true science of this philosophy and understandingly apply it; for it can be demonstrated as perfectly as a problem in mathematics, clearly showing that wrong belief in ourselves or progenitors is the first cause of disease.

"The work of the mental healer, when called to a patient, is to inwardly fix the patient's mental eyes on the goal of health to which the healer desires to raise the patient; the healer then seeks to disabuse the patient's mind of old beliefs, and lift the thought to the Infinite Good of all life and the wisdom of his harmonious creation. The ethereal or real body has its own organs, which are the essence or real basis of the outer senses.

"When truth asserts its sway in our thoughts, we acknowledge these molecular bodies as derived from the mineral, vegetable, and animal kingdoms of earth, formed from prepared dust of the ground; but our life is the breath of God, our heritage is dominion over all.

We shall, through this recognition, come into diviner rapport with the Infinite Soul of the Universe, and understand that our life is contingent on him though contiguous to the body.

"As we battle against the darkness of negative thought, which tells us of our suffering bodies, the finer lenses of the soul's consciousness to the realities of life are awakened, and we enter upon a truer and more positive understanding of the laws of our life, which understanding enables us to help the sick and afflicted, also the drunkard, the sensualist, etc.; for such conditions are all aberrations from, or ignorance of, the truth concerning which Christ came to convince the world, making plain to all his disciples the error of sin and disease, by eradicating it in his work and teachings, then sending them forth to do likewise.

"Our Master came to do our Father's will, which was his meat and drink. He came to fulfil all law, not to break it; *i.e.* the Father's law, not negative or man-made beliefs. Is it not strange that we have held on to the garments of negative or material conditions so long, placing life in the body and amalgamating the sensations of the body with the realities of the spiritual?

"Healing by the true spirit is a source of increased strength to the healer, for it carries him or her nearer to the true source of all life; still he or she must reserve time for growth, concentration, inward examination, and reflection.

"A study and application of mental healing enables a mother resolutely and fearlessly to control the health of her children and her household, for during the course of class instruction, the truth of the science of being so enters into her own soul that a new understanding of life is born within her which gives her power over that which she once feared, and she realizes that a true and perfect expression of God through man demands a sound body: we read in Holy Writ that Christ had a body provided for him.

"The positive thought of good-will manifests itself through the mental organization upon the outward body, and modifies the tenor of our lives, to the exclusion of all anxiety and fear.

"In reading this carefully you will perceive that sickness and suffering are due to material or Adamic thought, that the pills and potions administered express an Adamic or material understanding entailed upon us through previous generations. Through the science of spiritual thought we learn that we can overcome our material beliefs, in perfect love casting out fear, the truth of which in all its aspects I consider it of the first importance to understand, for it opens the windows of our souls to the reception of higher truths and a better understanding of the divine law of life.

"'If Truth, the inmost soul, a being share,
The universe becomes a book of prayer;
Prayer pushes prayer
E'en into heaven's sublimest air.'

"If from what I have said, any of you get a glimpse of how to commence to rid yourselves of any physical infirmity, I shall rejoice, I having fully realized and experienced it to be so great an alleviation of physical infirmities and suffering, as well as the true light of an exalted understanding of man's nature, descending from Infinite Love into the hearts of his children, saying to the suffering and weary, 'In returning and rest shall ye be saved; in quietness and confidence shall be your strength.' Isa. xxx. 15.

"As we receive the power of the healing influence of this science, and demonstrate its effects upon the thoughts and deeds of mankind, an intense desire for others to understand it must burn within us, and, as Whittier so beautifully expresses it, —

"'The heart of silence
May throb with soundless words,
And by the inward ear alone
The spirit voice be heard.'

"Those who are least anxious about their bodies invariably enjoy the best health.

"Our physical *needs* are very small. All over the world, in every clime, the hardest workers eat the plainest food, and their culinary department is of the simplest character; a study of which will teach us that all life and strength is an influx from the divine, omnipresent life of the universe, which fills all space.

"All space is permeated with an invisible life principle; we inhale this life with every breath we draw, and condition it according to the quality of our thought, which, if good and desiring good, produces that good in and around us. When God first sent forth his Word on this planet, it rested in chaos and darkness; but the Word had power, and transformed the chaos and darkness into form and light. We, possessing divine attributes of perfection ('Be ye perfect, even as your Father is perfect'), have power within ourselves, by the outworking of our thought in good, to transform the chaos and confusion around us into Light, Truth, and Harmony.

"We should seek earnestly to realize the responsibility of thinking rightly at all times, when we know that so much power is invested in us, and our capabilities and possibilities are so grand. Circumstances and conditions are constantly changing around us; but this power of thought always abides, for it was from the beginning, and who knows aught about the beginning? God ever was, and as we come forth from the breath of God, the power of thought must ever be, and it is a dynamic power in whatever way we use it, whether we are positive for good or negative to its opposite.

"As life unfolds, we find the law of growth ever active; not an atom in God's universe is at rest, and in harmony with this law our thoughts are never stationary. If we think rightly, the right use of things will be ours to possess. If we think wrongly, we create wrong conditions for ourselves. O soul, send out thy thought deep, long, and earnestly in the realization of man's noble and intrinsic nature; call into this body of earth all the harmonious conditions of thy heavenly birthright; tamper not with that over which thou holdest dominion, and so let it rule thee; but arise to a right understanding of thy privileges and unlock the mysteries of thy power over thine earthly heritage, and so disperse all thoughts of limitation by thy surroundings; in so doing thou shalt find that thou art not weary and heavy laden with the infirmities of sickness, disease, poverty, and the like; for, by positive knowledge and right attitude of thought toward the forces around thee, thou canst draw from the universe that which thou desirest, and thereby dwell in the harmony of thy interior nature, which is thine eternal life.

"Perhaps, some of you may say, God has ordained for us sickness and trial as a means to draw us nearer to him, and have I any right to take this positive attitude? To this I answer, God is a God of law; his laws change not. As we sow, we reap. He has given us the best in all creation, and we have no right to refuse it or hesitate to accept it. Our hesitation makes us fear; fear makes us negative to that which we fear, and while we fear we have not the power to think rightly of our birthright possessions; we do not see their intrinsic value nor are we able to use them.

"In all things let us learn from our blessed Saviour, who made himself a sacrifice that he might show us the way of life. We never find him fearing to do the Father's will in the non-exercise of his will. His thought went forth in the positive 'I will.' The will to do the will of God and so fulfil the law. In thus doing he harmonized the forces around him by casting out devils, healing the sick, cleansing the leper, etc., and bade his disciples do likewise: his disciples are those who do the will of the Father.

"Can we count ourselves his disciples, while we are crouching in fearful thought to the limitations of the flesh?

"Decidedly not! We must arise and put on the whole armor of God, regard well the dynamic power of thought, and send it forth for *Good* in the realization of freedom for the highest part of nature, to check and keep the lower in bondage. Then shall we behold not only a power for good in ourselves, but a power for good to all around us. Inharmonies, false belief, and unreality will have no part with us, for it will find no affinity in us, as we can only attract to ourselves that which we love, — love being the cause of attraction in all things.

"Knowledge is valuable, and to knowledge let us add wisdom.

"'Wisdom's ways are ways of pleasantness, and all her paths are peace.' May our peace and rest be found in following the steps of One who thought as never man thought, for in that precious thought has rested an adamantine power for the good and uplifting of humanity, constantly growing in intensity throughout the past eighteen hundred and sixty years."

When she ceased speaking she invited questions, and many were put to her, all of which she answered with the same holy dignity which characterized her appearance and her movement, no matter what might be the special phase of her immediate activities.

Lady Copleigh and her niece were well acquainted with Mrs. Katzenheimer, who had often visited them, and it was a great pleasure to Professor Monteith to find that *some* workers in a similar line of action can and do appreciate each other and fulfil the Golden Rule when their conversation turns upon each other in each other's absence.

Lady Copleigh, who was renowned for hospitality, cordially invited Professor Monteith to take tea in her private reception-room after the exercises had ended and the audience had dispersed. Though he had not utterly recovered from his doubts, which still sometimes harassed him, he was no longer a wilful or even willing sceptic; he desired to know the truth, that by its emancipating force he might be set finally free from all the clouds of uncertainty and error which still hung over him, though he rejoiced to realize, with far less density than formerly.

Lady Copleigh's private conversations were, if possible, even more edifying than her public lectures, as, unlike many eloquent orators, she had the happy faculty of appearing at her best in private, and by means of a singularly keen intuitive perception she knew how to minister directly to the precise need of almost every one who sought a consultation with her. From the rich stores of her deep and varied knowledge, gained by a wide practical experience with the world, in addition to the results of extensive, well-selected reading, and deep meditation, Lady Copleigh was the woman above all others engaged in her particular form of ministry, who could resolve doubts and reply to queries in a manner to interest and edify a man of science and an illiterate seamstress; her versatility and wonderful adaptability to widely dissimilar cases was the secret of her great success in reaching the widely sundered multitude, who, by letter as well as personal interview, sought her advice and received instruction and healing through her ministry.

Lady Copleigh differed widely from all the other ladies with whom Professor Monteith had conversed on psychic science. Mrs. Eastlake-Gore, though very cordial, was remotely placid; Madame Discalcelis was unquestionably romantic; Mrs. Katzenheimer was sparkling and oratorical; Lady Copleigh was understandingly appreciative, comprehendingly sympathetic, and knew just what note to touch to call forth the best that was in her companion. As they parted, after a two-hours conversation at the tea-table, Professor Monteith exclaimed inwardly: —

"I believe I have at last found the key to my own nature. I will henceforth work to apply whatever knowledge I may gain for the relief of those who are in suffering; we can well afford to let the incomprehensible alone: the world sorely needs workers, and I will be one of them."

As he rode on the top of an omnibus back to his chambers in Oxford Street, the old text of the previous summer Sunday evening when he had visited the New Jerusalem Church in Argyle Square came back to him, and the words seemed to sound out from the wheels of the moving vehicle as it glided across the asphalt pavement, "Happy shall be he who taketh and dasheth thy little ones against the Rock."

"I see it now," he meditated; "blessed are they who take to the rock of truth, the living stone of universal principle, the offspring of the mystical daughter of Babylon (all that makes for sensual greed and mammon worship), and bringing these falsities, results of erroneous thought and practice, to the touchstone of reality, destroy the love of wrong and the practice of it, through the living, vitalizing demonstration of truth in righteousness. Those old writers are very quaint, and often obscure in their imagery; I could wish they were less allegorical if the common people are to be their audience, but I see now they knew what they were talking about."

The omnibus left him at his own door, the professor retired early and slept soundly, to wake with the lark next morning to thank God for a new bright day.

CHAPTER XXIII.

A DARING HOPE FOR THE COMING CENTURY.

Now that Professor Monteith had become so thoroughly determined to devote his energies, which were great, and his talents which were ample, to the discovery and propagation of the highest knowledge to which he could attain, even though it should lead him far away from the old ruts and grooves in which he had persistently travelled for many years with obstinate, though almost despairing, pertinacity, it was a delightful recreation for him to catch occasional glimpses of the new wonders which were continually taking place in Aldebaran's marvellous laboratory, hewn out of solid rock and utterly retired from the very knowledge of the people, save only the very few who were highly privileged in being permitted occasionally to enter it; for his eager, restless nature must now receive for its needed sustenance the highest and truest revelations of exact science, on both its psychical and physical planes of demonstration, or suffer the agony that all earnest, enthusiastic, highly strung characters endure when they are denied an insight into the mystical arcanum of nature, which is, in truth, the native land of the aspiring spirit, and the only region where it feels truly at home and satisfied. Aldebaran, after the manner of mystics, was a quiet, plodding worker, prosecuting his researches, often quite alone and far into the night, into the mysteries of that stupendous occult lore which is to-day accessible only to the few who are in direct communion with the quiet, unobtrusive orders of real scientists, who are proceeding along the same lines as those travelled by the veritable magicians of ancient Persia, India, Egypt, and especially Chaldea.

Since the episode with Madame Discalcelis on board ship, and the narration of her singular vision of the present state of the planet Mars, Professor Monteith had been endeavoring to construct a telescope on a plan differing widely from all plans suggested by modern exoteric astronomers, and he was beginning to hope that his new invention might help to settle the existing controversies and resolve the prevailing doubts regarding the actual present condition of the earth's nearest brother in this planetary group. Aldebaran had on one occasion, in the course of an intensely interesting and instructive conversation with Professor Monteith, given out the following idea.

"A building," he said, "pyramidal in shape, two hundred feet high, one hundred feet at the base, and having at the apex a disc with a minute aperture in its centre, and a triple combination of reflectors, which must concentrate upon one centre which must be focalized upon the minute aperture in the disc,— the image being received at the base of the pyramid upon a white surface prepared to receive it,— would yield results beyond the dreams of the most sanguine astronomer of the present day. The distinctness of the image taken would be the most wonderful part of the phenomena, and the size of the magnification would be limited only to the diameter of the base of the pyramid. This probably explains the great Egyptian pyramid, with its circular opening through its centre and cavity at the bottom. The apparatus from its summit has probably been destroyed during some of the many ravages to which that land of strange vicissitudes has so frequently been subjected. The Great Pyramid proves that, among the ancient Egyptians, the knowledge of astronomy was amazingly great, although they need not necessarily have known of the modern telescope to have obtained it. The almost impossible labor of making lenses is done away with in this system, which embraces also a microscope on a similar principle without lenses, far superior to anything now in use."

With Professor Monteith, to hear of the possibility of anything was to feel incited to set to work as speedily as possible to render the dream actual; in accordance with which predominating impulse, whenever he had profited by an interview with Aldebaran, his old housekeeper, Mrs. Mittershoose, was perplexed anew with some fresh evidence of her employer's indefatigable attempts to render things "himpossible," as she phrased it, "right down rehalities, when God never intended as 'is creechurs should dabble in them there forces as belongs to 'Imself halone."

Mrs. Mittershoose and her school cannot be said to by any means monopolize the nonprogressive sentiments they thus inelegantly express; for, strange though it may seem to people who prize original discoveries and dare to think freely themselves, there are many who oppose every suggested forward step in science, while — inconsistent to the core, as they certainly are — they make haste to utilize to their own pecuniary and luxurious advantage every invention which, though now fashionable, was quite as "*impossible*" twenty years ago as an air-ship, or any other advanced contrivance of human ingenuity, is supposed to be to-day. Yesterday accounted the achievements of to-day impossible; to-day, in this respect no wiser than yesterday, pronounces the reasonable prospect for to-morrow equally impossible. But so invulnerable is truth, and so mighty are its demonstrations, that day by day science proves what nescience scorned; and so doubtless will it ever be, till this ball floats no longer in ether, and returns into the bosom of the Great Ring which gave it birth.

"In the next century," protested Professor Monteith, at Lady Porchester's first reception after his return from America, "we shall be able to converse as readily with the inhabitants of Mars as we can now talk with our friends and business acquaintances in remote places, through the agency of long-distance telephones. While I was in Chicago last summer I heard a singer, who was at that moment singing in New York, as distinctly as though she had been in an adjoining apartment instead of one thousand miles away. Theodore Thomas, the illustrious leader of one of the finest orchestras on earth, has engaged musicians with whom he has made artistic acquaintance solely through the agency of the marvellous electrical inventions which are now threatening to so completely supersede the old, slow, imperfect means of converse between men and nations, that we may well predict that in a very few years hence there will be no more difficulty in inter-planetary than there now is in inter-oceanic communication."

Lady Porchester was always interested in all that promised to fulfil any of the predictions which had been made to her through the mediumship of Miss Poyntz, and some others of her close friends who shared with Katherine the enviable endowment of clairvoyance; but for scientific tables she had neither taste nor comprehension. "Leave these," she would say, "to our experts and specialists; it is enough for the rank and file of us to follow where our generals bravely lead."

Mrs. Spottiswoode, who was a very progressive woman, never missed an opportunity to delve more deeply than she had yet done into the mysteries of the arcane; she loved mystery in one sense, but she craved utility even more. Thus the practical side of every discovery was to her its most important side, though she agreed with the Eastlake-Gores and Madame Discalcelis, that theoretical idealism is essentially the parent and forerunner of practical realism.

It was in answer to the query of the Reverend Bear Bare Bayre and his sister, Mrs. Stillmore Bayre,— who were guests of Lady Porchester's for a few weeks, during a period of severe financial strain in their own household,— concerning the application of the new discoveries to economics, that Professor Monteith undertook to show that nature's resources are, indeed, so boundless that destitution is quite needless, and will be completely mastered, directly the clergy and laity together co-operate to make actual the industrial teachings, as well as the purely spiritual precepts of the Christ they profess to serve.

On a recent Sunday evening, the Reverend Bear Bare Bayre had delivered a touching sermon, in a Mission Chapel, to about five hundred working people, on the miracle of multiplied loaves and fishes, in which he had tearfully expatiated upon the hundreds of thousands of able-bodied men and women in England and America, wishing to work, but almost starving because the labor market was closed against them. The sermon was, unfortunately, of a rather depressing type. Mr. Bayre was a sincere man, tender-hearted and compassionate, but not at all practical, and almost totally destitute of organizing ability; he and his family were hopelessly in debt, with which they patiently struggled year after year to very little purpose, while they attributed to the mysterious dispensations of the Divine Hand what was clearly due to their own shiftlessness and inefficiency so far as business was concerned,— though none could deny that they strove to do their religious duty according to their highest light, which some people ventured to say was not dazzlingly brilliant.

"How I wish we were living in Palestine between eighteen and nineteen hundred years ago! We might then be privileged to see some miracle wrought by supernatural power," pathetically exclaimed the clergyman, when some one asked him if he honestly believed all he had said in the pulpit the previous Sunday evening. "Believe it? How *can* I, how *dare* I, doubt it? But alas! the age of miracles is past; they were granted only once in the history of the world, and that was previous to our Saviour's resurrection."

"Indeed," expostulated Mrs. Spottiswoode, who dearly loved an argument when she felt sure of her ground and could readily discomfit the opposition, "you, a clergyman, who must be supposed, not only to have read, but to have studied, the entire New Testament, to say nothing of subsequent church history, what, pray, do you make of the book entitled Acts of the Apostles, which you, as a minister of the Anglican Establishment, of course include as a portion of the Sacred Canon?"

"What do I make of it?" queried Mr. Bayre, slightly, but not wholly, disconcerted by his fair antagonist's presumptuous appeal. "Why, I accept it, and preach from it, of course; and I do not see how you can prove from any portion of its contents that the Roman Catholic doctrine of continuous miracles, which I know you hold, is a correct one."

"We will let Roman Catholic doctrines alone, if you please," rejoined Mrs. Spottiswoode; "so far as this controversy is concerned, all I ask you is, how do you explain the obvious discrepancy between your statement that miracles were not needed after our Lord's resurrection, and the very decided asseverations in the Acts of the Apostles that they were performed many years after that event, in many places, by many persons, and on behalf of many persons?"

"Well, my first statement may have been a trifle unguarded," admitted Mr. Bayre, now clearly under hot fire; "but we usually believe, as clergymen of the Church of England, that during the first century, certain phenomenal attestations to the truth of the Gospel were considered necessary to establish the truth of Christianity among the Gentiles."

"Indeed," continued Mrs. Spottiswoode, smiling blandly and arching her eyebrows; "then *we* are simply consistent enough to maintain that, whenever and wherever what you call a miracle is of any real use in establishing truth in any part of the world, that miracle is capable of occurring in harmony with divine ordination. As to your last Sunday evening's sermon, which some of my friends heard, and reported to me afterwards, I can only advise you, when next you call together an audience of working people to hear you on 'Bible Miracles in the Light of Modern Needs,' to try to supply some of those *modern needs* a little more fully than you did when last you attempted to prescribe for them. Multiplied loaves and fishes are literally no chimerical delusion; they represent supply to meet demand, and were Christ on earth to-day, I think we should find him practically settling labor troubles, rather than sentimentally deploring, as so many clergymen and others do, what they are pleased to term the inexpressible sadness of the present situation. I, for one, believe that to-day were we to trust ourselves unreservedly to follow our best inclinations, and co-operate where now we compete, first in thought, then in action, we should soon see ushered in a bright, happy age of peace and plenty, which could well be described as a time when all could eat until satisfied, and leave over and above the limit of their consumption what is signified in Scripture by twelve basketfuls of fragments."

"I seldom argue," meekly retorted Mr. Bayre, "and when I do, it is rarely with a woman, but I must say there is ingenuity in your interpretations, and plausibility in your predictions; at the same time it must not be forgotten that the words are contained in Holy Scripture, 'The poor ye have always with you.' Our Lord said that; and 'The poor shall never cease out of the land.' David, I believe, declared the latter. I fear it is a part of God's inscrutable decree, that poverty on earth will continue as long as seedtime and harvest."

How long or how brisk this discussion might have become had it not been arrested by the entrance of Mr. Eastlake-Gore, full of purposeful animation and in his brightest mood, it would be difficult to conjecture, as Mrs. Spottiswoode had ready answers for all the clergyman might advance; but a happy turn was given to the conversation by Mr. Gore exclaiming, as he shook hands heartily with Professor Monteith:—

"I, too, have seen your mystic, Aldebaran, and I am greatly pleased with him; he told me more in an hour than one usually learns from inventors in a lifetime. I took notes of our conversation, and think I can by this time say without presumption that I can fairly state some of his amazing propositions, and, further, that I have witnessed more than a few intensely interesting demonstrations. In my opinion, among the most interesting experiments which can possibly be proved by the general experimentalist are the phenomena of color produced by vibration. Vibrations necessary to the production of colors are very high, reaching to millions of vibrations per second. The true relation between the vibration and the color can only be a harmonic one, as colors commence in the millions and end not lower than in trillions of vibrations per second. The conditions essential to this class of phenomena are, first, a condition relating to the structure in which they take place, free from all·extraneous vibrations; the experimenter's presence even influences to a great extent the motions of the molecules used in the experiments. A bath is employed, arranged so that light rays can be projected upon it at certain angles, and from that upon a screen. The bath must have what are termed centres of association and concentration, and suspended across its surface in such a manner that the centres approach very near the surface of the liquid, which is preferably water, whose surface must be free from all films. Upon this is dropped a single drop of naphtha dissolved in ether, which constantly spreads over the surface and gradually evolves most beautiful variations of color. The vibrations are transmitted from an instrument capable of producing vibrations of varying intensity and pitch, across the line of resonating centres, nine in number. The first centre shows a *light* straw color, condensing about the centre; the second shows a *very dark* straw color; the third exhibits an orange red; the fourth, a bluish red; the fifth is largely green. The entire gamut ranges from a very light yellow to a dark blue. The theory is that the vibrations produced gather certain numbers of the molecules together about the centres, which represent different ranges of motion, and which by the color evolved affords a demonstration of a certain connection between that vibration and the color it educes. Under different conditions, using films suspended in the air, and light passing through these films under polarization, (*polarized light*) the vibrations influence the molecules in the film, producing again exhibitions of varying colors when projected upon a screen. Experiments of this kind are most difficult, on account of the unstable conditions found everywhere.

"The experiments to which I have called attention thus imperfectly," continued Mr. Gore, "are by no means all that I have witnessed, but it seems that the directions necessary to be obeyed for securing more wonderful results are of so elaborate and intricate a nature that they suggest the laboratory of an alchemist, rather than a drawing-room table in Lady Tomlinson's house in Norwood, where I saw the fact demonstrated, in company with many others, one evening after dinner."

"What you say calls to my mind an incident concerning one of my parishioners," pursued the Reverend Bear Bare Bayre; "she was totally deaf, and used to tell me that, though she could not hear my sermons, she sometimes went to church to look at them and found them curiously interesting, though a trifle monotonous, as the colors I gave forth while preaching were not particularly brilliant and rather too much of a sameness;

but she told me that when I became unusually animated the sight was far more entertaining, as at such times, instead of drabs, grays, and browns in constant, unbroken succession, she would see bright, vivid amber, purple, green, and scarlet, and occasionally a charmingly variegated array of beautiful forms as well as colors. Another of my parishioners, who is also deaf, is acquainted with the experiments of Mrs. Watts-Hughes, and has been privileged to witness exquisitely convoluted shells, many-petalled flowers, and other pleasing forms appear in response to a singer's voice. Every tone, it appears, has its own special form, as well as color, and by increasing the volume of tone and raising the pitch, you can increase the brightness of the color and often the size and complexity of the form; and by lowering the pitch or decreasing the volume of the sound, you can render the color paler, and also contract the form it produces."

"My daring hope for the very early part of the next century," said Mr. Gore, when the Reverend Bayre had ceased speaking, "is that some of us will have learned to so perfectly master the mysterious force of vibration that we can destroy immense buildings, and even pulverize rocks and mountains if we desire to do so, entirely through the agency of sound. I do not regard the Bible narratives as myths; they are to me a scientific revelation, dim in places, I grant, but, nevertheless, storehouses abundantly filled with the vast knowledge accumulated by the truly learned in ancient times and distant lands. The walls of Jericho were made to fall through vibrating energy, directed against them by skilful experts in the use of machinery (intensely simple, but wonderfully effective) in use in those days; and I believe most firmly that when we come to know a little more than we know yet of how to manipulate the force of sound, we shall literally remove mountains through an application of the law of vibration. The omnipresent ether is at the service of any man who truly masters a few simple facts in mystic chemistry, and to the mastery of these facts I know our good friend Professor Monteith is now most earnestly devoting his best energies, and not in vain; for if I mistake not, it will be but a very few years (possibly only a question of months) before we shall see a result of his painstaking assiduity, the scope and wonder of which it would be impossible for me to state, at all events, till his invention has progressed a little further, or until he feels quite confident as to the outcome of his labors."

Mrs. Stillmore Bayre, who was a timorous woman, afraid of all new inventions,—one who honestly preferred a dip candle and a pair of snuffers to an electric light in her bedroom,— expressed mild interest, not unmixed with apprehension, while listening to the new theories which were so often and freely ventilated at Lady Porchester's. Like a celebrated Frenchwoman of a past century, she believed not in ghosts, but, nevertheless, she feared them. Does not this strange inconsistency characterize, in the present day, thousands, one might almost say millions, in the civilized portions of the world?

CHAPTER XXIV.

ELECTRO-HOMEOPATHY.

Lady Porchester was taken ill suddenly; no one knew what caused the attack, but one evening about half-past seven, before the cloth was removed from the dinner-table, Miss Poyntz, who was alone with her ladyship, was surprised by a faint, dull, gurgling sound, and looking up, saw that Lady Porchester's face was purple, her eyes distended, and her whole aspect one of strained, speechless agony. Heart-failure was her first thought, as it was a catastrophe she always feared; and now, in utter helplessness, she convulsively rung the bell and summoned all the servants she could muster, who were collectively even more powerless than herself to do anything but stare, and weep, and offer to fly for a physician, when Mrs. Spottiswoode appeared upon the scene as if by magic, and in her strong, peremptory manner insisted that her ladyship should be at once removed to her own chamber, and approached by no one save Miss Poyntz and herself. Mrs. Spottiswoode *commanded* the servants not to send for any doctor, and to answer no inquiries at the door which might concern her ladyship, further than to say that Miss Poyntz would receive all who might call on business.

Mrs. Spottiswoode had studied medicine in Paris; she was a thorough anatomist and physiologist, though she had never completed her medical studies to the point of receiving a physician's diploma. During a residence of several months in Bologna, she had thoroughly investigated the merits of Count Cesare Mattei's extraordinary medical discovery, and had personally enjoyed many edifying interviews with the Count himself at his magnificent castle, La Rochetta, to which only privileged guests are usually admitted. She had found this extraordinary, enterprising nobleman noble in every sense of the word, brave, philanthropic, cultured, sincere, and kindly, and what had impressed her as much as anything was that, though between eighty and ninety years of age, he was young, vigorous, and athletic, possessed of seemingly boundless vitality, fully demonstrating in his own person the truthfulness of the claim, so often maliciously or ignorantly denied, that he has made one of the very greatest discoveries of the century. The discovery of the Mattei remedies may be in some measure traced to the instinct of a dog; and this is not singular when one reflects upon with what perfection inborn instinct works in those lower creatures of the Almighty, who have no pride of self-reason, and act in no way against the impulses which God has graciously given them to preserve them in health and repair their wounds if they have met with misadventures.

Mrs. Spottiswoode never did anything by halves; she

was heart and soul in all she undertook; so, after thoroughly satisfying herself that the Count's remedies were indeed peerless, she enrolled herself as one of his warmest friends and most enthusiastic disciples and defenders. Lady Porchester's case she understood at a glance, and at once administered one of the remedies, which she always carried with her in case of need for their use arising. Without any difficulty, she succeeded in quickly overcoming the painful symptoms which had so terrified Miss Poyntz, and before many minutes were over her ladyship, though still unconscious, looked quite natural, and seemed to be sleeping peacefully.

"I shall stay here all night to watch the case and keep you company, Katherine; I must, therefore, ask you to dispatch a servant to my residence with a note, directing my maid to pack my Gladstone bag and include in its contents a full case of the Mattei remedies, which she knows exactly where to find, as I take care that they shall always be at my call whenever I require them. This is a *serious*, but in my hands not a *dangerous*, case," said Mrs. Spottiswoode to Miss Poyntz, as soon as both ladies were satisfied that Lady Porchester was in no suffering and needing no immediate attention; "but if her spectacled, bombastic nephew, or any other conceited medical puppy, were to try his bungling skill with her, it is very doubtful, in my opinion, if she would survive his mismanagement of the case. I do not intend to alarm you further, my faithful friend, but, on the contrary, to console you with the positive assurance, if you can but accept it, that your dear friend and mine is not in any danger whatever if she is judiciously treated, and as I know her as well as any one, and have a permanent invitation to make this house my home whenever I wish to, for as long a period as I desire, you and I must agree to be good comrades for the next six weeks at least. The Eastlake-Gores, Madame Discalcelis, and my brother can be admitted whenever they call, but further than this very limited number of visitors, I cannot allow callers to enter. How glad I am the Bayres left yesterday; for, good-hearted people though they are, their lugubrious countenances and pessimistic prophesyings, coupled with their ardent devotion to the oldest type of calomel-administering allopathy, would prove a detrimental element, against which it would be difficult to contend successfully without cruelly wounding the abnormally sensitive feelings of these long-time pensioners on her ladyship's bounty."

To administer the Mattei remedies in extreme cases requires patience and vigilance, though in all ordinary instances their administration is so simple that it is quite within the grasp of an intelligent child not over fourteen years of age. No difficulties attend the giving of the remedies at any time if they are placed in the hands of an intelligent person, but the directions are that, whenever the vitality is very low, the dilutions should be given regularly at very frequent intervals, necessitating, consequently, continual attendance upon the patient.

For this work Mrs. Spottiswoode was particularly well adapted, as she was the proud possessor of complete control over both her nerves and muscles. She could wake and sleep at will, at any hour of the day or night; her hands never trembled, her sight never wavered, and her intellect was amazingly perspicacious. Her great success as a journalist and reporter when she was only a girl, arose mainly from the fact that she could keep awake the whole night if need be, to report speeches or transcribe notes, and the work she did at such a time would be as good as her best, free from any important inaccuracies, and finished in as creditable a manner as though she had been working in the middle of the day, in the most accommodating circumstances. When this talented woman espoused the cause of electro-homeopathy, many of its unscrupulous enemies began to tremble, as with her legal intellect and singular command of logic, she could attack instantly and most effectively the vulnerable places in the armor of the opposition, no matter how clever the attempt might be on the part of its wearers to cover up its defects and unsoundness.

Lady Porchester slept from eight till ten o'clock, and then partially awakened, moaning slightly, and moving restlessly upon her pillow. When she found herself in her own bed, with Katherine and Lavinia beside her, she appeared only slightly confused, and asked in a dazed voice: —

"How did I get here, and what has happened to me? I must have fallen asleep at dinner and you carried me upstairs while I was insensible."

Though not in pain, Lady Porchester was very weak as well as drowsy, and soon fell asleep again under Mrs. Spottiswoode's careful attention; but it was plain to be seen that her ladyship was not long for this world unless the centres of vitality could be greatly stimulated, and that speedily, in her debilitated system, which had slowly but surely succumbed to the insidious invasion of a cancer in the stomach.

Mrs. Spottiswoode wisely refrained from making known, either to Lady Porchester or to Miss Poyntz, the nature of the disease she was evicting, as in most instances it is highly desirable to keep secret the results of a diagnosis, when the nature of the derangement is such as to cause grave fears in the minds of timid, superstitious people, and such people constitute an overwhelming majority in every community.

"It may be seriously questioned by mental healers, and all who are interested in mental healings, whether it is legitimate to employ remedies in any case, as, according to metaphysical teachings on the subject of therapeutics, all diseases are mental, and can only be conquered mentally. A reasonable, dispassionate view of this important subject seems to be that, so long as man exists on earth and operates through an external body, requiring food as well as raiment, all such varieties of food as may be best adapted to the varying needs of the system would be, in a perfectly natural condition, instinctively selected by the individual to supply his own necessities, but there is no warrant for assuming that in the most ideal condition of terrestrial existence we shall eat and drink nothing. The sensational professional faster, who succeeds in dragging out a morbid existence of a month or more, almost if not entirely without nutriment, is not in any sense a demonstration of man's ability to live without food, but quite the reverse, as his enforced idleness and emaciated condition prove that, though it may be possible to exist for forty days or more on mineral waters and cracked ice, the work of the world cannot be done by people whose *menu* is so restricted. Poisons should be entirely eliminated from the pharmacopœia; but not until we have all reached a plane of psychical development where we can successfully dispense with all external agencies are we justified in refusing the aids which nature offers in the almost boundless resources of the vegetable kingdom,— resources so copious that when we truly understand their powers and usefulness we shall turn no longer to the mineral for assistance, nor shall we dabble in poisons, the very mention of which strikes terror wherever they are introduced."

So spake Mrs. Spottiswoode when a brave, decided advocate of mental treatment pure and simple expostulated with her upon her advocacy of the Mattei remedies. Mrs. Fotheringill was an able advocate of mental therapeutics, and a fearless one; she had also been a patient of Dr. Notluf, the eminent homeopathic specialist of St. Catherine's Hospital, Mount Royal; and, to accentuate her position and prove that she was on firm ground, even in the estimation of some of the more advanced members of the medical fraternity, she produced and read the following letter, which she had recently received from this thoroughly competent and successful physician, to whom she had for experiment's sake presented, on Mrs. Spottiswoode's recommendation, the claims of the Mattei remedies. She was desirous of hearing what Mrs. Spottiswoode might have to say in answer to the learned doctor's position on the remedies she was so faithfully employing in her constant attendance upon the feeble, but convalescent, Lady Porchester.

ST. CATHERINE'S HOSPITAL, MOUNT ROYAL.

MY DEAR MRS. FOTHERINGILL: How is it you so emphatically indorse the Mattei remedies, and you a teacher of mental and spiritual science? Is it not easy to concede their virtues to the *faith* put in them, or the *spiritual* state of the one who *gives* them, rather than in the pilule itself? I must state for you a fact in my experience with them. During 1891 and 1892, I largely used Mattei remedies for cancer cases, without good results, for every case but *one* ended fatally, and that case has taken the remedies over two years, and abandoned the treatment at last as a bad job.

I have used the remedies in many other cases; in some cases with *fine* results, in others *no good at all* was derived. My conclusion is, they are not as effectual as ordinary homeopathic remedies *well* selected. For your own gratification I state, that during 1893 I have practised mental or spiritual healing with grand results, using *no medicine*, and curing *tumors* and *cancers* in *two weeks*, after the patient had suffered over two years and doctored all the time besides!

Such results transcend all drug experience of any school of medication that I know of. I seem to be obliged to use medicines in most cases to retain the patients. If the great central truth is, that mind is the cause of all phenomena, then the form of medication used is of little account in accomplishing results. I am a seeker for truth, and hope soon to be able to lay aside all medicines and use a more excellent way.

I and family are enjoying good health, and trust you are.

With best wishes, believe me sincerely yours for truth.

H. J. NOTLUF.

"Now what do you say to that?" exultingly exclaimed Mrs. Fotheringill. "Do you not see that we are all misled by appearances, so long as we believe there is any real efficacy in anything save spirit?"

"My dear friend," retorted Mrs. Spottiswoode, "in my judgment you are both right and wrong. I, as much as you, acknowledge that all potency is essentially divine, and that, apart from a recognition of divine immanence, we are blind materialists indeed; however, my experience teaches me that nature's myriad forms are all expressions of a subtle psychic force which, though unitary in essence, is manifold in operation and expression, and, as the wise men of old discovered, there are simples in nature which are most truly ordained by God to serve fit ends in sustaining the exterior existence of his children while yet they sojourn on the crust of this planet, prior to their removal to more ethereal and exalted stages of existence. But I am not answering your doctor's statements. Let me at least attempt to do so. In my judgment, Dr. Notluf failed to administer the remedies as I know they should be administered, and it is possible, though I will not say probable, that he secured some of the worthless imitations which at one time were freely sold to gratify the malice and cupidity of unscrupulous speculators. Granting, however, that the genuine remedies were in his hands, I can only cite my own experience as exactly the reverse of his; for since I have seriously taken up the work of introducing this great discovery to the world I have individually superintended nineteen cases of cancer, and of these seventeen have completely recovered; the remaining two were so far advanced that only relief could be given, but their sufferings were assuaged and great comfort given them. I, of course, may be said to possess a magnetic touch and to be a firm upholder of spiritual supremacy, but I have known several instances where the remedies were applied according to the directions, by persons whose mental attitude was even painfully agnostic, and still the results were extremely satisfactory, though I do not think the patients recovered quite so rapidly in their hands as in mine. There is an institution in Chicago where a specialty is made of treating cases by the use of these remedies alone. The institute issues a monthly paper, called the *Health Monitor*, and I am assured by the most reliable persons, who have thoroughly investigated the claims put forward in the pages of that periodical, that the cases reported cured are in reality as the declaration states."

."Well, I only hope you will be successful with our dear friend upstairs. I know Lady Porchester has been ailing for a long time, and though I love her dearly, I must say that a little indiscretion on her own part may have had something to do with her malady; but, dear good soul, it wrings my heart to think of her as suffering when she has been so good to us all, and so generous and charitable in all her dealings with humanity."

"Suffering! she's not suffering in my care. Miss Poyntz has been a little nervous on two or three occasions, and perhaps spread the report among the very few callers who have managed to enter the house without my sanction, that her ladyship is in pain, but I know better, and as she is now very much stronger I will let you see her for a few minutes if you wish to. Miss Poyntz is with her, and she is quite happy and able to take such food as that faithful companion prepares for her. Those two women adore each other; there is a sacredness about their attachment which reminds one of David and Jonathan, or of Damon and Pythias,— they are everything to each other; they are both noble natures, though I wish they were both a little stronger in the assertion of moral independence and freedom from conventionalities."

As Mrs. Fotheringill and Mrs. Spottiswoode entered Lady Porchester's room together they were both delighted to see her well enough to enjoy a good book, which Miss Poyntz was reading in a quiet but interesting manner to while away the hour and keep her ladyship from talking, as it was better that she should taste some of the sweetness of a rational rest cure for a few days longer, and then she would be stronger and healthier, Mrs. Spottiswoode declared, than she had been for twenty years at least. The remedies administered regularly, and at first incessantly, had secured one of their greatest triumphs, and thanks to kind care and effective nursing, a woman over seventy and not of robust constitution, was completely delivered from the ravages of cancer in the stomach and all its attendant afflictions in less than three weeks' treatment.

Mrs. Fotheringill rightly attributed much to the action of well-directed thought, and Mrs. Spottiswoode was not wrong in thanking the Mattei remedies for doing their part to purify the external structure, through which the spirit had to work.

"Paderewski and his piano are two, but when one wishes to listen to the ravishing strains of music the romantic Pole can draw from a well-tuned instrument, he knows that the piano must be of the best, and perfectly in tune. Our exterior bodies are machinery; they are fashioned and kept in repair, as well as operated, by the power of invisible, super-material intelligence, but they, as instruments, have necessities which true science knows how to meet. When we all grow to that high state of perfection that we obey the law of health in its entirety, and therefore never transgress any divine commandment, the time for sickness and remedies will have gone by forever; but till then we may well be thankful for all that nature yields us in the way of specially adapted foods for times of special need. God reigns in and through, as well as over, all things, and though to him alone we must give glory, we will not despise any of his humblest messengers." So spake Mrs. Spottiswoode, and so agreed Mrs. Fotheringill, as the two ladies parted in the drawing-room.

CHAPTER XXV.

WHAT OF AERIAL NAVIGATION?

AMONG the problems which most intensely interested Professor Monteith, after his return to London, that of aerial navigation occupied first rank. It was at the retreat of Aldebaran, one cold January afternoon, that he received the following remarkable instruction from the lips of the mystic scientist, who was then in the act of constructing an aerial navigator which he declared would, in the course of from three to five years, be quite ready for presentation to the world. The method of constructing this wonderful machine was explained in the following demonstration, which took place under the eyes of the professor.

A small instrument, having three gyroscopes as a principal part of its construction, was the object exhibited to the professor as the instrument for demonstrating the facts of aerial navigation. These gyroscopes were attached to a heavy, inert mass of metal, weighing about one ton. The other part of the apparatus consisted of tubes, enclosed in as small a space as possible, being clustered in a circle. These tubes, the mystic went on to explain, represented certain chords, which were coincident to the streams of force acting upon the planet, focalizing and defocalizing upon its neutral centre. The action upon the molecular structure of the mass lifted was based upon the fact that each molecule in the mass possessed a north and south pole, — more strictly speaking, a positive and negative pole, — situated through the centre, formed by the three atoms which compose it. No matter which way the mass of metal is turned, the poles of the molecule point undeviatingly to the polar centre of the earth, acting almost exactly as the dip-needle when uninfluenced by extraneous conditions, electrical and otherwise. The rotation of the discs of the gyroscopes produces an action upon the molecules of the mass to be lifted, reversing their poles, causing repulsion from the earth in the same way as like poles of a magnet repel each other. This repulsion can be diminished and increased according as the mechanical conditions are operated. By operating the three discs, starting them at full speed, then touching two of them, so as to bring them, according to the tone they represented by their rotation, to a certain vibratory ratio, the weight then slowly swaying from side to side left the floor, rose several feet in the air, remaining in that position, and as the discs gradually decreased their speed of rotation the weight sank to the floor, settling down as lightly as a thistle-down. Where one molecule can be lifted, there need be no limit as to the number in a structure that may be operated upon as easily as one. The vessel in contemplation, the aerial navigator, will be over two hundred feet long, over sixty feet in diameter, tapering at both ends to a point, made of polished steel, and will be capable of being driven under the power of depolar repulsion, at the rate of three hundred miles an hour. It can be far more easily controlled than any instrument now in use for any phase of transit. Another very remarkable feature connected with this strange revelation of aerial navigation, is that the vessel is not buoyed up or floated in the air through the medium of the air, so that if there were no atmosphere it would float just as readily; hence, under mechanical conditions most certainly capable of production, involving massive strength of resistance to interstellar vacuity this can be made capable of navigating even the remote depth of space, positions between planets where polarity changes being controlled by other adjuncts of concentration for that purpose.

Safely enclosed within this structure, a man possessing the chemical knowledge these new laws give, with sufficient supply of material from which to make oxygen, by the enormously increased rate of speed attained by such navigator where atmospheric friction is avoided, the time occupied in travelling from one planet to another would be amazingly brief, and one can travel to other planets in this system of worlds as easily as the same ship could navigate the depths of the ocean.

The great obstacle hitherto preventing the solution of this problem has been the strength of structure needed under conditions above presented. With this knowledge of matter, the size of structure is unimportant; the heaviest can be as easily controlled as the lightest.

The results following the advent of such wonders as are here represented must closely approximate the long-foretold millennium, or more properly golden age: the disarming of nations, the ennoblement of man, the universality of the realization of brotherhood, and the true elevation of womankind; since man, possessing all that may be obtained, need no longer fear the development of woman to perfect equality with himself. In that time it shall be the search for the divine ideal which must engage the faculties of all to their utmost extent. This other great law of universal consciousness is most aptly expressed in "The Finding of the Gnosis," by a very learned brother mystic, where the soul's answer to the query of the Nameless, asking if to such heights he can ever attain, is expressed in the following words:—

"Ever the starlit eyes
Shall gaze on the unattained;
Ever the rainbow ahead,
Subtly elusive, is shifting.
Think'st thou arrival is never,
Or is't hid in the scan
Of the newer endeavor?"

CHAPTER XXVI.

THE PROFESSOR IN HIS STUDY.

LADY PORCHESTER had quite recovered her health — indeed, she had done far more; for when she appeared on the Monday afternoon following her first outing in the Park, after her three weeks' retirement, every one remarked upon her wonderfully improved appearance, the almost transparent whiteness of her skin (formerly very sallow), and the quiet animation which pervaded all her movements. Professor Monteith was one of the first to offer congratulations; but he was so very busy, working upon an air-ship of which he had procured a perfect working model from Aldebaran, that he had become almost as complete a recluse of science as that exceedingly retiring worker, who scarcely ever allowed himself an evening, much less a day, in which to pay tribute to the social amenities, without which life would be such a complete blank to the devotees of fashion, and not to them only, but to many kindly natures whose gregarious instincts are strong, and who have little interest in life outside their fellowship with others.

Aerial navigation promises to be interesting; there is a great fascination for most people in the prospect of flying through the air; consequently, as soon as it became noised abroad that a mutual friend was actually engaged in perfecting a flying machine, many were the importunate entreaties made to Lady Porchester to induce the "dear professor" to let them take just a peep at his "*heavenly*" invention. The subject of aerial navigation was the one topic at Lady Porchester's reception on Monday afternoon, Jan. 29, 1894. Colonel McVickers, of the 67th Highlanders, a man of much learning and keen observation, had made the matter something of a study and had collected many interesting facts concerning it, which in the course of the afternoon he gave to his fellow-guests. In answer to an attempted sneer from a youthful popinjay, who had far more carefully arranged hair on his head than cultivated brains within, he called attention to the fact that Professor Alexander Graham Bell, the distinguished inventor of the telephone, has been grappling with aerial locomotion for some months past in Nova Scotia, and, like all other experimenters in that science, he is very hopeful of success. He is not a believer in extreme lightness, but thinks that the solution of the problem lies in proper balancing. He has made machines that will fly to a height of several hundred feet, but the motive power is acquired externally, and motion cannot, therefore, be long continued. Moreover, there is no method of directing the apparatus while in the air.

Also that Professor S. P. Langley, director of the Smithsonian Institution in Washington, has much the same ideas as Professor Bell, and has followed very similar lines. In fact, these two investigators have worked together to some extent. Various means of propulsion have been tried, and among them slow-burning gunpowder, which has been used successfully in propelling torpedo boats.

And he added, "Here in London Hiram Maxim is still busy with his great air-ship. The principle he has adopted is that of the kite, sufficient surface being provided to enable the ship to float in the air when a minimum speed of twenty-five miles per hour has been attained. The propelling force consists of two screws, operated in the usual fashion by a boiler and steam-engine."

After stating these well-known facts, he turned his attention to the ethical advantages of this great question, and pursued his conversation thus: —

"What important purpose can flight in air serve? Maxim, Langley, and all who have studied the subject thoroughly, agree that the speed of aeriation will greatly exceed that of any terrestrial locomotion.

"From this must follow an entire economic change in the direction of rendering immense tracts of comparatively worthless territory, at distances of twenty to forty miles from cities, much more available.

"There would also result the relegating of city property in large measure to business and storage purposes.

"This would to a large extent accomplish what Henry George sighs for, and by means which do not involve any wrong to the land-owner by the wage-earner.

"With flying navies, capable of carrying unseen at night large quantities of explosives to the centre of a city, war would become so destructive that it would be soon supplanted by arbitration, as a matter of common sense and self-preservation.

"Arbitration once established, an international police system, controlling nations as we do individuals, and enforcing the decrees of boards of arbitration, would be enormously assisted by this power of rapid and, if necessary, destructive patrolling.

"Immense areas of country, now well-nigh impenetrable, would be opened to usefulness. Large sources of wealth would thus be added to the civilized world, and would result in the amelioration of the condition of the savages of such regions as central Africa.

"We should have to give up selfish legislation and restriction upon the commerce of other nations, and be obliged perforce to stand on a broader heritage than that of a nation or of zone."

Two or three clergymen who were present, and notably Mrs. Northafriker, an earnest missionary to foreign lands, expressed an intense desire to witness the progress already made by Professor Monteith; but as the work was not sufficiently completed to admit of close inspection, without disturbing the professor too greatly in the midst of his laborious, but beloved, undertaking, he declared himself obliged to content himself, and trusted they would be contented, with seeing the model which was the pattern he was faithfully determining to copy on a much larger scale. Though his own work was as yet immature, he assured them that others had made great progress, though he was only in the infancy of his herculean task.[1]

[1] The model is accurately described, as far as it can be at present, in a previous chapter of this book. See page 280.

"The propeller of this wonderful aerial navigator," said the professor, "is now actually in existence in Philadelphia; for I have seen it there and I have, therefore, the authority of an eye-witness for this statement, as well as the word of many distinguished scientific investigators, whose judgment and veracity are entirely beyond dispute. It is a stupendous fact, of colossal magnitude, that the above navigator has associated with it all the conditions requisite for interstellar communication, it being *positively* proven that this wonderful vessel can navigate the air under all varying atmospheric conditions, from the calmest to the most perturbed, and is capable of travelling with amazing velocity, as well as at the lowest possible rate of motion, and that with perfect safety to the vessel and its inmates, making due allowance for atmospheric friction."

The professor's study was a simple attic in a house in Bloomsbury; his workshop was an adjoining attic, and there, with no companion and no attendant save his faithful old housekeeper, he was spending his days and nights tirelessly at work, on what is doubtless the greatest mechanical labor of the nineteenth, and will prove the greatest victory of the twentieth century. Sometimes he had a fit of depression, and something of the old cynical gloom returned to him, but these lapses were rare, and whenever he felt particularly depressed, some sweet, assuring message from the unseen would come to cheer his solitude, revive his drooping courage, quiet his nerves, and what was more, with words of wise, practical counsel whispered into the inmost ear of his soul, tell him again, and yet again, of the certainty of his triumph and the fadeless crown of immortality.

On one particularly dreary day, when all the elements seemed at war with each other and fighting desperately against man, Aldebaran felt impelled to come from his eyrie in Tower Heights, Islington, to the professor's humble dwelling in Bloomsbury, a distance of several miles. When he entered the workshop and saw that his friend was literally unable to greet him (so overcome was he with what seemed to him a new and formidable obstacle, though in reality the phantom was conjured up from his temporarily distracted brain), Aldebaran, in his peculiarly sweet, penetrating, earnest voice, spoke as one inspired, saying: —

"You long, my brother, to reach that goal which you think will give you peace; to attain to those heights of wisdom that shall place you beyond the dark valleys of pain; to enter the holy temple where the All is worshipped, and you a glad devotee; to still the strife within you, to be as one emancipate. You cry aloud in your despair, Oh! give me light who am so blind; naught but your voice you hear till the storms have washed the tangled cobwebs from your eyes; then you see, not the far-off stars, but the earth, which offers itself humbly at your feet. Let it be your teacher, let it show you the lesson of Pain. Poor, sad-eyed pain! had you not known her sister Pleasure and loved her best, you could not have known Pain. Why love her best, since Pain makes your love? Get you away from such folly; these are the things of life, as needful as the air you breathe, not to be dispensed with in any case. Your peace! Why think of it? Could you desire it without the strife? What could you rest from? Let strife alone; much do we need the *hateful* thing (is not that strange?) to show us what peace is, and hate, that we may know love. You long for growth, development, for wisdom, and freedom; have I said aright? You have naught to do with the ordered eternal laws of immortal living; your wishes and desires are as they have been, only to enjoy the play of the senses as they throb under the unceasing force of exhaustless action, never capable of being brought to rest; your desire a little higher in the scale, but desire still. Small need have you to think of these except to know them as they are, as inseparable from life and consciousness as death from life. You have your freedom here and now, for you cannot ever have more than here and now. Your heaven here, you enter Nirvana here, and when you will; do not look to that time to come, your time has come. You insatiate, do not be deluded; if you cannot live in the present now, you cannot in the future then, nor can you labor if not now, nor be content or happy. What, pray, will tell you when you have reached that time looked for? shall a guide-board be there placed by whom? The Incomprehensible One speaks to you day by day, giving you work to do, which you never seem to think you do right. You are grieved, you despair, and that, too, in that future then, which is that far-off time become the now and here. Your heavenly days you fill with foolish joys that make you say, Oh! give me peace, and longingly you dream that time will come some day. Ay, and will come surely if you can say,

Ah! it is here now, and let the things which belong to life alone. You ask then, what have I to be happy for if no rest from strife will come, no love supreme, no heaven of unending joy. Will you tell me what you are who ask, or even tell yourself? Yet you say, *I* am sad, *I* am glad, *I* am angry, or *I* am compassionate; how could you say *I* am anything, if you separate that *I* from all these phases of passing *consciousness* which makes up that *I*'s existence? That *I* is the main point and the conscious point which all else sustains, and sustains it for an eternal life of consciousness, not for negation and nothingness, which would result if some desires were gratified. It satisfies me wholly to say *I am;* it is my peace. I hear you say I am, and I have my joy, and when I look at you, and the covers are removed from that *I am* of yours, I veil my eyes, blinded by its awful majesty."

As the mystic orator ceased speaking, Professor Monteith raised his eyes (which he had kept almost closed and downcast during the strange and touching address), beaming with a light of perfect comprehension. As his full orbs met the steady gaze of the lustrous eyes of his teacher, he said fearlessly and unfalteringly: —

"Yes, I know you are right; not one struggle do we have to undergo for naught. Tennyson hoped and tried to believe, what all some day will KNOW, and that perfectly; I may well say I have been long blind, but now I am beginning to see clearly; trees and men walking are no longer confounded to my vision as they were before. Thanks to you, my noble friend, and thanks to all who have pointed me to something beyond this transitory sphere, I can say confidently at last, 'Nothing walks with aimless feet.' I am even coming to trust 'that not a worm is cloven in vain,' and I am already satisfied 'that somehow good will be the final goal of ill.' There is no ill when the scales are off our eyes; we call that evil which we think is not right, because we fail to understand its origin, its ministry, and its outcome." * * * A sweet, silvery voice, like the sound of a far-off belfry chime, drawing nearer and ever nearer, swept through the barely furnished room, and a vibration of sound, audible, perhaps, only to the intensified perceptions of those whose hearing had become attuned to the melodies of registers beyond the limits of those ordinarily compassed by mortal hearing, chanted, "Blessed shall he be who taketh thy little ones and dasheth them against the rock." * * * A pause, silence for a breathing-space, and then the same sweet voice rang out louder and clearer this time, "Upon *this* rock I will build my church, and the gates of the underworld shall not prevail against it." * * * Another brief silence, and then a still firmer tone-vibration, echoing in a harmony of enchanting fulness, "The stone which the builders rejected is become the headstone of the corner. This is the Lord's doing, and it is marvellous in our eyes. Grace, grace, grace unto it."

The voice ceased; all was still, but from that hour the professor *knew* the meaning of holy Scripture, and read the purpose of the Infinite in the checkered career of **man**.

CHAPTER XXVII.

IDEAL MARRIAGE AND ITS RESULTS.

A BEAUTIFUL marriage ceremony had just been performed at Gore Towers, Hants. Arthur Selwyn Eastlake-Gore and Visalia Discalcelis had become man and wife. The ceremony was strictly private; only a few very choice friends knew of it, and they were surprised at the apparent suddenness of the event. Mrs. Eastlake-Gore was delighted to welcome so fair and loving a daughter as the talented Visalia to her heart and home. The newly married couple, with their mother (no hideous " in law " was ever tolerated even in thought) were going straight to Sicily, to spend the honeymoon and bring home the charming sister with them two months later, who had been spending fully six months in that romantic island, with a company of true gnostics who had formed a little settlement there, in a delightful retreat "far from the madding crowd," where they might give themselves to study and spiritual development ere they returned to actual life in the outer world, where they expected to use all the knowledge they had acquired in their quiet, natural sanctuary for the greatest good of a perplexed and sorrowing humanity. The voyage to Italy, even though it was midwinter, was delightful, and when, after the rigors of an exceptionally cold English winter, they landed in the lovely island off the southern coast of Italy, they felt their hearts dilate with thankfulness to the bountiful Giver of all good for making this poor vestibule of heaven so fair and bright.

Mr. and Mrs. Eastlake-Gore, Junior, as they were formally addressed, intended to devote themselves to joint literary and musical activities. Arthur intended to unite journalism with art, and Visalia was determined to incorporate in her amazingly well-written novels all the highest dreams of human progress she could receive in her most exalted moments, and accompany her literary life with the sweetest song. Their plan was to bring the gospel of beauty home to the very heart of the tried, sad workers of the world, who suffer literally because they have so little faith and hope, and whose career can be so immeasurably ennobled by introducing into it the sunshine of heavenly peace. "Worship the Lord in the *beauty* of holiness," was the life motto of this gifted and devoted couple, but how they carried out their aims and gratified their high ambitions will be the subject of the sequel to this tale.

Since Madame Discalcelis had become Mrs. Eastlake-Gore, Junior, she had been the recipient of a large pile of congratulatory and expostulatory letters from friends and literary acquaintances from far and near; for though her private residence was not open to unsolicited invasions at any time, she received and read every fragment of correspondence addressed to her in care of her publishers, Signori Leoponti and Vulperini. A woman holding remarkable views on many subjects, and never fearing to express them in public print, must naturally in these days, when discussion of the topic is so rife, be prepared to become the recipient of numberless astonishing inquiries regarding the law of heredity, which is agitating the minds of the public in many circles, more even than the labor problem, or any other important question vitally affecting the interests of the present, and of coming generations. A newly married woman, whose ideals of marriage are exceptionally high, can reasonably be looked upon as a source whence ideas worth considering relative to family life may be expected to emanate, even though as yet the privileges attendant upon maternity have not fallen to the lot of that woman; for the wise woman is she who knows before marriage what course she intends to pursue after it, and is therefore spared the misery of discovering, when too late, that she has made a fatal misstep, involving herself and others in frightful wretchedness.

Ursula Gestefeld's *Woman who Dares*, Sarah Grand's *Heavenly Twins*, and other popular novels with a decided purpose, dealing frankly with delicate, and too often hidden subjects, have done, and are still doing, much to arouse public sentiment on one of the most important subjects with which human intelligence can possibly become engaged; but these books and many others, good though they are, deal more extensively with the sorrows consequent upon ill-assorted unions and false standards of ethics, than with the sovereign panacea for all these woes, which is nothing less than perfect frankness before marriage as well as after it.

Arthur Selwyn Eastlake-Gore and Visalia Discalcelis were two very unusual people, in all respects; for they were morally, mentally, and physically so far above the average development of men and women to-day, that their extreme healthfulness on all planes constituted them a phenomenal couple. Two such singularly natural and harmoniously cultured persons would of necessity find it far easier to discuss the most vital questions fearlessly and intelligently, than those who would bring to the discussion a far slenderer share of ability to cope with its far-reaching consequences; still, there are no people capable of feeling in the least deeply, who have not the requisite ability, if they will but use it, to grapple with the greatest difficulties which can possibly beset the question of the right relation of the sexes in marriage. A woman as thoroughly independent financially as Madame Discalcelis must have advantages, in respect of unfettered sense of personal freedom, which no woman dependent on marriage for support can possibly feel; but, thanks to the industrial education of women, now becoming universal, all women will soon be able to realize and practically demonstrate their equal ability with their brothers to earn an honest, noble living by their own properly remunerative occupations, before they have reached what may reasonably be called the marriageable age, which in common reason cannot fairly be placed *under* twenty-one, and had better be *over* that period.

Mr. Gore and his bride were almost exactly of an age, and that age was twenty-five; they had both achieved remarkable success in their chosen career, which was literature of the highest stamp, though one was a journalist and the other a novelist. This distinctness in literary action was better than identity of line of occupation, as two persons who are to harmoniously co-operate in any undertaking must each have his or her decided specialty. The old adage, "Two of a trade seldom agree," need not have reference to the detestable and unreasoning jealousy which so often undermines society, and renders mutually antagonistic those who, if rightly instructed in the science of co-operative industry, would be mutually helpful; but where jealousy is, as it should ever be, entirely absent, there is often a lack of mental satisfaction on both sides, when two individuals are constantly thrown together who can do little more than merely echo each other's sentiments. That kind of sympathy in thought which causes one to say to the other when a remark is made, "That is exactly what I was going to say myself," becomes irksome, if it is too continuous, for the real joy of companionship and the true profit to be derived by it, is that one hears from his companion exactly what he could not have voiced himself. Complementary or supplementary associations are what we need to round out our lives, and keep us perpetually fresh in thought and young in feeling. The married state, therefore, when ideal, is a union of equals and a blending of contrasts, without which there may be good unison, but no perfect harmony.

Mr. and Mrs. Eastlake-Gore, Junior, had fully expressed themselves to each other on all vital subjects, not only before marriage, but previous to betrothal; for it was the conviction of both that one's word should be one's bond, but no word should ever be hastily given; and in no case is a pledge given less thoughtfully than where two young persons, superficially attracted, but lacking anything approaching to knowledge of each other's character and sentiments, agree to take each other for better or worse, without knowing much, if anything, more about each other than the most external details regarding physical appearance, social position, and business prospects. It is necessary to happiness that the two who are to become one in the eyes of the civil law, should know that they are already one in spirit, before they take upon themselves to declare their purpose to live as one before the world. The marriage laws do not need as much revision as the prevailing conduct of those contemplating marriage, before they have recourse to the operation of the marriage laws. No law can ordain that two shall be one in spirit, except the law of God, which has made those one who rightfully belong together, and though the highest ideal of spiritual marriage set forth in earlier pages of this volume is an exceptionally high standard, and probably beyond the present realization of nine hundred and ninety-nine people out of every thousand, at the lowest calculation, still there is an approximation toward this high ideal which is by no means unpractical.

On the question of hereditary influences, our hero and heroine were perfectly agreed; they accepted the theory that every soul has a mission to fulfil on earth, and that the divine secret of maternity is far beyond man's present intellectual comprehension; but with the deep, hidden mystery of infinite purpose we have not to deal; the part assigned to us to perform is a very comprehensible one, if we will but study it. To secure a healthy, harmonious surrounding for an unborn child, it is essential that the father and mother should be one in all their highest desires and life purposes. Maternity should always be voluntary, and the mother should rejoice in her glorious prerogative. With regard to the special moral and mental influence which should afford the occult matrix for the unborn, both parents should contribute psychically to the orderly construction of this, each giving a special impetus to a desired attainment. The best of the old Greeks understood this necessity, and strove to live up to it; and in all cases where they were faithful to their noblest ideals, they brought forth offspring whose moral, mental, and physical development was so phenomenally high, that they are to-day among the best models of human expression the world's literature and art contains. Madame Discalcelis had said in *Askalon*, that it is a truth recognized by Rosicrucianism, and by all occult orders entitled to prominence on the score of dignity, that any soul contains what any other soul holds infolded; the difference between souls in expression arises from the sole fact that one manifests what another conceals, or that one excessively exhibits the opposite qualities to those which are especially apparent in another; by reason of this, a system of ante-natal, as well as post-natal, training, will suffice to call into prominent activity, qualities which would without this appeal to them remain dormant, though they are never non-existent.

Arthur Gore, before his acquaintance with the authoress, had been forcibly struck with the reasonableness of this theory, and had commented most favorably upon it in his extended review of the book. Now that he was the husband of the lady whose writings he had so greatly admired before he met her, he resolved to work with her in perfect sympathy, whenever the time came to make in their own family life a practical test of this encouraging and sensible theory. It was the dearest wish of this exemplary couple that, should a son or daughter be born to them (they cared not which, believing so entirely as they did in the absolute equality of male and female), he or she should be a great musician, — a really great master of harmony, like unto Handel or Mozart, — and it was, moreover, their deepest prayer that should they, under Heaven's guidance, be the instruments for ushering into objective terrestrial existence, a soul capable of flooding the world with deathless song, that this gifted son or daughter of the great musical circle in the skies, should devote his rare talents of composition and rendition to the furtherance of all that is really highest and worthiest to endure in human expression. Music, to those who can interpret its divine inner meanings, is no mere art wherewith to tickle transient fancy, or please for the hour natures whose emotions are but shallow and vain. Music is the vibrant effluence of the great solar centre of every planetary system, and they who are learning to trace out the truth, long buried in the mystic verbiage of the astrologers and alchemists, concerning the music of the spheres, are commencing to see that through vibration, and through vibration only, can diseases be permanently driven out of the social and individual communities, now so grievously afflicted with such morbid distempers as result from perverse devotion to sense, to the almost total neglect of spirit. The youthful David, playing dexterously on his harp, can charm away the aberration of Saul, when all other means have been tried and proven useless. The true musician of to-morrow will be he or she who has so interpreted and translated the divine meanings of song, that Christ will indeed be found in music vastly grander even than Wagner's "Parsifal," though that, as Albert Ross Parsons has truly said, is at least a key to something of the treasure concealed within the sacred adytum where the goddess of melody sits among the immortals.

To rear an infant yet unborn, in the paths of harmony, needs that the mother be herself, before that child's conception, attuned to the rhythmic vibrations of the central sphere; and as in that divine abode there can be no jars of feeling, no discordances in thought, how is it possible for a holy temple to be prepared and consecrated to divinest uses of maternity, when the woman who is priestess at the shrine, defiles her inner chambers of affection with harsh thoughts or sordid misbeliefs. The purer a woman is, and the more active in worthy mental undertakings, the less likely is she to be even tempted to harbor a single suspicion of wrong concerning any one, and as she, being healthy herself, detests disease, its causes and concomitants, she cannot be expected to deal gently with those who treat her as though she were a vulture or buzzard in human shape, and proceed forthwith to regale her with carrion. A woman's safety is not in knowledge of sin, but in the strength of virtue, and what is true of woman is true of man also. Knowledge of disease will never prevent contagion, but sound, vigorous organisms afford no chance for microbe culture.

The calm retreat which the newly married pair who are now our hero and heroine had chosen, was selected chiefly because of its almost entire remoteness from any place where tourists stray, and where the air is filled with the psychic emanations from gossiping, discordant, mismated misanthropes.

"For the first few weeks of our married life let us be where we can breathe heaven's unpolluted air, and forget that 'Mrs. Grundy' and '*they say*' ever had existence. Let us learn through nature how to blend our lives, so that when we return to London, and take up the thread of our accustomed occupations and meet the world, as meet it we must, we shall be above it, even though in it."

Such were the words of his treasured bride, in answer to Arthur's first question as to where they should spend their honeymoon, and how.

"Give me," she continued, "the songs of nightingales, not the cackle of geese; the odor of sweet outdoor plants and fragrant garden flowers, not the stale mustiness of patchouli and musk; the freedom of the brown earth and the verdant fields, not the dust from Daghestan rugs and Axminster carpets. Nature unperverted, true, pure, and versatile, is the source whence, on the outer side of life, I wish to draw my first inspiration in preparation for maternity."

The thought of shirking motherhood, or contemplating it as distasteful, would have been as impossible to the pure-minded Visalia, as for the unfallen angels in the heavenly hierarchies to seek to avoid fulfilling the high and glorious privileges of ministry vouchsafed to them by their Creator. It is one of the surest signs of deep-seated degradation in the present day, that cultured women think with fear, if with no worse emotion, of approaching maternity, for such a feeling must proceed from moral or physical disorder, and is frequently the result of both. The "curse of Eve" theory, which has been studiously fostered by mistaken and deluded theologians, has robbed the prospect of motherhood of most of its joy for such women as are yet held in the chain of bondage to the superstitions attaching to religion; and outside all ecclesiastical precincts, utterly false medical ideas make life a burden to women who, through disgraceful ignorance of psychology and physiology alike, combined with slavish devotion to pernicious fashions, fail utterly to study and apply the principles of a sound gynecology or tokology, which is now happily dawning upon the world for the most part through the agency of those very "irregular" health doctors, whom "regular" bunglers would consign to the inferno of imprisonment, for daring to teach truth in place of administering poison. There are in all professions many excellent, conscientious people, but, alas! there are charlatans everywhere, and nowhere is charlatanism practised to a greater extent than in connection with the most sacred functions and responsibilities of life. Shakers and others who have made the fatal mistake of counselling the best and purest men and women to forego parentage, cannot of course be expected to do anything whatever to improve the race through hereditary transmission, because they leave the work of race propagation entirely in the hands of those whom they declare to be worldly, unsaintly, and unspiritual. Truly intelligent reformers hold that whenever we find an exceptionally noble man or woman, there do we find a model father or mother; therefore, if any steps are to be taken to check parentage, the check must be applied, not to the healthy and aspiring, but to the diseased and the debased. It is impossible for any, save the few who are intensely sensitive to psychic influences, and that knowingly and normally, to understand anything like how large an extent of mental sympathy between wife and husband is essential to the harmonic raising of a family or a single child.

Mr. and Mrs. Eastlake-Gore, Junior, were one day talking, in presence of their beloved mother, with a young married lady whom they met in their retreat, concerning the phenomenal precocity and extraordinary healthfulness of her little boy, a child of two, who was in many respects as mature mentally as most children are at seven; and what astonished every one who saw him was that he was so perfectly good-natured, and so entirely free from the symptoms of transmitted and reflected hysteria, under which almost every child one meets is groaning in greater or less degree.

Signora Electra Monterini was the wife of a young Italian artist whom she had met in Florence and fell in love with, as he did with her, literally at first sight.

They were married three weeks after their first meeting, but on the day of their first meeting they engaged themselves to each other, in the clear light of a full assurance that they were truly each other's already, and had ever been so, — though they had not discovered it outwardly till then, — in heart and soul. Signor Pietro Monterini was at this time — when his wife met the Gores — in Vienna, executing a commission for the Emperor of Austria, and though he would gladly have taken his wife and child with him to the gay capital, they had agreed that it was best for the young mother and their little one to remain far away from the bustle and mixed atmosphere of a feverish metropolis. When there is such union as existed between this happy pair, there can be no separations; for thought, on swifter wings than light, can conquer every obstacle of distance, and almost instantly convey to the beloved one at the other end of the globe, if need be, whatever tidings are considered of sufficient value to transmit.

Electra Monterini and Visalia Discalcelis Gore were at once on terms of perfect intimacy; the two women understood each other immediately the one felt the atmosphere of the other, and it was from the radiant Electra that Visalia gathered the few further hints she needed on the question of a practical outworking of the truth she had never doubted, viz., that a child can be psychically educated before and after birth through the united influence of the parents' thoughts. Little Bernadino Monterini had never been taught his letters, he had never been taught to speak, to walk, to count, or to do any of the many things which it is generally supposed young children must learn in a formal way, or they would never know them; but he was already something of a little Buddha, for he *knew* what he had never *learned*. He could talk the purest Italian and a little English and French, he knew a good part of the multiplication table, and he walked with a grace and dignity of bearing so remarkable in a little child that it provoked mingled merriment and admiration among all who saw. This wonderful little fellow had not been ill a minute since his birth, and he had never cried, though he often laughed, a soft, sweet, silvery peal of perfect laughter. He was a musician, and that was what made him doubly dear to Visalia, and when she saw him, utterly without training, go to the piano, and occasionally pick up a violin and evoke ravishing though simple harmonies, and then run away and play with flowers and chase butterflies,— who, by the way, were not in the least afraid of him, and he never injured one, — the thought welled up in her own bosom that she, too, would be the mother of such a messenger of the mighty Israfil. Music such as this child played was in no sense technical, and it could be traced to no "school." It was voluntary as the songs of larks and thrushes, its perfect spontaneity gave it its deepest charm, and when he sang, he simply let the sound escape through his lips, and it was free as a wild-bird's note and quite as tuneful.

"How did you raise him?" questioned Visalia. To which, with beaming countenance, lit with more than earthly love, Electra answered:—

"My husband and I are one, we breathe together; our

hopes, joys, pleasures, ambitions, interests, are all the same; therefore, whether we are together or not in body, we are always together in spirit. Before my babe was conceived, I knew he was coming; I saw the heavens open to me one night, and a fair, dazzling cherub appeared at the furthest end of a shaft of light, which reached to the very spot where I was reclining under the trees; in a lovely garden I heard the sound of many instruments of music, mingling with a mighty concourse of voices. I have sung in La Scala in Milan and other great theatres, where the music seemed as near an approach to the harmonies of heaven as could be caught and imprisoned below, but never till the night when heaven really opened to me did I, or could I, imagine what celestial song might truly be. My husband had just completed a wonderful painting, an ambitious attempt to portray the angel Israfil surrounded with a legion of celestial choristers, and as I gazed admiringly, almost worshipfully, into the canvas to read the soul of what was depicted thereon, I saw the face of the cherub who had appeared to me in my vision out of doors. The bright, fairy-like creation of my husband's brush answered exactly to the child of my enraptured dream. I was about to speak; the tiny hands of the pictured angel were stretched toward me — a thought filled my bosom with rapture too great for words. * * * My husband articulated what I could not utter, and with a countenance illumined with light, but one degree less brilliant than that of the shining company of my vision, softly whispered to me, 'He is our own, he came to me and told me so; you will yet press him to your bosom.' * * * The next day I knew that I should be a mother. * * * Nine months passed swiftly, happily away; no jar even for an instant marred the intense, unutterable fulness of our rapturous mutual affection. During those nine months we were all in all to each other, and when at length the hour of my child's nativity approached, I passed into a trance of rapture; no one but my companion was near me,— he alone tended me, and I know not if I needed tending,— and when I awoke from my trance there were three of us on earth, for he who was erstwhile in heaven had descended, and I knew that an angelic embodiment was drawing physical sustenance from my bosom. I cannot tell you, even you, dear lady,— to whom I can open my very soul and relate experiences at which the world would scoff and pronounce me raving,— all that I have enjoyed in the past two years. I cannot thank God; I am too happy in the glory of His blessing to praise Him verbally. I know He sends His messengers in human guise to earth, and I am privileged to be the mother of one of them."

Though to most minds such rhapsodies would sound meaningless, in the ears of Visalia, who had had many strange and glorious experiences of her own, they were words of truth and soberness, and before she and those nearest to her returned to resume their life in England, there came to her also an intimation of a joy that was in store. Very slowly but very sweetly it dawned upon her, that before another year had completed its course, her high prerogative might be like unto Electra's, and she become the happy mother of a child whose earthly strength and loveliness should prove but a shield for heavenly brightness sent down to illuminate and bless an all too dreary globe. * * * Two months of exquisite enjoyment soon pass; time which is laden with happiness seems to fly on fleetest wings, while time weighted down with care and sadness moves as on leaden feet. Thus do we realize, if we reflect, that time is as long or short to us as our mental condition makes it; we are therefore arbiters even of the length of our days.

When Mr. and Mrs. Eastlake-Gore, Junior, returned to London, they took up their life together in the charming villa with their treasured mother and sister, and lived much as before, only more perfectly knit together in every feeling than when their now ripened union was only in its bud. One of the first visitors whom they received was the mystic Aldebaran, who greeted them quite unexpectedly, and brought with him as a wedding gift a magnificent illuminated scroll, bearing the legend: "Glory be to God for the briefness of man's terrestrial career, for the joy of transition and for the certainty of life immortal. Glory for ever and ever. Amen."

Professor Monteith also called, and he, too, brought an offering, which was an exquisite model of an air-ship, accompanied by an explanatory and prophetic treatise, the cover of which contained the text: "Happy shall he be who taketh thy little ones and dasheth them against the rock." Beneath the text there loomed up out of the sea a tall, massive rock, on which an angelic form was seated, emitting rays of brightness which fell on the waters beneath in the form of a cross surmounted by a crown in the shape of a seven-pointed star; and following the light and rising by its aid out of the water, was a weather-beaten seaman, with a look of hope and trust on his somewhat careworn face, while his breath proceeded through his nostrils in the form of a prayer, which took shape in the supplicatory words, "Lead me to the rock which is higher than I."

Many were the gifts poured upon the beautiful young bride and bridegroom, but none did they value quite so highly as these two suggestive tributes of high esoteric import, presented affectionately and understandingly by friends who deeply realized the import of the tokens they bestowed.

Visalia at once began work on a new book entitled, *Christ in Life's Song of Triumph;* her husband resumed his post of honor and influence as literary director of one of the largest and most important weekly papers published in any part of the world. Health, beauty, and prosperity were theirs, and what made these possessions doubly sweet to them, was that they consecrated all they had and were to the service of God in work for His offspring.

FINIS.

www.ingramcontent.com/pod-product-compliance
Lightning Source LLC
Chambersburg PA
CBHW030011240426
43672CB00007B/912